M000118274

Generalist Social Work Practice

Intervention Methods

JOSEPH WALSH
School of Social Work
Virginia Commonwealth University

BROOKS/COLE
CENGAGE Learning™

Australia • Brazil • Japan • Korea • Mexico • Singapore • Spain • United Kingdom • United States

BROOKS/COLE
CENGAGE Learning

Generalist Social Work Practice: Intervention Methods
Joseph Walsh

Assistant Editor: Stephanie Rue

Editorial Assistant: Caitlin Cox

Technology Project Manager: Andrew Keay

Marketing Manager: Karin Sandberg

Marketing Assistant: Andy Yap

Marketing Communications Manager: Shemika Britt

Project Manager, Editorial Production: Christy Krueger

Creative Director: Rob Hugel

Art Director: Caryl Gorska

Print Buyer: Paula Vang

Permissions Editor: Roberta Broyer

Production Service: Newgen–Austin

Copy Editor: Michele Chancellor

Cover Designer: Lisa Buckley

Compositor: Newgen

© 2009 Brooks/Cole, Cengage Learning

ALL RIGHTS RESERVED. No part of this work covered by the copyright herein may be reproduced, transmitted, stored, or used in any form or by any means graphic, electronic, or mechanical, including but not limited to photocopying, recording, scanning, digitizing, taping, Web distribution, information networks, or information storage and retrieval systems, except as permitted under Section 107 or 108 of the 1976 United States Copyright Act, without the prior written permission of the publisher.

For product information and technology assistance, contact us at
Cengage Learning Academic Resource Center
1-800-423-0563

For permission to use material from this text or product, submit all requests online at
www.cengage.com/permissions.
Further permissions questions can be e-mailed to
permissionrequest@cengage.com.

Library of Congress Control Number: 2007938730

ISBN-13: 978-0-534-64130-6
ISBN-10: 0-534-64130-X

Brooks/Cole Cengage Learning
20 Davis Drive
Belmont, CA 94002-3098
USA

Cengage Learning is a learning provider of customized learning solutions with office locations around the globe, including Singapore, the United Kingdom, Australia, Mexico, Brazil, and Japan. Locate your local office at **international.cengage.com/region**.

Cengage Learning products are represented in Canada by Nelson Education, Ltd.

For your course and learning solutions, visit **academic.cengage.com**.

Purchase any of our products at your local college store online store **www.cengagebrain.com**.

Printed in the United States of America
2 3 4 5 6   17 16 15 14 13

*To all of my undergraduate students, past and present,
at Virginia Commonwealth University, and to my first five students
at Ohio Dominican University*

Brief Contents

Contents

Preface

Generalist social work practice can be defined as the comprehensive assessment of a problem situation in a client system, followed by planning and intervention at any of five levels including those of the individual, family, group, organization, or community. The generalist perspective assumes an interdependence between individuals and their social environments, and requires that social workers have a broad base of knowledge about the functioning of individuals, families, groups, organizations, and communities, and the ways in which they may reciprocally support or inhibit functioning. *Generalist Social Work Practice: Intervention Methods* is a textbook that provides undergraduate social work students with a wide range of specific intervention strategies for use with client systems at all levels of generalist practice. Six of the 12 chapters are so focused, and all of the other chapters include sections on practice implications of the topic material as well. Thus, the major strength of this book is its emphasis on intervention.

Regarding practice applications, this book is based on a strengths-based problem-solving model that can apply across all levels of intervention. Students are introduced to *cognitive* and *behavioral* theory for use with individuals and groups, and *structural theory* for use with families. These approaches have been selected because they are clearly understood by undergraduate students, practical in most social work settings, and have demonstrated effectiveness with a range of problems in living. Students are also introduced to the *contingency, community systems,* and *social support* theories for larger scale interventions. All of these intervention perspectives are consistent with each other, and thus provide the social work student with a systematic set of strategies for generalist practice. Each chapter also includes a list of classroom discussion topics and ideas for assignments.

Generalist Social Work Practice: Intervention Methods is divided into three sections, as follows:

- An introduction to generalist practice, including attention to the special nature of social work, the problem-solving process, and the process of managing professional relationships

- Intervention theories and applications, with special attention to behavior theory, cognitive theory, and social support theory

- Specific intervention methods for use across all five levels of generalist practice

ORGANIZATION OF THE BOOK

Parts I and II consist of seven chapters that lay out a theoretical perspective for generalist practice. The well-known problem-solving model, with a clear strengths focus, is presented as the underlying conceptual framework for intervention. This model is practical for generalist practice because it is applicable across the five levels. Another advantage of the problem-solving model is that it provides a basis for client empowerment. A major theme of the book is that clients are always helped by the social worker to become better problem solvers. The cognitive, behavioral, and social support theories for practice are introduced in Part II. These theories and their related intervention strategies help practitioners to focus their work on a client system's cognitive, emotional, and behavioral functioning, including its development of new knowledge or new ways of approaching the environment. Concepts of community are also given special attention in Part II. Social support theory is presented with this material as it provides a link between work with smaller and larger systems.

Part III, focused more specifically on intervention methods, provides sets of strategies for use with client systems at all five levels of generalist practice. Each chapter includes at least four distinct strategies, and many of them build on each other. There are three reasons for taking this approach. First, it enables the instructor to cover as much material in each chapter as fits with the scope of the course. Thus, instructors who teach a practice course for only one semester may use half of the intervention strategies covered in each chapter. Secondly, an instructor may choose to emphasize some levels of practice more than others, if such an approach fits with the nature of his or her program. Thirdly, the instructor may want to cover some intervention strategies at all levels of practice early in the academic year, and then go through the sequence again to teach additional strategies later in the year. This way, students who are given caseloads or other practice assignments in their agencies early in the year (agencies are quite variable in this regard) do not have to wait long before getting to course material that lends guidance to their field activities.

An in-depth discussion of agency-based practice is reserved for Part III. The first half of that chapter is theoretical and may be used earlier in the semester. At that time students will be adjusting to their field placement agencies and will probably experience many orientation activities before they are in a position to provide interventions. This content will help the students to make a successful adjustment to the field, and the recommended assignments and questions for discussion will help the instructor take advantage of the opportunity to teach students about large-systems practice. This concept is emphasized in the chapter on agency-based research, which provides students with the ability to develop empirical rationales for their interventions at that level.

PROFESSIONAL VALUES AND ETHICS

Many textbooks include separate chapters about professional values. *Intervention Methods* incorporates attention to a single social work value principle in each chapter of Part III. This enables the instructor to place the teaching of values into a context of the other text material, and students can integrate this learning into their range of practice activities. A case vignette representing a value dilemma is included in each of the last six chapters, based on the intervention principles from that chapter, for student reading and discussion.

A RANGE OF INTERVENTION METHODS

Figure 1 outlines all of the theories and intervention activities for generalist practice that are described in the book. Each theory and activity is listed beneath the target of intervention to which it applies. If a line moves from the topic across a portion of the page, that topic is intended to be applicable to several levels of intervention. What should be evident from this table is that each level of intervention may call for the practitioner's application of different roles and interventions. A major principle of *Generalist Social Work Practice: Intervention Methods* is that, while generalist practice provides an overarching perspective for service delivery, the effective practitioner needs to be able to call on special knowledge and intervention skills to help clients resolve problems and challenges at each of the five levels of practice.

Social work is a challenging profession, one in which even the most seasoned practitioners face new dilemmas every day that test their abilities to help clients solve problems. This book can help new social workers develop the competence, confidence, and sense of optimism to embark on a lifelong career in service to others.

F I G U R E 1   Generalist Social Work Practice Interventions

Target Systems

Individuals   Families   Groups   Organizations   Communities

Theories and Interventions

*Problem-solving theory*_____

  Problem-solving model, Task-centered practice

*Cognitive–Behavior theory*_____

  Cognitive restructuring, Skills training,
  Stress management, Stress prevention,
  Behavioral reinforcements,
  Crisis intervention

*Social support theory*_____

  Formal and informal linkage development and maintenance

          Family systems
            Structural (includes communications)
            Educational

                    Group process
                      Five types, Four stages,
                      Leadership strategies

                            Contingency theory
                              Changing: People,
                                          Processes,
                                          Structures
                              Approach: Policy, Program,
                                          Project, Personnel,
                                          Practice
                              Strategy: Collaboration,
                                          Campaign,
                                          Contest
                              Research: Needs assessment,
                                          Evaluation

                                    Social action
                                      Collaboration,
                                      Campaign,
                                      Contest

ACKNOWLEDGMENTS

I have enjoyed teaching undergraduate social work students throughout my 15 years in academia. Writing this book has been a dream of mine, and many people have helped me in the process. First I want to acknowledge my most influential mentor in teaching and working with undergraduate students—Jane Reeves, former BSW program director at Virginia Commonwealth University. For their assistance with preparing the manuscript I want to recognize the contributions of colleagues Lori Thomas, Jeanne Crowell, and Jacqueline Corcoran. From Cengage Learning and the Newgen–Austin production team I want to thank Marcus Boggs, Stephanie Rue, Dan Alpert, Christy Krueger, Michele Chancellor, Caitlin Cox, Bharathi Sanjeev, Rebecca Logan, Debra DeBord, and Randa Dubnick.

A special thanks goes to Lisa Gebo, formerly of Thomson Brooks/Cole, who offered me the contract for this book.

The reviewers listed in the following section provided excellent suggestions for improving early drafts of the manuscript.

REVIEWERS

Roseanna McCleary (California State University, Bakersfield)
Kenneth Hermann (State University of New York)
Santos Torres (California State University, Sacramento)
Barbara Rio (Stephen F. Austin State University)
Andrew Scharlach (University of California, Berkeley)
Ronald Polon (Ball State University)
Diane Calloway-Graham (Utah State University)
Sabrina Sullenberger (Indiana University)
Frederick Stephens (University of North Carolina, Pembroke)
Margaret Elbow (Texas Tech University)
Phillip Ortiz (Eastfield College)
Anthony Mallon (Virginia Commonwealth University)
Sandy Cook-Fong (University of Nebraska)
Jay Bishop (University of Maryland, Eastern Shore)
Freddi Avant (Stephen F. Austin State University)

About the Author

Joseph Walsh is a professor of social work at Virginia Commonwealth University. He has been a direct service practitioner in the field of mental health for many years, first in a psychiatric hospital and later in community mental health center settings. He has mostly specialized in services to people with serious mental illnesses and their families. Since 1993 Joe has been at VCU, teaching courses in generalist and clinical practice, human behavior, research, and social theory. He was the 1998 recipient of the National Mental Health Association's George Goodman Brudney and Ruth P. Brudney Social Work Award, given annually to recognize significant contributions to the care and treatment of people with mental illnesses. Joe is the author or coauthor of six other books related to social work practice.

PART I

Introduction to Generalist Practice

Chapter 1

Defining Generalist Practice

G eneralist social work practice is the specific province of BSW (Bachelor of Social Work) and BSSW (Bachelor of Science in Social Work) practitioners. Only people with those degrees are educated in this complex form of professional practice that requires a broad knowledge base, the utilization of many intervention skills, and the application of a specific value base, all of which have evolved through the 100+ years of the social work profession. Generalist practice also provides a strong foundation for MSW (Master of Social Work) students who need to develop an appreciation for the scope of interventions within the profession. Students who complete a course of study in social work and embark on a practice career should feel proud of the humanitarian values for which the profession stands, and for its unique contributions to human service delivery.

The complexity of generalist social work practice is sometimes underappreciated, because practitioners must know a lot about a lot of things. The purpose of this book is to provide students with the knowledge, skills, and values they will need to work effectively as generalist practitioners. This first chapter is devoted to defining generalist practice. We will also review social work's person-in-environment perspective, consider the various roles of the generalist social work practitioner, and become familiar with the profession's code of ethics.

DEFINING GENERALIST PRACTICE

As a starting point in defining generalist practice, it is helpful to understand how social work is unique from other, somewhat similar professions. For many years I began my practice courses by asking students to participate in the following exercise. I asked them first to develop a list of professions that have some similarity

3

to social work. They always produced a list of 15 or so professions including psychology, psychiatry, rehabilitation counseling, occupational therapy, art therapy, the ministry, education, and others. Interestingly, bartending and hairdressing often made the list! Next, I organized the students into small groups and divided the list of professions among them. They were asked to consider ways in which social work *differed* from these professions, in that way identifying unique aspects of social work practice. In the final part of the exercise, the students shared observations with each other and compiled a complete list of defining characteristics of generalist social work. Over the years, my students summarized social work practice as featuring:

- A "person-in-environment" perspective on human functioning rather than a strict medical or psychological one
- Sensitivity to the broad needs of people (material through spiritual)
- A focus on family and other interpersonal systems, rather than individuals in isolation
- A broad range of practice roles and interventions
- Flexibility in interventions, rather than relying on "set" procedures (social work is often utilized in unstructured, uncontrolled settings, permitting creativity)
- A specific set of values and a code of ethics
- A specific educational base (and an ability to use the undergraduate degree for employment right away)
- An emphasis on close working relationships with members of client systems that facilitate a sense of safety and trust, including a nonhierarchical stance in those relationships (and with that, unique challenges regarding professional boundaries)
- Self-awareness regarding personal biases
- Attention to the spiritual concerns of clients without working from a specific religious orientation
- A desire to promote cohesion among coworkers and other agency staff (an interdisciplinary approach)
- A desire to empower client groups
- Unique licensure standards
- An "action" orientation (*doing* things with, rather than merely *talking* with, clients)
- An understanding and appreciation of diversity in client populations
- A strengths orientation, including a refusal to "blame the victim"
- Interest in problem prevention
- Excellent interviewing skills

- Access to formal and informal resources to facilitate linkages
- Skill in multidimensional assessment
- Policy development skills
- Crisis intervention skills
- A commitment to client outreach, including a willingness to work in natural environments, such as making home visits
- Client advocacy, from the level of the individual to the legislature
- The use of the "human instrument," or minimal material technology
- Working with a full spectrum of voluntary and involuntary clients
- Avoidance of the use of diagnostic labels when possible
- A career so varied that practitioners can *never* burn out

The last item was offered by enthusiastic students who were convinced that social workers receive unique internal rewards for their work. We should all hope to be so fortunate! It may be argued that some of the items on this list are not unique to social work practice. Taken together, however, they illustrate the breadth of elements of practice, which has implications for our definition of generalist practice.

A Model of Generalist Practice

There is no single definition of the term, but generalist practice has been defined by the program faculty at my school of social work as the comprehensive assessment of a problem situation in a client system, followed by the social worker's planning and intervention at any of the five levels noted in the chart in Figure 1.1.

The generalist perspective assumes an *interdependence* between individuals and their social environments (a *systems* perspective), and thus requires that social workers have a broad base of knowledge about the functioning of individuals,

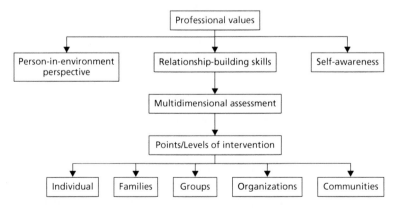

FIGURE 1.1 Components of Generalist Social Work Practice

families, groups, organizations, and communities, and the ways in which social institutions support or inhibit functioning. Figure 1.1 will be referenced throughout the book as we address each of its components in detail.

The social worker's choices about level(s) of intervention ideally result from a comprehensive (multidimensional) problem assessment, which will be explored in more detail in Chapter 2. After examining the presenting situation and deciding that intervention is appropriate, the generalist social worker focuses on the level that is most changeable, or offers the greatest potential for long-term benefit for the client system. These decisions are guided by professional values and the practitioner's self-awareness. Practically speaking, however, level of intervention is also a function of the social worker's prescribed role in an agency. Social workers are often formally limited to working with individuals, families, groups, or communities, or some combination of those systems. Even in these situations, however, the generalist practitioner must be aware of *potential* interventions at other system levels for the purpose of making appropriate referrals for additional services. In every situation, the generalist practitioner must maintain flexibility to transfer his or her knowledge, values, and skills across diverse client populations and settings.

Generalist practice, particularly among non-social workers, is sometimes described with other terminology. It may be called *direct practice,* or even *clinical practice,* when referring to interventions with individuals, families, and groups. *Case management* is a term that refers to practice focused on small systems but featuring the social worker's service linkages and client advocacy (Frankel & Gelman, 2004). Sometimes distinctions are made between direct practice and *macro practice,* with the latter term describing interventions designed to bring about change in organizations and communities. We will use the term "generalist" throughout this text, recognizing that in particular practice settings social workers may be given other designations.

ELEMENTS OF GENERALIST SOCIAL WORK PRACTICE

The Bio-Psycho-Social-Spiritual Perspective

Generalist practice incorporates attention to broad aspects of human functioning, and people are never considered in isolation from their surroundings. We are all continuously interactive with our external environments, and the quality of our social functioning (defined as the ability to successfully carry out our roles as family member, friend, significant other, student, employee, and community participant) is determined by interactions with our family, group, organization, and community surroundings. The bio-psycho-social-spiritual perspective helps social workers to organize this broad perspective for purposes of client assessment and intervention. No social worker can be expert in all of these areas, of course, but practitioners should attend to each of them in assessment.

The "Bio."   The biological perspective respects the fact that heredity, physiology, physical capacity, and all material body processes create and influence emotions, thoughts, and behavior in all people (Ginsberg, Nackerud, & Larrison, 2004). The focus of the biological perspective in social work includes:

- Health and wellness
- Body image and awareness
- Proper "use" of the body
- Care of the body
- The meaning and consequences of vulnerability (including death and dying)

Challenges to social workers from the biological perspective include helping client systems experience physical wellness, preventing and intervening with regard to physical illness, respecting the regenerative capacity of people, and respecting the strengths that allow people to accept and deal with illness and impairment. Strengths of the biological perspective include its promotion of the role of physical processes in social functioning, a reduction of cross-cultural or class bias (which are often less problematic in biology), acknowledgment that people are limited by their physiology, and crediting people with being ill when they are so. Its limitations are that it may unfairly attribute many problems to medical causes, promote a disease model for interpreting diversity and deviance, and promote an overutilization of medications.

The "Psycho."   Psychological perspectives on human behavior highlight the role of one's *cognitive* and *emotional* status in adaptive social functioning. Social work has long been interested in developmental theories of psychological development (Walsh, 2003a). Examples of these theories include Freud's psychosexual theory, Erikson's psychosocial theory, Piaget's theory of cognitive development, and Kohlberg and Gilligan's theories of moral development. Developmental theories assume that all people pass through sequential states of emotional, cognitive, and moral development, along with their physical development. Personal maturity implies successful passage through each stage of a developmental sequence, and problems in living can result if one becomes stuck at, or regresses to, a lower level of development.

The strengths of the developmental perspective are that it provides a framework for social workers to understand human potential, helps social workers appreciate challenges faced by people at various stages of life, and provides a focus for assessment and intervention by tracing one's history to periods when difficulties may have originated. The limitations of this perspective are that no single theory can apply to all individuals or groups. Few developmental theories come out of traditions that embrace diversity, and they tend to be influenced by the theorist's cultural biases (Harper & Lantz, 2007). In fact, developmental theories have fallen into disrepute in recent years. An "ideal" theory would apply to broad populations but not be so rigid as to promote the negative labeling of deviant people. Such a theory may unfortunately never exist. Social workers, then, should view theories of development as useful frameworks rather than facts.

The "Social."   The social perspective includes all aspects of the world outside one's family—the neighborhood, school, larger community, workplace, and other organizations with which the person is associated. The major focus of the social work profession during its early years was the development of supportive communities to meet members' needs (Ehrenreich, 1985). Practice eventually became more focused on small systems, but social workers continue to rightly assume that social influences on human behavior are the equal of biological and psychological influences. *Social support theory* is one useful perspective for addressing a client system's social environment. This will be considered in detail in Chapter 7. Here we review the National Association of Social Workers' (NASW) formal person-in-environment (PIE) system, one example of a small systems assessment tool that attends to social aspects of a client's functioning.

Social work's PIE classification system (see Table 1.1) formally organizes the assessment of individuals around the four themes of social functioning problems, environmental problems, mental health problems, and physical health problems (Karls & Wandrei, 1994). Such a broad classification scheme helps to insure that a client's range of needs is addressed. The authors of the PIE system state that it "seeks to balance problems and strengths; it delineates problems pertinent to both the person and the environment and qualifies them according to their duration, severity, and the client's ability to solve or cope with them" (p. 3). While a limitation of the PIE is the lack of a place for noting strengths and resources, it represents a positive step by the social work profession to systematize its perspective on social functioning.

The "Spiritual."   This component of human functioning represents a relatively new focus of attention in social work practice. Although spirituality and religion have always been important aspects of most people's lives, and the social work profession itself has roots in American religious traditions, those topics have tended to be considered private—outside the sphere of formal intervention. As the profession has become more strengths-oriented and sensitive to issues of diversity, however, the potential for clients' spiritual traditions to be utilized as a resource in problem resolution has been recognized.

Spirituality can be understood as one's search for, or adherence to, meanings, purposes, and commitments that lie outside the self (Lantz & Walsh, 2007). Examples can be seen in the desire of many people to make a difference in the world, from participation in neighborhood associations to political activity. Many social workers are driven by the value of serving other people. The concept of *religion* is narrower, including any system of thought shared by a group that gives members of that group a frame of orientation and an object of devotion (Angrosino, 2004). Catholics, Protestants, Muslims, Jews, and others all share particular religious beliefs, but a person's spiritual life may transcend the beliefs of his or her religion. A challenge for the social work profession is to consider

T A B L E 1.1   The Person-in-Environment Classification System

Factor I: Social functioning problems

T A B L E 1.1   The Person-in-Environment Classification System (Continued)

Factor I: Social functioning problems

A. Social role in which each problem is identified
1. Family (parent, spouse, child, sibling, other, significant other)
2. Other interpersonal (lover, friend, neighbor, member, other)
3. Occupational (worker/paid, worker/home, worker/volunteer, student, other)

B. Type of problem in social role
1. Power
2. Ambivalence
3. Responsibility
4. Dependency
5. Loss
6. Isolation
7. Victimization
8. Mixed
9. Other

C. Severity of problem
1. No problem
2. Low severity
3. Moderate severity
4. High severity
5. Very high severity
6. Catastrophic

D. Duration of problem
1. More than five years
2. One to five years
3. Six months to one year
4. Two to four weeks
5. Two weeks or less

E. Ability of client to cope with problem
1. Outstanding coping skills
2. Above average
3. Adequate

4. Somewhat inadequate
5. Inadequate
6. No coping skills

Factor II: Environmental problems

T A B L E   1.1   The Person-in-Environment Classification System (Continued)

Factor II: Environmental problems

A. **Social system where each problem is identified**
    1. Economic/basic needs
    2. Education/training
    3. Judicial/legal
    4. Health, safety, social services
    5. Voluntary association
    6. Affectional support

B. **Specific type of problem within each social system**

C. **Severity of problem**

D. **Duration of problem**

Factor III: Mental health problems

---

human behavior within a context of meaning represented by spirituality and to help people identify meanings and purposes that can guide them in making decisions to enhance their lives.

There are many spiritual frameworks that social workers may use in practice. For one example, Frankl's (1988) *logotherapy* asserts that all people have a drive to create or discover meaning and purpose in their lives. Creation of meaning implies that either some or all purposes are arbitrary, while discovery implies the belief that some purposes are absolute. Frankl states that both positions should be respected. Logotherapy asserts that in all cases people aspire by nature to make commitments to values beyond their mere existence and survival. Five categories of meaning include:

- Creative (music, art)
- Experiential (responding to natural beauty or to works of art)
- Social (engagement in a variety of social activities to advance some value)
- Religious
- Defiant (resisting oppression)

In some cases it may be helpful for the social worker to assess a client's spiritual sense and help the client more clearly identify his or her sense of purpose. This is because in the everyday stress of life many people become detached from their ultimate values.

The strengths of the spiritual perspective are that it promotes the dignity of all people, a nonmechanistic view of people, and the identification of personal strengths that clients can bring to managing challenges in their lives. A potential problem is that the social worker may be biased by his or her own spiritual perspectives and perhaps unwittingly impose those on clients.

Thus far we have considered generalist practice and the bio-psycho-social-spiritual perspective that encourages broad client system assessment. Next we will consider the concept of *theories* to guide the social worker's interventions in generalist practice.

THE RELATIONSHIP OF THEORY TO PRACTICE

Generalist practice is not a theory, but an orientation to practice. Within the generalist practice perspective several theories for guiding assessment and intervention will be presented in this book. For this reason we need to consider the nature of a practice theory. It is essential that social workers understand their theoretical orientations so that they can provide interventions in a thoughtful, systematic manner.

Theory is an abstract concept, but it is often described in a more confusing way than is necessary. For example, from simple to more complex, a theory can be defined as:

- An attempt to explain something
- An orderly explanation for confusing experiences
- A systematic but speculative explanation for an event or behavior
- A set of propositions linked by logical argument that is advanced to explain or predict an area of reality

We could go further with definitions here, but my eyes will begin to glaze over! In every case, a theory involves the imposing of an arbitrary structure on a reality that is too complex for easy understanding. The world is such that we must always narrow our focus, or limit what we pay attention to.

A *practice* theory is a coherent set of ideas about human nature, including concepts of health, illness, normalcy, and deviance, that provides explanations for behavior and rationales for intervention (Frank & Frank, 1993). Practice theories usually include concepts about what internal and external factors help people to change. There are dozens of practice theories available for use in the human services, such as ego psychology (change through insight), cognitive theory (change through more rational thinking), behavior theory (change through new reinforcers), narrative theory (change through a new life story), and social support theory (change through the reworking and acquisition of resources), to name just a few. They have developed in different eras, different countries, and with respect to different client populations. The variety of practice theories reflects the fact that there are many ways to view people and the change process. How, then, does a practitioner decide what theoretical perspective to use in practice? Some criteria for theory selection may include (Turner, 1996):

- Its effectiveness is supported by evidence-based practice research. This is defined as empirically tested and validated theory-based intervention.

- It implies clear and practical techniques for intervention that are consistent with the client's goals.

- It produces positive results with the least amount of time, money, and effort. This refers to efficiency, so that the social worker can assist a greater number of clients.

- It is consistent with the practitioner's ethics, knowledge, and skills.

- It is consistent with the practitioner's own worldview (that is, it makes sense to the practitioner).

- It is consistent with the practitioner's agency policies about intervention.

The value of the practitioner's taking the time to think about, experiment with, and select theories and their related intervention strategies for practice is that they help the social worker to explain and predict the behavior of client systems, bring order (versus randomness) to the social worker's activity, help the social worker speculate about how he or she will intervene in future practice situations, and also help the social worker identify his or her knowledge gaps (What more do I need to know? How else might I act in a situation?).

Every practice theory, however, includes limitations. Human beings have greater diversity and complexity than any single theory can accommodate. If adhered to rigidly, a practice theory can be reductionistic (ignoring certain aspects of human behavior) or antihumanistic (seeing people in a mechanical fashion).

A challenge for social workers is to learn about many practice theories and select several with which they can practice comfortably and effectively. We should always be open to new ideas, never forgetting that all practice theories must evolve to accommodate new generations of clients and new types of practice situations. We will focus on a limited number of practice theories in this book, as described in the forthcoming chapters.

ROLES OF THE GENERALIST PRACTITIONER

Social workers in generalist practice may occupy a variety of professional *roles*, or positions within which they carry out certain service activities. The following list of seven roles has been adapted from Hepworth, Rooney, Rooney, Strom-Gottfried, and Larsen (2006), Kanter (1989), and Neugeboren (1996):

⌐ *Service accessibility advocate.* Makes sure that clients who seek intervention are able to acquire it. (Example: Providing bus passes to older adults who wish to attend a community center.)

⌐ *Direct practitioner with individuals, families, and groups.* Develops relationships, makes comprehensive assessment and intervention plans, and provides specific educational, problem-solving, behavioral, and cognitive interventions. (Example: Teaching social skills to delinquent adolescents in a group setting.)

⌐ *Environmental practitioner.* Links individuals and families with organizational and community resources, connecting organizations with each other, and mediating between clients and other people or agencies. (Examples: Providing respite care but also service referrals to women who walk into a battered women's shelter, and then following up on the success of those referrals. A hospice social worker follows up on clients who have been referred to nursing homes and public health agencies to see if their expressed needs are being met.)

⌐ *Information manager.* Documents client activities and gives this information to providers when appropriate. (Example: A social worker in a homeless shelter makes information about a client's service activities available to a potential landlord, with the client's permission.)

⌐ *Agency program and policy developer.* Creates services within his or her own agency when unmet client needs are identified. (Example: A mental health agency initiates a new support group for the families of its clients who have major mental illnesses.)

⌐ *Community resource developer and advocate.* Creates services outside his or her agency when unmet client needs are identified. (Example: Staff at an urban family services agency participate in the development of a foster care agency in a nearby rural area in response to an increasing incidence of child abuse cases there.) Represents the interests of client systems among organizations, within communities, and with political bodies, and promotes client empowerment and self-determination. (Example: Working for medication price discounts with a local funding organization on behalf of clients.)

⌐ *Outcome evaluator.* Tracks all of the above intervention activities to determine whether the client system's goals have been met.

It should be apparent that effective generalist practice demands the application of a range of skills. In fact, helping clients to change requires different skills than changing policies, programs, and community practices (Neugeboren, 1996). Environmentally focused practice requires "sociopolitical" skills, in contrast to "socioemotional" skills (relationship development, assessment, and planning). Some practitioners may be more skilled at one type of intervention than the other, but this merely underscores the importance of generalist social workers receiving ongoing professional development in all areas of practice.

Systems in Generalist Practice

When considering the roles of the generalist practitioner, it is important to also recognize the systems, or types of people, with which the social worker may be involved in the course of practice (Netting, Kettner, & McMurtry, 2004). We will refer to these seven systems throughout the book. They include:

The initiator system. The person (or people) who first recognizes the existence of a problem and brings attention to it.

The referral system. The person (or people) who represents a client's significant others or another institution and who refers the client to the social worker with an interest in the outcome of the change effort. For example, a judge may refer a client for substance abuse intervention in lieu of a jail sentence. This person has the right as a member of the legal system to be apprised of the client's progress and possibly to use the information in making future decisions about the client's legal status.

The change agent system. The person (or people) who is responsible for leadership and coordination of the change effort. This would include (and might be limited to) the social worker.

The client system. The primary and secondary beneficiaries of change. A primary beneficiary may be an individual, with the family or employer being a secondary beneficiary. Likewise, in cases of child abuse, a family might be a primary beneficiary with the community as the secondary beneficiary (in that a larger social problem is being addressed). The social worker does not always have contact with secondary beneficiaries during the change process.

The target system. What needs to be changed (an individual, family, group, organization, or community) for the intervention to be successful.

The action system. The people who will see the change effort through to completion. This would include the social worker but possibly other professionals and other significant people in the client system.

The professional system. Those professionals who are members of the social worker's agency or service network and who participate in the change effort. This includes the social worker's own agency and the ways in which its policies and procedures either facilitate or hamper the change effort.

Now that we are familiar with some basic professional terminology in generalist practice, we can move on to a topic that may account more than anything else for the distinctiveness of the social work profession—its values.

THE VALUE BASE OF SOCIAL WORK PRACTICE

All professions espouse distinct value bases that are intended to define their purposes and guide the actions of their members. *Values* are principles concerning what is right and good, or beliefs about the preferred conditions of life. *Ethics* are principles concerning what is right and correct, or rules of conduct to which a person should adhere in upholding his or her values (Dolgoff, Loewenberg, & Harrington, 2005). Values are the principles that define ethical behavior in professional situations. It is often said that professions are most clearly distinguished by their codes of ethics.

All people adhere to values. Shared values are necessary to the peaceful functioning of a society. We may adhere to several sets of values in different life roles, and these may be generally consistent with each other or sometimes conflicting. *Personal* values reflect our beliefs and preferences about what is right and good for an individual. *Societal* values reflect a consensus among members of a community that has been reached through negotiation, often politically, and reflect what is right and good for the group. These may be different from one's personal values. We maintain standards of behavior because of our membership in a society although we may not agree with them all. A person's values may also be inconsistent. For example, most people would agree that lying is unethical as a general rule, yet they may feel justified in lying at times to promote their individual interests.

Professional values specifically guide the work of a person in his or her professional life. Professional ethics are the obligations of a person in relationship with other people encountered in the course of work, including clients, other professionals, and the general public. Social work's values are intended to help practitioners recognize the morally correct way to practice and decide how to act correctly in any professional situation. The NASW Code of Ethics (1999) is intended to serve as a guide to the professional conduct of social workers. The primary mission of the social work profession, according to this code, is "to enhance the human well-being and help meet the basic human needs of all people, with particular attention to the needs and empowerment of those who are vulnerable, oppressed, and living in poverty" (p. 1). The six core values of the profession relate to *service, social justice, dignity and worth of the person, the importance of human relationships, integrity,* and *competence.* We will examine all of these core values in detail in this book.

Many value systems converge in social work practice—those of the society, its subcultures, the profession, the individual social worker, and the social worker's agency. *Agency values* emerge from its philosophy, mission, and funding sources. The social services agency needs to be concerned with its own survival as well as the status of its clients. Social work values may conflict at times with agency values (for example, with a different emphasis on the quality versus quantity of services), and also with the values of other professions within the agency. For example, social workers and physicians may have different perspectives about the value of client confidentiality or the value of nonmedical interventions.

Social work values need to be concretized for daily practice so that they take on practical meaning. Consistent support of these helps the social worker to improve the quality of life for clients.

Strengths-Based Practice

The strengths orientation to practice is an overarching value in the social work profession. It implies that practitioners should assess all clients in light of their capacities, talents, competencies, possibilities, visions, values, and hopes (Saleebey, 1996).

This perspective emphasizes human *resilience,* or the skills, abilities, knowledge, and insight that people accumulate over time as they struggle to surmount adversity and meet life challenges. It refers to the ability of clients to persist in spite of their difficulties. Strengths-based practice is evident when the social worker interacts collaboratively with a client, and both parties recognize their expertise in resolving a presenting challenge.

Dennis Saleebey (2002), the profession's foremost writer on this topic, asserts that social work (and other helping professions) has been historically guided by a *deficits* perspective that exists in opposition to humanistic values. This orientation encourages attention to *individual* rather than *ecological* accounts of psychosocial functioning, which is contrary to social work's person-in-environment perspective. Saleebey adds that several negative but still-dominant assumptions in social work practice need to be adjusted toward the development of a more "balanced" strengths perspective. These include notions that the person is the problem (rather than person-environment interactions) and that certain social conditions and interpersonal relationships are so toxic that they invariably lead to problems in functioning for people, families, groups, and communities.

Saleebey's work is constructive in offering positive concepts for social workers to use that will more adequately identify client strengths. The major principles of strengths practice include the following (Saleebey, 1996):

- All people have strengths.

- Problems can be a source of challenge and opportunity.

- Practitioners can never know the "upper levels" of clients' growth potentials.

- There should be greater collaboration between practitioners and clients, to replace the traditional worker–client hierarchy.

- Every environment includes many resources (many of them informal) that can be mobilized to help clients change.

Strengths-oriented social work practice mandates that social workers give attention to both the risk and protective influence in a client's life. Another concept closely related to strengths-oriented practice is *empowerment.*

Client Empowerment

In keeping with the profession's values and mission, social work practitioners desire to enhance the capacity, or *power,* of clients to address their life concerns (Lee, 2001). Power can be understood as including a positive sense of self-worth and competence, the ability to influence the course of one's life, the capacity to work with others to control aspects of public life, and an ability to access the mechanisms of public decision making. Many clients do not, or perceive that they do not, have power, either over themselves, their significant others, or the agencies and communities in which they reside. This sense of powerlessness underlies many problems in living. It can be internalized and lead to learned helplessness and alienation from one's community. An empowerment orientation to practice represents the social worker's efforts to combat the alienation, isolation, and poverty of content in clients' lives by positively influencing their sense of worth, sense of membership in a community, and ability to create change in their surroundings (Rose, 1990).

Empowerment incorporates three themes (Parsons, 1991). It is a *developmental* process that can be experienced along a continuum from individual growth to social change. Secondly, it is in part a *psychological state* characterized by feelings of self-esteem, efficacy, and control over one's life. Thirdly, it may involve a client's *liberation from oppression,* a process that begins with education and a politicization of his or her presenting problems. In every case of empowerment practice the social worker helps clients become aware of the tensions within themselves and their surroundings that oppress or limit them, and also helps them become better able to free themselves from those restraints.

Social workers may perceive this concept to be more relevant to practice with large systems (organizations and communities), but it has implications for intervention at *all* levels. From the person-in-environment perspective, even the most "individual" of problems, such as physical illness, have intervention implications that may include helping the client to create a more facilitative environment for recovery. In summary, clients may be empowered at a *personal* level (changing patterns of thinking, feeling, and behaving), an *interpersonal* level (managing their relationships more effectively), or perhaps a *political* level (changing their manner of interacting with larger systems) (Adams, 1996).

Ethical Dilemmas

Despite the existence of values in the profession, there is no "recipe" for ethical social work practice, and ethical dilemmas in social work practice are routine. These are situations in which "the social worker must choose between two or more relevant, but contradictory, ethical directives, or when every alternative results in an undesirable outcome for one or more persons" (Dolgoff, Loewenberg, & Harrington, 2005). Ethical dilemmas may at times cause the social worker great discomfort. Some common sources of ethical dilemmas include:

- Professional knowledge versus clients' rights (Who knows best?)
- Conflicting obligations to different members of the client system (an individual, family, employer, or referring agency)
- Conflicting obligations to the client and the social worker's agency
- The adequacy of "informed consent" practices (actively informing clients of their service choices, the possible benefits and limitations of each of them, and the right to refuse services)
- Truth telling even in the face of possible harm to a client (such as dealing with a parent's request that a child not be told about a serious illness he or she has)
- Confidentiality and its limits

- The need to distribute limited resources among many clients in an agency (time, services, financial support)
- The clash of the social worker's personal and professional values (strongly disapproving of a client's behaviors)
- Managing relationships with colleagues during disagreements about services to clients

The following questions may help the social worker resolve ethical concerns when they arise (Dolgoff, Loewenberg, & Harrington, 2005):

What are the specific ethical issues in this situation? Do I need other information to clarify the personal, professional, agency, and societal values that may be influencing the situation?

What criteria can I use to resolve the ethical dilemma? Is the NASW Code of Ethics sufficient, or does the value conflict persist even after reviewing the code?

Who should resolve the ethical problem? Should it be me, the client, a member of the client's family, another practitioner, or a supervisor?

Who should benefit from the resolution of an ethical situation when there is a conflict of interest? To whom am I most accountable?

What are the ethical consequences of the various options? What are the long-term as well as the short-term consequences? Which decision risks the least harm possible?

When a social worker experiences an ethical dilemma that cannot be satisfactorily resolved by reviewing the NASW Code of Ethics, he or she may refer to a personal *ethical values hierarchy* for guidance. This is a list of the practitioner's professional values, in order of their inviolability. It should be constructed only after careful reflection about one's personal and professional values, and it may be revised over the course of one's life. Included next are two examples of value hierarchies, the first based on the work of Reamer (1998) and the second taken from Dolgoff, Loewenberg, and Harrington (2005).

Values Hierarchy #1:

1. Client self-determination takes precedence over everything else, including basic well-being (when one is judged competent to make choices).
2. Physical health, well-being, and basic need-meeting take precedence over confidentiality.
3. One person's well-being takes precedence over another's privacy, freedom, and right to self-determination.
4. A client's right to well-being *may* override certain laws, policies, and agency procedures.

Values Hierarchy #2:

1. The protection of human life (food, shelter, income, health needs), including that of the client or anyone else, takes precedence over every other

obligation. Meeting the basic survival needs of individuals or social groups is primary.

2. Autonomy, independence, and freedom are of secondary importance. A person does not have the right to harm himself or anyone else as part of these values.

3. Equality of opportunity and equality of access for all people is vital.

4. Quality of life for all people takes precedence over the individual.

5. The client's right to privacy (confidentiality) cannot be excluded.

These two hierarchies are different, and it follows that their proponents would not make the same decisions when faced with certain ethical dilemmas. For example, a social worker using the first hierarchy (focusing on the first principle) might support a seriously ill client's end-of-life decision, or refuse to intervene when a physically ill homeless client refused shelter on a frigid winter's night. (Much more information would be needed about both these scenarios, of course.) Another social worker, using the second hierarchy, may not support any client's end-of-life decisions and may attempt to involuntarily detain the homeless client if it appeared that he or she was at risk of death.

Every social worker's professional value hierarchy is likely to be unique. Although it always needs to be based on the profession's code of ethics, it takes into account one's interpretation of those values in particular circumstances and the social worker's field of practice and expertise. It also reflects the practitioner's personal values to an extent, recognizing that these can never be completely separate from professional values. Throughout this book we will discuss a variety of ethical dilemmas and how they might be resolved.

Professional Value Principle: Service

In every chapter of this book we will review the six value principles highlighted in the NASW Code of Ethics (1999). We begin with a review of the *service* value. The related ethical principle states, "Social workers' primary goal is to help people in need and to address social problems" (p. 5). Social workers are ethically bound to place service to others above self-interest in the context of their work. They are also encouraged to engage in some professional volunteer service as a part of their career work.

The service value is an overarching one reflecting the profession's humanitarian basis. It is addressed specifically in some code principles but is implicit in all of them. For example, regarding their ethical responsibilities to clients social workers should set reasonable fees (when applicable), make reasonable efforts to ensure continuity of services, terminate services when they are no longer required, avoid abandoning clients who are still in need of services, and notify clients promptly when an interruption or termination of services must occur. Regarding responsibilities to the broader society, social workers should promote its general welfare at all levels, advocating for suitable living conditions for all people. They should facilitate citizen participation in shaping public policies and institutions, provide service during public emergencies, and engage in social and political action that supports the purpose of the profession. Social workers should support high standards of practice. Their services should be of the highest possible quality with regard to helping client systems meet their goals.

CHARACTERISTICS OF EFFECTIVE PRACTICE

To conclude this overview of generalist practice, we step back and look more broadly at the characteristics of effective practice across all forms of intervention and all client populations. Several authors have conducted literature reviews to identify these trans-theoretical and cross-cultural factors. Most of these apply to work with individuals, families, and groups, but they underscore the importance of relationship development regardless of the level of intervention. In a world-wide study of professional helpers, Frank and Frank (1993) identified the following factors that seem common to all effective interventions:

- *The client perceives that the practitioner is competent and caring.* Their relationship enhances the client's morale, and promotes the determination to persist in the face of difficulties.

- *The setting of the intervention sometimes includes elements that arouse the client's expectation of help.* This also refers to the social worker's personal presentation to the client, especially because many practitioners work in noisy, crowded, and Spartan surroundings. An example of this factor is the parent who visits his child's school guidance counselor. The counselor's office, with book-lined shelves and degrees on the wall, inspires the parent's confidence in that professional.

- *Interventions are based on a rationale and procedures that include an optimistic view of human nature.* The practitioner's explanations are compatible with the client's view of the world and in that way help the client make sense of his or her problems.

- *Interventions require the active participation of the practitioner and client,* both of whom believe them to be a valid means of improving functioning. The client is provided with new opportunities for success experiences to enhance his or her sense of mastery. The intervention demands effort from the client.

Two social work authors have also looked at cross-cultural factors in effective human service practice (Harper & Lantz, 2007). They specify that the nature of client empowerment derives from the development of self-understanding, opportunities to use physical interventions (medications) when indicated, enhanced social networks, the capacity to affect the environment through social action, enhanced self-management capability, and the acquisition of social skills. All of these outcomes are within the purview of generalist social work practice.

SUMMARY

In this chapter we have covered much ground in reviewing the nature of social work and generalist practice, the relationship of practice theory to generalist practice, the various roles of the social work practitioner, and the value base of the profession. What should be evident is the broad sweep of the social work profession and the many opportunities for the generalist practitioner to affect the social functioning of clients as well as the functioning of organizational and community systems. While the scope of generalist practice may appear daunting, we now embark on the task of studying a variety of practice models, theories, and intervention strategies that will bring a focus to practice, and make the process manageable.

TOPICS FOR DISCUSSION

1. Is it possible to be a skilled generalist practitioner at all five levels of intervention? Why or why not?
2. What does the social worker mean who says, "I don't use any practice theories. I just do what works for my clients."
3. What are some ways that clients in different types of human service agencies are treated so that they are *not* empowered?
4. All people have qualities and limitations, good points and not-so-good points. Why do you think that social workers (and many other human services professionals) did *not* practice from a strengths perspective prior to the 1980s?
5. How might social workers attend to a client's spirituality in ways that are helpful and harmful? How can the social worker exercise appropriate caution when addressing this area of a client's life?

ASSIGNMENT IDEAS

1. Interview social workers in their agencies about which intervention theories they use, and why.
2. Ask other class members to identify any ethical dilemmas they have experienced or observed as university students. How were they, or would they be, conflicted about how to deal with these dilemmas? How did they, or might they, resolve the dilemma?
3. Select someone you know personally, and write as much as you can about the biological, psychological, social, and spiritual aspects of the person's life. Is it difficult to distinguish between any of these four aspects of functioning? Are any of the four aspects easier to document? If so, why?

Chapter 2

Problem Solving in Generalist Social Work Practice

It was emphasized in the last chapter that social work intervention should be a thoughtful, systematic process. This requires an understanding of practice theory and a capacity to use intervention strategies in a disciplined manner. Practice should never be a random process in which the social worker looks at each situation in isolation or makes decisions purely on what "feels" right (although feelings and self-awareness certainly have a role in practice). In this chapter the problem-solving approach to practice is introduced, an approach that underlies all of the intervention strategies that follow. That is, regardless of the specific practice theory that a social worker might use, his or her thinking should follow the logic of the problem-solving approach. Problem-solving theory has an extensive history in the social work profession (Turner & Jaco, 1996). The profession has moved in recent years from a focus on problems to a focus on solutions, but the approach presented here incorporates attention to client strengths and potentials. Along with the logic of problem solving we will consider the nature of stress and coping, and the types of problems that generalist practitioners address.

PROBLEMS IN LIVING

Before we focus on problem *solving,* it is important to consider how the social work profession conceptualizes the problem *experience.* Remember that, with its systems perspective, social work focuses not on people but on transactions—their relationships and interactions with their environments. The purpose of social

work is in fact to facilitate better matches between people and their environments (Karls, 2002). The PIE figure in Chapter   illustrates this process.
Problems represent imbalances between the demands on people and their ability
to meet those demands. The social worker's interventions may of course be
more focused on the person or the environment, depending on his or her desig-
nated role in an agency and the nature of available resources. While all problems
in living are transactional, they can be conceptualized as resulting more from *external pressures* (a primarily environmental focus), *ineffective personal functioning* (in-
dicating the needs of people, families, or groups to acquire greater coping capacities), or normal stresses that accompany *life or role transitions* (Germain &
Gitterman, 1996).

Any list of life transitions is arbitrary, but the social work profession generally
considers that the stages listed next create adjustment demands that may result in
problems in living for people (Germain & Gitterman, 1996). This first list represents critical developmental stages of life:

Infancy (early attachments and a nurturing environment)

Preschool (first experience leaving home)

Primary school age (socialization)

Early teens (separation from family, peer influences)

Late teens (identity formation)

Early adulthood (establishing life direction, making relationship
    commitments)

Middle adulthood (changing life course)

Early old age (easing away from career and other necessary commitments,
    putting more energy into personal interests)

Later old age (managing physical and perhaps cognitive limitations)

This second list includes less predictable role transitions that may create either
transient or long-term stress:

Work changes	Single parenthood	Death of partner, significant others
Career changes	Widowhood	
Marriage/Partnering	Post-parenthood	Institutionalization (prison, hospital, nursing home)
Parenthood	Retirement	
Moving	Managing health issues	
Separation/Divorce		

These lists are intended to illustrate that problems in living are ubiquitous in
normal human development. People who experience these life stage stresses are
not inadequate in any fundamental way. The concept of role functioning helps
to explain how people who must make adjustments in their social roles are always challenged to implement new behaviors associated with those roles. Some
people manage role transitions more successfully than others do, but this may be

due to their available supports. Generalist social work practitioners should consider in their assessments that many presenting problems are partially caused or complicated by these transition points.

STRESS AND COPING STYLES

Problems by definition are discomforting and produce stress to which the affected person or system must respond with reparative efforts. *Stress* can be defined as any event in which environmental demands, internal demands, or both tax or exceed the adaptive resources of an individual or system (Lazarus, 1999). Stress may be *biological* (a disturbance in the body's systems, such as the experience of a physical disease), *psychological* (cognitive and emotional factors that are involved in the evaluation of a threat, such as excessive worrying about one's safety), or *social* (the disruption of a social unit, such as the closing down of a community organization that employs many people). Anxiety, guilt, shame, sadness, envy, jealousy, and disgust are sometimes characterized as "stress emotions."

Three Categories of Stress

Stress can be broken down into the categories of harm, threat, and challenge (Lazarus & Lazarus, 1994). *Harm* refers to an event that has already occurred to a person or system in which some damage has been done. An example is a person losing his job due to company downsizing. *Threat* is probably the most common form of psychological stress. In this condition a person or group perceives a potential for harm, but such an event has not yet happened. Stress is experienced because the people involved are apprehensive about the possibility of the negative event. People can of course be proactive in managing threats so they are less likely to occur and result in harm. An example is the person who is concerned about losing his job because of the threat of cutbacks by agency administration. The event has not, and may not, happen, but the possibility creates high anxiety for the employee. *Challenge* consists of the appraisal of possibly negative events as opportunities rather than occasions for alarm. The person or system is mobilized to struggle against the obstacle, as with a threat, but the attitude is quite different. In the former situation the person is apt to act defensively to protect the self. The person does not want to change. In a state of challenge, however, the person or people are excited, expansive, and confident about the task to be undertaken. The challenge may be perceived as a productive experience. An example is the employee who has some concerns about losing his job, but this concern serves as a motivating factor to seek an alternative career about which the person is excited.

Lazarus emphasizes that stress is not so much an outcome of an event, but a transactional process that is dependent on the characteristics of the people and the environment. *Coping* can be defined as efforts to manage the demands of stress, and includes the thoughts, feelings, and actions that constitute those efforts (Lazarus, 1993). Stress management may require adjustments in lifestyle, perceptions, or one's physical condition.

Biological Coping

The body seeks to maintain physical equilibrium, or a steady state of functioning (Selye, 1991). According to Selye, stress is less transactional than a consequence of any demand on the body (specifically, the nervous and hormonal systems) that occurs during perceived emergencies to prepare for fight (confrontation) or flight (escape). A stressor may be any physical process, emotion, or thought that calls forth the *general adaptation syndrome*. This includes the stages of alarm (when the body first becomes aware of a threat), followed by resistance (which signifies the body's efforts to restore homeostasis) and exhaustion (the body's termination of coping efforts due to its inability to sustain the state of disequilibrium). In this context, resistance has a different meaning than is generally used in social work. It is an active, positive response of the body in which endorphins and specialized cells of the immune system fight off stress and infection. The immune system is constructed for adaptation to stress, but there is a cumulative wear and tear after each stress episode that can gradually deplete the body's resources. Common outcomes of chronic stress include stomach and intestinal disorders, high blood pressure, heart problems, and emotional problems. For this reason, among others, stress must be combated and prevented to preserve healthy physical functioning. People who cannot access basic resources for living, such as food, housing, clothing, and medical care, and who are at risk for certain medical conditions are particularly at risk for physical illness that test the body's ability to cope.

Psychological Coping

Psychological coping, which involves a person's thinking, emotional processing, and behaviors, is considered by some theorists to be a stable personality characteristic (or trait), and by others as a process that changes over time depending on the stress context (a transient state) (Lazarus, 1993). The first perspective sees coping as an acquired cognitive style of information processing. Cognitive distortions, described in Chapter 6, are automatic responses that enable people to minimize perceived threats and sometimes keep them out of awareness entirely. Cognitive distortions may be adaptive or maladaptive depending on the extent to which they promote or impede our quality of functioning. It must be emphasized, too, that there are always environmental reasons for these responses.

The second perspective sees psychological coping as a process, which is consistent with a systems view of social functioning. Coping strategies by individuals, families, groups, agencies, and communities change in different situations because perceptions of threats, and what becomes the point of focus in a situation, change. For example, if a neighborhood restaurant discriminates against people of color, an African American resident may choose to cope with that issue in several ways. If he perceives the neighborhood to be generally supportive of equal rights, he may organize a small group to confront the restaurant owner. If he perceives the neighborhood to be nonsupportive, he may maintain a position of less visibility by working through legal channels or avoiding the restaurant entirely. It should be evident that the context of the stress situation has an impact on people's perceived and actual abilities to apply effective coping mechanisms. The trait and state approaches can be combined to summarize coping as having *both* components, or featuring a general pattern that may incorporate some flexibility across diverse contexts.

Coping Styles

The previous example demonstrates how one's coping efforts may be *problem focused* or *emotion focused* (Lazarus, 1999). The function of problem-focused coping is to change the problem situation by acting on the environment (such as developing assertiveness skills so that a person's needs can be more clearly communicated). This method may be most effective when a person views situations as controllable by action. The function of emotion-focused coping is to change either the way the stressful situation is attended to (by vigilance or avoidance) or the meaning to oneself of what is happening (such as dealing with the presence of gang members at school by keeping away from them). The external situation does not change, but a person's behaviors or attitudes change with respect to it, and he or she may thus effectively manage the stressor. When stressful conditions are assessed as unchangeable, emotion-focused coping may be a more appropriate strategy.

There is a tendency in our culture to venerate problem-focused coping and the independently functioning self, and to distrust emotion-focused and relational coping. From the relational perspective, a person's coping ideas take into account actions that maximize the survival of others as well as the self, such as families, children, and friends (Banyard & Graham-Bermann, 1993). Feminist theorists propose that women are more likely to employ the relational coping strategies of negotiation and forbearance. Social workers must be careful, then, not to assume that one type of coping is generally superior to the other.

Lazarus (1993) has outlined a set of coping styles reflecting each of the functions noted (see Figure 2.1). These include confronting the stressor and engaging in proactive problem solving (both problem-focused); distancing oneself from, or ignoring, the stress; physical or psychological strategies to escape or avoid the

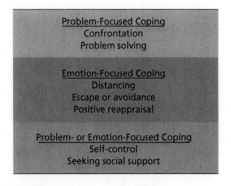

Problem-Focused Coping
Confrontation
Problem solving

Emotion-Focused Coping
Distancing
Escape or avoidance
Positive reappraisal

Problem- or Emotion-Focused Coping
Self-control
Seeking social support

FIGURE 2.1 Coping Styles

stress; and positive reappraisal of the stress as growth-enhancing (emotion-focused). Other styles include learning to control one's feelings and seeking social support (which may be problem- or emotion-focused, depending on the context). All people utilize any or several of these mechanisms at different times. None of them characterizes any person's sole means of managing stress.

You are certainly aware that college students face many predictable stresses when attending to the demands of academic work. A few years ago I wanted to learn more about how my social work students used problem- and emotion-focused coping styles in responding to stress. I surveyed undergraduate social work students in several practice courses at the midpoint of an academic year about their stresses, the probable effects of those stresses, and how they coped with them. The results of this informal survey are summarized in Table 2.1 (although I can't be sure that they were completely open about their coping responses that involved misbehavior). I have categorized the students' coping strategies into problem- and emotion-focused styles. It should be apparent from this table that both types of coping were selected almost equally and indicated (mostly) healthy planning on the part of the students.

T A B L E 2.1   Stress and Coping Among Social Work Students

Source of Stress	Effect of Stress
Academic demands	Physical
Computers	Ulcers
Classroom demands	Other physical illnesses
Field placement demands	Poor eating habits and feeling "sluggish"
Pressure for grades	Psychological
Managing group projects	Irritability
Assignments and deadlines	Anxiety, panic
Money concerns	Poor concentration
Relationships	Depression
Relationship strain	Guilt
Less time with family	Insomnia
Less attention to marriage	Procrastination
Planning my wedding	Chronic tension, pressure
Lack of sufficient time	Rumination
Role overload	Social
Driving/Parking	Tension due to relationship problems
Wear and tear on car	Poor academic performance
Time spent looking for parking spaces	Isolation
Professional job search concerns	Life becomes no fun
Personal concerns	No time for recreation
Attention to personal interests	No time to socialize
Personal problems	
Conflicts with peers	
Unanticipated stress events	

Coping Strategies

Confrontation
  Learning to say "no"
Distancing
  Denial
  Procrastination
Self-control
  Pushing too hard
  Bearing down and "gut it out"
  Taking on a job
Escape-Avoidance
  Drinking
  Smoking
  Giving up
  Venting to others
  Overeating, under-eating
  Cursing at other drivers
  Watching too much television
  Neglecting significant others
  Caffeine
  Neglecting other important concerns
  Isolation
  Using charge cards
  All-night study sessions
Positive reappraisal
  Money produced by one's job
  Maintain perspective ("It will end soon")
  Reframe frustrations as growth opportunities ("I can learn to deal with pressure")
  (Items from other categories may apply)

Seek social support
  Talking
  Intimacy
  Sex
  Processing the day with others
  Therapy
  Networking with others
  Demanding support from others
  Reserving time with family
Accepting responsibility
  Crying (possibly)
Problem solving
  Exercise
  Working with other students
  Talking with professors
  Going to the beach (for relaxation)
  Time management
  Proper self-care
  Reserving time for self
  Staying ahead
  Relaxation techniques
  Walking
  Cleaning the house
  Carrying own lunch (to save money)
  Good nutrition
  Taking breaks
  Looking for "free" social activities
  Pursuing art interests
  Task organization
  Careful budgeting of finances
  Planning for a job search
  Developing flexibility

Now that we have considered the issues of stress and coping styles, we move into the topic of the problem-solving process that can be used by social work practitioners.

THE PROBLEM-SOLVING PROCESS

Social workers are in the business of helping clients to solve problems (or, put another way, to resolve challenges). It is thus imperative that the generalist social worker adopts a model of problem solving that can guide his or her thinking about practice situations at all levels. Problem solving is an orderly, systematic means of evaluating concerns, formulating problems, and seeking solutions. It is a skill that people implement frequently in their everyday lives.

A *problem* can be defined as a stimulus situation for which a person does not have a ready response (Meacham & Emont, 1989). The person must experience a feeling of discomfort with the situation as a means of generating motivation to resolve it. Problem resolution may be difficult when there are significant obstacles to the person's response. It may require a *creative interpretation* of situations and possibilities. In fact, many problems persist because people rely on old, repetitive solution patterns ("ruts") that are no longer functional. Successful problem solving at all levels of generalist practice involves a breaking out of patterns that impede appropriate problem definition or the discovery of new solutions. The underlying assumptions of problem solving are as follows (McClam & Woodside, 1994):

- Problems are routinely experienced by all people.

- Problem solving is a structured but not always linear process, and it is not culture-bound.

- Problems often have more than one solution.

- People can learn to be more effective problem solvers.

- Problem solving may be interrupted due to personal and environmental factors or changing life circumstances.

- Teaching effective problem-solving skills empowers clients by producing both immediate and long-term benefits.

The Roles of Critical Thinking and Creativity

The activities of critical thinking and creativity are integral to the problem-solving process. *Critical thinking* is thinking that is purposeful, reasonable, goal directed, and evaluative of its outcomes (Gambrill, 1990). It is a process in which a person reflects on the assumptions that underlie his or her thoughts and actions and considers alternative perspectives. Critical thinking is characterized by flexibility, persistence when solutions are not obvious, and a willingness to plan and self-correct. It is not easy because it requires that a person question his or her knowledge and values, and take risks to think differently.

Effective problem solving also requires creativity to produce imaginative and innovative solutions. *Creativity* refers to a person's ability to generate diverse and original ideas for resolving problems (Lubart & Mouchiroud, 2003). Problem solving, while systematic, should not be perceived as a rigid process but as a means to facilitate a person's thinking "outside the box." There are four aspects of creative thinking that are helpful to problem solving. *Content knowledge* refers to the base of knowledge that is relevant to a problem. *Divergent* thinking is the ability to entertain or generate new ideas from that knowledge base. *Critical analysis,* discussed earlier, is the ability to separate promising from unpromising solutions and consider alternatives. *Communication skills* include the ability to make others clear about the product of one's problem solving.

For the social worker, using creativity in problem solving means encouraging clients to look beyond the boundaries of their personal, social, and cultural conventions and being open to adopting new ideas. There is no particular virtue in doing things the way they have always been done. Of course, the social worker needs to be aware of this as well in his or her practice!

Before moving on, let's summarize the characteristics of the creative and critical thinker:

- A willingness to question basic assumptions

- Continual efforts to be objective (looking for supporting *and* opposing evidence for ideas)

- Specificity in asking questions

- The ability to imagine and explore alternative ways of thinking

- An understanding of the importance of social and cultural context in addressing concerns

- Distinguishing between questions of fact and questions of value (facts can be identified with research but values pertain to beliefs and feelings)

- Caution about inferring causality or making generalizations from one situation to others (as this may promote rigidity)

THE PROBLEM-SOLVING MODEL
OF GENERALIST PRACTICE

Problem solving is an orderly, systematic means of evaluating a client system's concerns, formulating problems, setting goals, and implementing strategies to achieve those goals (Turner & Jaco, 1996). It requires the client and social worker's attention to the following steps.

Problem Identification and Exploration

The social worker and client should always consider the validity and reliability of all information in making decisions about the nature and causes of the problem. The social worker and client also must:

Elicit a problem statement from the referring system, which may be the client or some other source

Consider accounts of the problem from different perspectives, if available, including members of the client system, the referral source, and any significant others

Use input from the above sources to formulate a focused problem statement with the client (processes of assessment will be described in later chapters of this book)

Determine whether it is appropriate for the social worker and client system to work together, based on the nature of the agency program and the social worker's areas of expertise

Maintain a strengths perspective about members of the client system throughout this process

Planning for Problem Resolution

The social worker and client identify the most critical problem areas and the resources that can be devoted to their resolution. Then the social worker sets one or more goals with the client, specifies points of intervention, considers a range of intervention strategies that may be utilized for goal attainment, including their benefits and limitations, and develops a concrete plan for intervention, selecting change indicators that can be identified and monitored.

Implementation of the Plan

The social worker and client access the resources and services to be used, carry out the resource activities as noted in the intervention plan, and ensure that the responsible parties (client, social worker, and perhaps others) carry out their assigned activities.

Evaluation of the Plan

The social worker and client determine the intervention's *effectiveness* (outcome) and *efficiency* (required time and effort), and either end the intervention or develop a new plan of action.

Problem solving in generalist practice may be directed toward individuals, families, groups, organizations, or community environments. Ideally, the social worker and client focus on the system that is most accessible to change within the constraints of their mutual expertise and the mission and programs of the employing organization.

A "PROBLEM" FOCUS VERSUS
A "SOLUTION" FOCUS

We need to address one of the criticisms of problem solving—that the social work profession has moved away from a problem focus toward a strengths and solution focus in its philosophy of intervention. In fact, these two approaches are not contradictory. People routinely experience problems, and social work clients seek services because they are facing problems or challenges. We emphasize here that in problem solving, strengths and solutions need to be highlighted, and that people can be helped to become better problem solvers. Thus, problem-focused and strengths-oriented social work are not dichotomous, but complementary (McMillen, Morris, & Sherraden, 2004). Our focus on strengths and solutions should be apparent in our discussions of practice throughout the book.

Having considered the steps of the problem-solving process, we now turn more fully to the elements of assessment and goal setting, which occur during the first two stages of that process. In Part III of this book we will introduce more specific assessment models that are applicable to each of the five levels of intervention.

CLIENT SYSTEM ASSESSMENT

Assessment is a process in which the social worker gathers, analyzes, and synthesizes information about a prospective client system into a problem and needs formulation. It is the first activity of the generalist practitioner when he or she encounters a new client system. Only after the initial assessment does the social worker know whether the *prospective* client system will become an *actual* one. The social worker needs to complete the assessment to decide, among other things, whether the prospective client's concerns match the goals and capacities of the service setting as well as the skills and knowledge of the social worker. If so, the social worker and client may proceed to formulate goals and objectives and undertake the intervention process. Assessments are equally important for small (individuals, families, or groups) and larger (agency-based and community interventions) client systems. In fact, the decision about what level of intervention to pursue is ideally one outcome of assessment, regardless of the nature of the presenting client system. That is, the social worker and client may conclude that the client's concerns may best be met with a group or community intervention. Still, as we have pointed out, the agency mission and social worker's job description may limit choices about the level of intervention in advance of an assessment.

Goals of the Initial Social Worker–Client Meeting

During the initial assessment the social worker should attempt to build a constructive rapport with the client system. This can be achieved through empathy—trying to understand what it is like to be the client and see situations through the client's eyes—and by promoting a sense of partnership, or shared sense of responsibility for addressing the client's concerns. Another task for the social worker and client is to decide who should ideally comprise the client system. For example, should it be an individual intervention? Will it involve family members? Is there a group of people from the client's home or work environment who may be appropriately involved? Will any agencies be involved in the process, such as a school? Will the social worker be contacting anyone from the community to help secure necessary resources for the client? Finally, the social worker and client should try to speculate about the anticipated length of the intervention, recognizing that this could change as the work proceeds.

Components of Problem Assessment

In generalist assessment the social worker should always be concerned with the status of the client system in the following areas (Germain & Gitterman, 1996):

The concern as presented by the client system. The perspectives of any referral sources, other professionals, and significant others are important, but to support the values of empowerment and self-determination the client's own perspective should take priority during the initial stages of intervention. This may later be negotiated among the relevant other people involved.

The impact of environmental factors on the presenting situation, such as the family, social networks, other service providers, social institutions, and community characteristics. The client system may or may not be sensitive to the influence of these factors, so the social worker may need to help the client explore them.

Developmental stage of the client system. While it is usually acknowledged that individuals, families, and groups move through certain stages through the life cycle, it is also true that organizations and communities evolve over time. They may, for example, be challenged to respond to predictable changes in size, bureaucracy, staff composition, and mission.

Any significant role transitions. These were described in Chapter and include moving into adolescence or adulthood, becoming a parent, beginning a career, moving from one location to another, losing parents, and so on. Developmental needs and life transitions are important to assess because the client's presenting issues may directly result from efforts to adjust to one of these.

Sources of Assessment Information

When conducting an assessment, the social worker may rely on one person's input or utilize a variety of information sources, although client confidentiality must always be respected. Appropriate sources may include (Murphy & Dillon, 2003):

- Verbal reports from members of the client system (other individuals, the family, or relevant groups)
- Collateral information from referral sources and past service providers
- Formal assessment instruments available through the social worker's agency

- The social worker's observations of the client's interactions with significant others when in the social worker's company

- The client's self-monitoring of his or her own behaviors (as requested by the social worker)

All of these may be useful sources of information, but the social worker must always evaluate their validity. It is generally useful to access more than one source of information to minimize the possibility of informant bias. Archival information (records from previous providers) is useful, especially about matters of fact (demographic information), but the social worker should always approach a new client system with an open mind and avoid the danger of forming impressions in advance of meeting the members of the client system.

Because assessments are always expected to conclude with an intervention plan, we will now consider some principles of goal setting and contracts. Goal statements must be articulated prior to intervention.

GOAL SETTING AND CONTRACTS

The purpose of articulating intervention goals is to specify what the client wishes to accomplish, and how the client and social worker will know when those outcomes have been achieved (Murphy & Dillon, 2003). Goals may be short-term (including one-time actions such as determining client eligibility for a public support program) or longer-term (ongoing participation in a community recreational center development project). The functions of establishing goals are to:

- Assure social worker–client agreement about the work to be done

- Provide direction to the helping process

- Facilitate the selection of interventions

- Help the worker and client monitor their work over time

- Provide evaluation criteria for how thoroughly, or how efficiently, the goal has been achieved

It is often useful to specify one or more objectives with each goal (the concrete steps that indicate progress toward the goal). All goals should be written down and the document shared when possible, so that all parties are clear about them.

Guidelines for Goal Selection and Definition

When constructing goals and objectives, the social worker and client should attend to the following issues, which are consistent with the problem-solving and cognitive–behavioral perspectives on generalist practice (Franklin & Corcoran, 2003):

A collaborative process to promote the client's motivation and hope for success. Goals should reflect the client's action potential, not that of the social worker. "I will learn new methods of child discipline" implies that the client will be active in the process, although tasks to achieve that goal will also reflect, for example, the social worker's teaching role.

Focusing on goals that are realistic and attainable. A foster parent who has problems with child discipline may want to "eliminate conflict in the household," but a more appropriate goal might be to "learn and use new methods of behavior control."

The client's motivation to work toward a particular goal, with regard to interest, resources, and capability. Does the client in fact want to learn new behavior control methods? Perhaps he or she thinks that existing methods are appropriate, but that a children's service agency is pressuring them to change.

Specific, measurable objectives. These may include overt (observable) and covert (thoughts, feelings) targets. One objective for our foster parent might be to increase the child's presence at the family dinner table (which he has been avoiding due to conflict) from two to five times per week.

Stating goals and objectives in positive terms, with a strengths orientation. The client should work toward something positive rather than move away from something negative. This is why the previous goal was not stated as, for example, "a reduction in arguments."

Possibly including significant others (parents, partners, friends, coworkers, other agency staff) in the process. The children's services worker might be a useful participant in the goal-setting process because she will be monitoring the foster parent's household.

Consistency of goals with practitioner's capability and the agency's functions. Quite simply, the social worker should have the experience, credentials, and resources to work toward the client's goal. If the agency rarely works with families, and another agency across town does so routinely, it might be appropriate for the social worker to make a referral. But this issue is a tough one because social workers also have a professional responsibility to expand their expertise to meet the varying needs of their clients.

The social worker should make sure that the client is clear about the terms included in each goal and related objective. Sometimes practitioners are prone to using broad terminology ("increase independence") rather than practical language ("secure own apartment"). The social worker should also discuss the potential risks as well as benefits of working toward goals, since they may require risk-taking by the client. A community organization that wishes to develop an older adult services facility should be aware of any risks for failure or loss of funding for existing programs (that is, establishing a new program may require the downsizing of another one). Finally, the social worker should try to acquire some concrete measures of a problem situation prior to intervention to establish a comparison point for monitoring goal attainment. If a school system is concerned about the problem behavior of a bully, the social worker should know as specifically as possible what kind of "bullying" behavior has occurred, as well as its duration and frequency. Any increase in positive behaviors will thus provide evidence of goal attainment. The client can provide this information through self-report or self-monitoring, or the social worker might rely on other sources for this information as described earlier.

Contracts

A contract is a written agreement between a social worker and client system about their plans for working together, including goals and objectives (Maguire, 2002). It is not a legal document, but a formal means of focusing the work that follows. Contracts should specify the roles of the participants and establish the conditions of intervention. There are many types of contracts used in agencies. Some are quite lengthy, others are brief, and other working agreements are not written down at all. In general the elements of a thorough contract include:

- Statement of the presenting problems, challenges, or needs
- Statement of goals and objectives
- Roles of participants
- Interventions to be employed
- Time frame, frequency, length of meetings
- Means of monitoring client progress toward goal attainment
- Stipulations for renegotiation

A sample client contract is included in Figure 2.2. We will see other examples in the coming chapters that are more specific to client system levels.

Moving away from the issue of problem solving, we conclude this chapter with a discussion of another value principle from the NASW Code of Ethics.

VALUE PRINCIPLE: SOCIAL JUSTICE

According to the NASW Code of Ethics (1999), social workers "promote social justice and social change with and on behalf of clients" (p. 1). The ethical principle corresponding to this value states that "social workers challenge social injustice" (p. 5), and that they do so "with and on behalf of vulnerable and oppressed individuals and groups of people. Social change efforts are focused primarily on issues of poverty, unemployment, discrimination, and other forms of social injustice." Social workers support all people's access to information, services, re-

Problem areas
1. _____
2. _____

Goals
1. _____
2. _____

Objectives (include time frames)
1. _____
2. _____

Skills/Capabilities to develop
1. _____
2. _____

Anticipated obstacles
1. _____
2. _____

Intervention modality (include frequency)
1. _____
2. _____

FIGURE 2.2 Sample Intervention Plan/Client Contract

sources, equality of opportunity, and participation in decision making in areas that affect their lives.

The social justice value is explicitly addressed in several of the code's ethical standards. In their ethical responsibilities as professionals, social workers should not practice or condone any form of discrimination. This standard has direct implications for social workers in their interactions with clients and coworkers at every level of practice. It also recognizes the responsibility of social workers to combat discrimination in their own agencies. This ethical standard is a serious mandate, because discrimination occurs in many subtle forms, often unintentionally, and the social worker may sometimes be in the uncomfortable position of needing to confront coworkers, supervisors, and other agency staff about such practices.

Consider the following example. Marwood Counseling Center was an outpatient mental health facility that for the first 10 years of its existence provided services to primarily middle-class adolescents and adults with nonpsychotic emotional problems. After policy and funding changes in the regional public mental health system, however, a growing number of people with severe mental illnesses such as schizophrenia were referred to the agency. The direct service practitioners were uncomfortable with these changes because of their preferences for long-term psychotherapy interventions that were not feasible with the new client population. The changes prompted many spirited but respectful discussions among staff about the future and appropriate mission of the agency.

The executive director became concerned that the clients with serious mental illnesses, who were sometimes unkempt in appearance and hygiene, were offensive in the waiting room to many of the traditional clients. He perceived that the new clients were negatively affecting demand for agency services by the "traditional" client groups and that service requests from private-pay clients were decreasing. His solution was to open a separate waiting room for the clients with serious mental illnesses in a comfortable annex that was located behind the main agency building. Most staff felt that this was appropriate due to the agency's needs to satisfy several types of clients and to meet its budget demands.

One social worker, however, saw this "separate but equal" strategy as demeaning to the newer clients. Not only were the "less attractive" clients kept out of sight, but over time the quality of the new waiting room deteriorated, as it did not seem to get the same attention from agency support staff as the primary waiting room. The social worker confronted the director privately about the matter, not questioning his motives but pointing out that a discriminatory practice had inadvertently occurred. The situation was amended in her favor, with more resources being allocated to the new area, but it alienated the social worker somewhat from her peers and the director. It could not be denied that the economic future of the agency required attention, and separating the waiting rooms might have been only a short-term solution to the perceived problem. But she had attended to her ethical need to combat discrimination and uphold social justice values.

Regarding their ethical responsibilities to the broader society, social workers should promote the general welfare of citizens at all levels, local to global. They should advocate as professionals and also in their personal lives for living conditions that promote the fulfillment of basic needs for all people and are compatible with social justice along social, economic, political, and cultural lines. As an example of this value, many social workers (as well as private citizens) in my city of residence serve as volunteers in relief efforts for victims of the hurricanes that occasionally pass through the area, damaging homes and businesses. Social workers should also engage in political action as appropriate to their jobs and their personal interests to promote standards of social justice. An example of this practice, also from my hometown (a state capital), is the participation of many social workers in the activities of the NASW political action committee, Mental Health Association, and other formal groups that lobby state senators to increase mental health funding for services to children. Such action should promote all people's access to resources, choice, and opportunities.

Social workers have a mandate to promote social justice, but they do not have a mandate to become political activists in the sense that these activities consume their personal lives. Like all people, social workers have different talents and interests, and they will be differentially inclined to participate in political life. However, they must always be alert for situations in their work and personal lives where social injustices exist and support initiatives that combat them. We must recognize, too, that at times people may reasonably disagree on what social justice means in a given situation. As discussed in Chapter , ethical dilemmas abound in one's work and can often be resolved only after much reflection and consultation.

SUMMARY

Social workers are professional problem solvers. As they help client systems articulate their problems or challenges they identify needs and also strengths, including the unique resources that derive from clients' cultural backgrounds. Social workers consider normal role transitions and human developmental processes in understanding how problems develop in people's lives, maintaining flexibility in assessing how people experience these challenges. Social workers are aware that stress can be biological, psychological, or social, and that coping strategies vary depending on the client system and the environment. Finally, social workers maintain their value perspective, including the principle of social justice, when assessing problems and helping clients formulate solutions. The process of problem solving is empowering in nature, helping client systems improve their abilities to resolve problems they may face in the future.

With this introduction to the problem-solving process, we turn in the next chapter to a consideration of the development of positive social worker–client relationships, which is a prerequisite to any constructive problem solving.

TOPICS FOR DISCUSSION

1. List examples in two columns of common types of stress that people may experience, based on whether they seem to be primarily biological or psychological in origin. Afterwards, discuss how many of these stresses can overlap the two categories.

2. Discuss a work situation (in contrast to the school-related situations included in the chapter) and describe the kinds of common problems that may occur there for employees. What kinds of situations may require problem-focused or emotion-focused responses, and why?

3. A person's capacity for critical thinking appears to be a positive characteristic. What are possible disincentives to the practice of critical thinking? Discuss whether human service organizations tend to encourage or discourage critical thinking.

4. The problem-solving process represents a structured, rational method of addressing problems. What other ways might people address their problems in living? Use several examples of life transition issues in responding to this question.

5. Discuss a situation at your university that may reflect a social injustice to some subgroup of students. How might social workers respond to this

situation? Do you believe that social work students or faculty have a professional responsibility to respond? Why or why not? What ethical concerns
may arise in addressing these issues?

ASSIGNMENT IDEAS

1. Select a problem in living related to a life transition that is predictable for
    many people. Devise a prevention strategy for helping people anticipate and
    thus cope more effectively with that problem than they otherwise might.

2. Select a client (or other acquaintance) with whom you have discussed a
    significant (to him or her) problem of some type. Write about the nature of
    stress that the person experienced and his or her coping style. Describe
    whether the specific coping practices were productive toward the person's
    problem resolution. Might an alternative coping strategy have been more
    productive for him or her?

3. Select another client or acquaintance for whom you have attempted to help
    solve a significant problem. Describe how you could have used the
    problem-solving model of generalist practice to help the person solve the
    problem. As a part of this exercise, write a tentative client contract for
    dealing with the problem.

Chapter 3

Relationships with Client Systems

There is a great emphasis in generalist practice on such activities as client empowerment, service linkage, and advocacy, but these should not obscure the primary importance of the social worker's relationship development skills. In any relationship with a client system the social worker must have the ability to form an attachment and earn the client's trust. The purpose of this chapter is not to introduce relationship-building skills, but to review some special challenges that emerge in social work interactions with client systems and even with other professionals. Topics include establishing the social worker–client relationship, the evolution of that relationship over time, working with reactant clients, the importance of boundaries in professional relationships, and the social worker's management of personal reactions to client behaviors. Most of the material in this chapter is based on generalist practice with small systems (individuals, families, and groups).

BEGINNING THE SOCIAL WORKER–CLIENT RELATIONSHIP

Relationships develop on the basis of each person's understanding of the situation in which they come together (Hewitt, 1997). The manner in which a social worker begins work with any new client system is based on his or her past experiences of beginnings with clients. The worker hopes that the client will openly disclose the presenting need, problem, or challenge. The social worker also hopes that the relationship will be a collaborative one in which both parties feel comfortable and able to focus openly on the issues at hand. This may or may not match the expectations of the client, however, who is new to the setting, may feel uncomfortable, and perhaps has had positive or negative experiences with helping professionals in the past. The client may, for example, assess the situation as one in which he or she should be acquiescent and avoid disclosing any negative attitudes. One example is the adolescent who is referred to an agency group intervention due to oppositional behavior at school, but who has no investment in the referral and distrusts authority figures. Still, he doesn't want to get into any more trouble so he keeps quiet about his reservations. The social worker's encouragement of the client's disclosure, in an atmosphere of comfort and trust, may help the client decide to share his honest feelings.

In accordance with the NASW Code of Ethics, social workers should strive to promote self-determination and honor the dignity of their clients. However, it must be recognized that workers and clients often have unequal power in the relationship. Social workers often possess resources that clients cannot access on their own. In an effort to receive these desired resources (such as medication, public subsidies, housing, sanctions for family reunification, school readmission, and so on) clients might feel a need to be cooperative rather than completely honest. The client with a substance abuse problem who is referred for assistance as a condition of keeping his job may be reluctant to express his disagreement about how his drinking behavior is being classified.

Likewise, many people who come to the attention of social workers experience a negative stigmatization that is demoralizing (Traub & Little, 1994). Stigma can have negative effects on many clients' willingness to invest over time in service activities. Many older adults, for example, grew up in an era when accepting formal help was a sign of weakness. As a result they may refuse independent living support services to which they are entitled. The social worker must be careful that his or her behaviors, and also the procedures at the employing agency, provide a welcoming atmosphere for the client. Long waiting lists, complicated eligibility requirements, and extensive paperwork are just a few examples of policies that clients may perceive as degrading.

The Client's Orientation to the Service Setting

Without encouraging the client's assertive participation, or openly addressing power imbalances and worker and agency expectations, the social worker may never learn what is most central to the client's life. Positive outcomes are enhanced when initial client/worker contacts include attention to their mutual expectations (Fischer, 1978). They are further enhanced when the social worker describes his or her mode of intervention with the client (Frank & Frank, 1993). Some authors recommend integrating formal client education about the process of intervention during the beginning stage (Germain & Gitterman, 1996). For example, whenever I meet a new client at my counseling center I make a point, as part of my self-introduction, to provide details about how I typically work with clients, the limits of my availability, and where the client can go (perhaps with my assistance) if they have additional service requests.

Prior to any in-person interactions between the social worker and client system, the nature of the agency setting itself (and perhaps the referral process) will have an effect on the unfolding of that relationship. The client's attitude about the social worker begins to form with observations about the physical appearance of the facility and the nature of the client's interactions with other staff (professionals or support staff) on the phone and when in the building. The appearance of the agency generates positive or negative attitudes within a client. An agency that invests little effort into its appearance may (perhaps mistakenly) communicate to clients that their overall well-being is not important. Likewise, the courtesy, helpfulness, and professional demeanor of support staff are important for creating positive impressions.

The social worker should be aware of any agency-related activities experienced by the client prior to their meeting. One of my clients once filed a complaint against the agency related to insensitive treatment by staff. I was ill one day and the receptionist was not able to contact the client to cancel the intake meeting. Upon arriving at the agency she was left waiting for 20 minutes before another staff member, on his lunch break, came out in a torn shirt and mouthful of food to tell her that she'd have to come back another time. The client never returned to the agency.

If the social worker constructively manages the relationship he or she can have a positive effect on a client's self-esteem. The client may perceive the social worker's positive attitude and expectations as reflecting his or her potential for growth. In the following section we review more specifically the key elements of the relationship process.

Communication Skills

Essential communication skills for social workers include empathy, authenticity, and focusing (Hepworth, Rooney, Rooney, Strom-Gottfried, & Larsen, 2006). These skills can be refined throughout the course of a social worker's career—they can never be "mastered."

Empathy is the ability to perceive accurately and sensitively the feelings of the client, and to communicate understanding of those feelings to the client. The second step in the process is critical because in order for empathy to be useful the client needs to be aware of the social worker's sensitivity. The functions of empathic communication are to accurately assess the client's concerns and related thoughts and feelings, set the stage for constructive confrontation (to be perceived as supportive rather than critical), and manage any obstacles presented by clients. A high level of empathy is characterized by the social worker's ability to accurately reflect both verbal and nonverbal messages back to the client. The social worker may be able to tap into thoughts and feelings about which the client is not fully aware. The social worker might say:

> "You say that you are not concerned about your ability to get your child back from the children's service agency, but I hear anxiety in your voice when you talk about this."

> "I know it's hard to admit to the other people in this group that you hit your spouse. You sit there denying that it was serious, but I see the pain in your face. This is tough to talk about, isn't it?"

Authenticity is the social worker's sharing of self with the client by relating in a natural, sincere manner. Social workers may demonstrate authenticity in many ways depending on their natural personality styles. When the social worker shows genuine concern, the client will feel comfortable and more likely to trust the worker. Like other communication skills, however, this requires balance. An excess of informality may convey to a client that the worker is unprofessional or overly intrusive. Authenticity may include self-disclosure, or the worker's admission of certain feelings in the relationship. Self-disclosure will be discussed in the later section on boundaries. Following are a few examples:

> "I'm pleased that you've been able to ask your father for help with your academic problems."

> "I had trouble keeping a job five years ago, similar to what you are describing. I can share with you some of my efforts to resolve the problem that seemed to have been helpful."

> "It frustrates me when you don't let me finish making my point before talking."

Focusing is a process of giving selective attention to aspects of the client's problem situation. This is an important skill in which the social worker directs the process of problem exploration and resolution. Clients may have many issues that they wish to discuss with the social worker, only some of which are related to the social worker's helping role. The social worker focuses when he or she:

- Selects topics for exploration that are consistent with the client's goals ("You said you were interested in supported housing, so why don't we talk more about that now, rather than the arguments with your in-laws.")

- Explores those topics in depth ("Before we move on to your current finances, tell me more about difficulties you've had in managing your own housing in the past.")

- Elicits open ended rather than short responses to questions about relevant topics ("You say that you often have arguments with your landlords. Okay. But tell me more about that. What are they about?")

- Explores the basis of the client's conclusions ("You've said that your partner won't contribute to the mortgage, but from what I gather she hasn't actually said that. How do you know this?")

- Elicits specific details of the client's experiences, feelings, and behaviors ("When you argue with the landlord, exactly what happens between you? Do you shout? Fight? When some time has passed, can you try talking to him again?")

- Summarizes the client's responses by reviewing their most critical aspects ("So let me recap. And tell me if I'm wrong. You want to look into supported housing because your family is asking you to leave, you have a limited income, and your partner won't help you financially. Is that right? Have we left anything out?")

Counterproductive Communication

Barriers to effective communication with clients include anything the social worker says, or perhaps fails to say, that interferes with the problem-solving process. These are rarely intentional. That is, all social workers have unique ways of communicating, with strengths and limitations. Some common barriers include, (Kadushin & Kadushin, 1997):

- Failure to clarify the purpose of the conversation
- Prematurely advising a client (before understanding the client)
- Persuading or lecturing (rather than listening and collaborating)
- Judging or labeling negatively
- Intimidating the client (inappropriate use of authority)
- Dominating the conversation or interrupting excessively
- Responding passively
- Anticipating what the client will say
- Assuming to understand the meaning of a client's unclear messages

Social workers may at times inadvertently behave in ways that are counterproductive to the relationship development process. These include both nonverbal and verbal behaviors. Nonverbal behaviors include the social worker's physical attending to the client. As examples, the social worker may show appropriate posture, eye contact, and facial expressions to demonstrate active listening. Problematic nonverbal behaviors may include the social worker's yawning (a problem that I sometimes experience), looking away, or fidgeting in the chair.

WORKER–CLIENT DIFFERENCES
IN GENERALIST PRACTICE

In generalist practice, working with clients from a different culture, class, or race, or with clients who are different from the social worker in other significant ways, is both potentially productive and potentially harmful (Lantz & Walsh, 2007). It is potentially productive because the differences between the social worker and client can facilitate the client's increased knowledge, insight, and coping skills. It is potentially harmful if the social worker does not have cultural sensitivity and specific knowledge about the client's worldview.

Cross-Cultural Intervention

There are four types of generalist practice situations that can be described as cross cultural, defined as addressing the merging or converging cultural positions of the social worker and client. These situations include a dominant culture (for example, Caucasian) social worker and a minority culture (for example, African

American) client, a minority culture social worker and a majority culture client, a minority culture client and a different minority culture social worker, and also a majority culture social worker and majority culture client who have experienced different processes of acculturation (Harper & Lantz, 2007). Although it is possible to conduct effective intervention in all of the above situations, it should be noted that the greater the cultural differences between client and social worker, the greater the difficulty the parties will have in developing a facilitative relationship (Lee, 2002; Lum, 1999).

It is important to emphasize here that research on the effects of similarities and differences between social workers and their clients on intervention outcomes does *not* support matching on such variables as age, gender, sexual orientation, race, or ethnicity. Clients desire social workers with cultural competency and sensitivity, rather than cultural "sameness." This is consistently found in studies regarding gender (Hatchet & Park, 2004; Parker-Sloat, 2003), sexual orientation (Burckell & Goldfriend, 2006), Hispanic clients and Caucasian social workers (Flicker, 2005), Asian American clients and Caucasian social workers (Ito & Marimba, 2002), and African American clients and Caucasian social workers (Negy, 2004; Liu, 2004; Sherman, 2000).

We will now consider each of the four types of worker–client characteristics noted here.

Dominant Culture Social Worker and Minority Culture Client.   In this situation a client from a minority race or culture is provided with services by a member of the dominant culture (in the United States this generally means a Caucasian helper). There is often a great difference in the worldviews of the parties, which in turn gives rise to opportunities for misunderstanding, distraction, and prejudice (Harper & Lantz, 2007; Van Voorhis, 1998). In such situations the social worker is responsible for:

- Actively researching and developing knowledge about the client's culture and race
- Actively engaging the client in the helper's self-education process by asking questions and being open to the client's efforts to help the practitioner improve his or her understanding of the client's heritage
- Utilizing self-awareness skills to monitor and evaluate his or her own possible distortions and prejudices about the client's cultural and racial heritage (Harper & Lantz, 2007; Lee, 2002; Van Voorhis, 1998)

Described next is one example of how this process can work.

In an intervention related to housing assistance, a middle-aged Caucasian male from a small midwestern city was working with a 21-year-old client named Connie who originally came from Puerto Rico by way of New York City. Following the first visit he reviewed two textbooks for information about people from Puerto Rico (Fong & Furuto, 2001; Green, 1999). The social worker learned that Puerto Ricans are the second-largest Latino subgroup in the United States. Their culture emphasizes spirituality (sometimes out of the frame of formal religion), the importance of extended and cross-generational family ties, and the values of community, children, respect, and cooperation. Interestingly, and significant to his client's presentation, Latino children tend to have a heightened sensitivity to the nonverbal behaviors of others. Latino people also value personalism in relationships—informality and warmth rather than observances of formal roles.

Interestingly, the social worker recognized over time that his client, Connie, displayed some personality characteristics that were different from what might be expected of a woman with a strong Puerto Rican ethnic background. She certainly was sensitive to nonverbal behaviors and maintained an informal relationship with the social worker, but on the other hand her family background featured conflict and splintering rather than the close ties that are attributed to Puerto Rican families. Connie had also moved far away from her extended family and she was willing to seek professional intervention, whereas it is often described that those with Puerto Rican origins are more likely to get help from informal sources (Garcia-Preto, 1996). Further, Connie did not seem guided by a spiritual frame of reference. Thus, while understanding the client's unique cultural background was important, the social worker learned that he must be careful not to use this information to stereotype the client.

Minority Social Worker and Dominant Culture Client. In this situation a minority culture practitioner provides services to a client from the dominant culture. The minority culture social worker may discover that client distortions about the practitioner's culture, or simple client prejudice, threaten to disrupt the intervention process. The social worker is thus responsible for monitoring client distortions to help the majority culture client gain a more accurate view of the practitioner's world. The social worker may also have to overcome or control damaged feelings that have resulted from episodes of prejudice and discrimination by dominant culture people in the past. The minority culture social worker's task is to avoid defensiveness even if the dominant culture client is treating him or her in a manner that is perceived to be unfair (Harper & Lantz, 2007).

Minority Culture Social Worker and Minority Culture Client. In this situation a minority culture social worker and a client from a different minority culture attempt to work together to develop an adequate working alliance. Minority culture social workers are sometimes surprised at how hard it can be to connect with members of a different minority group, because they may assume that being from a minority group gives them special insight into the differences of living in any minority culture. The truth is that people from different minority cultures and races all face special problems in a heterogeneous society, and to compare minority culture situations often results in inaccurate assumptions (Lee, 2002). In this situation the social worker may exhibit adequate cultural sensitivity but inadequate cultural knowledge of the client and the client's cultural heritage. The social worker must be aware of his or her responsibility to learn about the unique characteristics of each different minority group encountered in practice, in the same way that was described earlier.

Majority Culture Social Worker and Majority Culture Client. It is sometimes assumed that when a majority culture social worker is working with a
majority culture client, this cannot be considered to be a cross-cultural helping situation. This is an incorrect assumption, as similarities between client and social
worker that appear on a surface level often cloud awareness of the many possible
differences that might disrupt the quality of the intervention process (Harper &
Lantz, 2007). Such differences are likely to be present because surface characteristics
are not always the primary culture determinant. Every cultural movement has
within it many different migrating paths, and every culture and racial heritage incorporates differences based on religious heterogeneity, migration path differences,
family history, and historical accident. In summary, it is most constructive to assume
that *every* practice situation is in reality a cross-cultural clinical situation.

UNDERSTANDING CULTURALLY COMPETENT PRACTICE

One useful model of cross-cultural education has been developed by Lee (2000,
2002). In this model, two dimensions of competence, *cultural knowledge* and *cultural sensitivity,* are understood to be the primary factors involved in providing
effective intervention (see Figure 3.1).

Cultural knowledge refers to the social worker's ability to acquire specific
knowledge about his or her clients':

- Cultural background
- Racial experiences
- Historic experiences
- Values
- Behaviors
- Attitudes
- Spiritual beliefs
- Worldview beliefs
- Resources
- Customs
- Educational experiences
- Communication patterns
- Analysis patterns
- Thinking patterns
- Coping skills
- Previous experiences when requesting help in a dominant culture setting

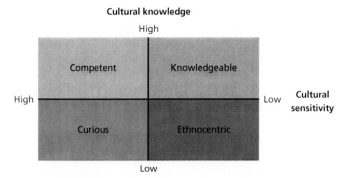

FIGURE 3.1   Competence in Cross-Cultural Generalist Intervention

Cultural sensitivity refers to a person's attitudes and values about cross-cultural generalist practice (Lee, 2002). In cross-cultural intervention it is hoped that the practitioner will manifest cultural sensitivity by developing the qualities of openness, empathy, respect, acceptance, and flexibility when working with people of a different race or culture.

The factors of cultural knowledge and cultural sensitivity can be utilized together to identify four potential personal responses to the cross-cultural practice situation. These responses can be identified as the *ethnocentric* response, the *knowledgeable* response, the *curious* response, and the response of *competence*.

The Ethnocentric Response

In this response to the cross-cultural practice situation the social worker has a low degree of cultural knowledge about his or her clients and also manifests little cultural sensitivity or empathy for the client. *Ethnocentrism* is the tendency to look at the world primarily from the perspective of one's own culture. It is the viewpoint that one's own group is the center against which all other groups are judged. The ethnocentric social worker manifests little motivation to either gain increased cultural knowledge or cultural sensitivity and holds to the worldview that his or her own cultural practices are superior to those of people from a different cultural or racial group. A social worker from any racial group, gender, gender preference, or cultural heritage can manifest such a response. The ethnocentric social worker seems to believe that "difference is dangerous" and he or she is not frequently motivated to change that stance. Ethnocentric people generally do not function well as generalist practitioners. All clients deserve a helper who is, if not sensitive and knowledgeable, at least willing to grow in those ways.

The Knowledgeable Response

In the knowledgeable response the social worker is willing to expand his or her knowledge and awareness about different cultures, worldviews, and patterns of coping and growth. Although the knowledgeable social worker generally has a high level of cultural knowledge, he or she also has a low level of cultural sensitivity. Such social workers often become stereotypical when working with minority culture clients, as they utilize knowledge about "general minority client patterns" to avoid contact and empathic concern with specific minority clients. The knowledgeable social worker requires close supervision but is often able to grow into a more culturally sensitive and competent practitioner over time. Below is a vignette that demonstrates the problems that may ensue when a practitioner assumes the knowledgeable response.

A Caucasian male social worker at a mental health agency occasionally felt uncomfortable with African American male clients. He did not think of himself as racist, but he understood that racial differences could negatively affect practitioners and clients who work together. He always raised the issue of racial difference with new clients when it existed to see if they had concerns about it. Usually his clients did not express any reservations. The practitioner's problem, though, is that he was reluctant to raise the issue of race again during the intervention if he perceived that it might be a barrier between the client and himself. He didn't want to risk insulting the client or imply that he was preoccupied with race.

Leon was a middle-aged and unemployed single African American male who came to the agency because of depression related to chronic job problems. He was rather well known around town as a talented jazz pianist. During the first session he raised the issue of race himself, seeming suspicious that the practitioner might not be able to understand his life experiences. It was a constructive conversation and they both seemed satisfied with its outcome. Every so often, though, he would challenge the practitioner again, wondering openly if he could empathize with him. This became difficult, because the social worker did think that in many situations the client placed himself in the victim role more than the evidence warranted, using race as an excuse. But the practitioner was not comfortable saying this because he was not sure that his perceptions were valid. Leon dropped out of intervention after three visits. The practitioner suspected that Leon questioned his awareness of, and comfort in addressing, the African American experience. The practitioner decided afterward that he needed to learn more about managing differences with his clients.

The Curious Response

In the curious response the social worker has high cultural sensitivity but little knowledge about minority culture clients. The social worker is highly motivated to learn more about minority culture clients' reactions to his or her basic cultural sensitivity and ability to develop empathy for the client. This is an open response that craves knowledge, and the social worker is motivated to use such knowledge in clinical work with minority culture clients. Such social workers are able to effectively utilize books and articles about minority culture clients for their professional growth.

The Competent Response

The competent response to the cross-cultural helping situation includes high cultural knowledge and high cultural sensitivity. In addition to acquiring considerable culture-specific knowledge about minority culture clients, the competent social worker also demonstrates openness, empathy, and care with minority cultural clients and is able to maintain an informed and empathic response to them. The competent response to the cross-cultural helping situation should be a primary educational goal in the education experiences of all helping professions and should also be a primary goal in competent supervision. When a social worker has developed a competent response to the cross-cultural helping situation, he or she is able to make sound intervention judgments from an informed point of view, is open and sensitive in the cross-cultural helping situation, is not bounded by conceptual knowledge, can connect with a client at an individual empathic level, is aware of his or her own personal experiences that might distort judgment in the cross-cultural helping situation, and is able to step outside the self in order to view the minority client from a multi-perspective frame of reference.

We end this chapter with another case vignette, an account that illustrates the competent response to the cross-cultural helping situation.

Case Illustration: The Apache Tear

Rebecca, age 40, came to the substance abuse treatment agency to get help with anxiety and depression. She was a recovering cocaine abuser. Her anxiety seemed to be rooted in a fear that she was going to lose control of her life. To prevent this she tried to be perfect and in complete control, because she had been so out of control several years earlier.

Rebecca was born on a reservation in the western United States. Her parents gave her up for adoption when she was seven. Her adoptive parents were Caucasian but they encouraged Rebecca to stay involved with her Native American culture. She visited her natural father every year on the reservation and interacted with Native American groups in her current area of residence. The social worker wondered if it would be difficult for Rebecca to work with a Caucasian female, but the racial difference did not appear to be a barrier. This was largely because the social worker asked Rebecca to help her understand Native American culture, and she read several books about her tribe. The social worker often shared with Rebecca what she learned from the reading, and Rebecca seemed to enjoy helping the social worker in this way. The social worker also talked with her supervisor often about her work with the client, to help insure that she was not "overlooking" anything important as a result of their differences. Rebecca and the social worker worked together for about six sessions, and the client learned to control her anxiety through a variety of behavioral activities. She made excellent progress.

When they met for the last time, Rebecca presented the social worker with a polished gemstone, a smooth, dark stone that she called an "Apache tear." The stone was dark but became transparent when held up to light, and a small "tear" could be seen in its center. The stone had been given to her by a friend many years before, and she wanted to pass it on to the social worker. She explained that the Apache tear symbolized both struggle and one's hopes for a better future. Rebecca wanted to give the social worker the stone as a thank you. She added that she had the stone blessed recently by a tribal healer. The social worker thought it was a wonderful gesture. It was very important to the client to give the gift and also to explain its history and significance. Agency policies often prohibit or discourage clinical staff from accepting gifts from clients. Sometimes, though, it is important for the client to give a gift and refusing it would be destructive to the relationship.

Having briefly considered barriers to relationship development, we now turn to a discussion of how social workers can approach clients who do not appear willing to engage in the relationship at all.

REACTANT CLIENTS

Relationship development is complicated when the client is involuntary. This term refers to any client who is forced to seek, or feels pressure to accept, contact with a social worker (Rooney, 1992). It applies to a majority of clients in some settings (prisons, drug treatment centers, and child protective agencies) but to many clients in all settings. Involuntary clients include those who are mandated by court order as well as those who are pressured to receive services by a referral source, family member, or significant other (such as an employer or guidance counselor). We prefer the term *reactant* to describe clients who are for any reason reluctant to engage with the social worker. They may be involuntary, distrustful, or ambivalent about change.

Social workers need to come to terms with their general discomfort about working with mandated clients. The process raises power issues that are inherent in all worker–client relationships (Rooney, 1992). It runs counter to the professional value of self-determination and puts the social worker into an authoritarian position. Reactant clients will attempt to manage the impressions that the social worker has of them by trying to covey an impression of competence, seeking exoneration from the social worker (and his or her help in dealing with the outside source of pressure), selective disclosure, and intimidation of the social worker with hostile comments.

The involuntary client may try to indirectly sabotage the relationship process by, for example, not attending scheduled meetings or following through with expected tasks. In these ways the client may test the social worker's resolve to follow through with any external mandates regarding the intervention. If the client determines that the social worker is not inclined to follow up, the client may drop out of the intervention. For example, some truant children are threatened with time in a detention home if they do not meet regularly with a social worker. The child may test the limits of this participating to see if the threat will be enforced.

The social worker can be proactive in helping the reactant client work through feelings about service participation in the following ways:

- Allow the client to state the cause of referral from his or her own viewpoint
- Express empathy for pressures experienced

- Avoid labeling the client in negative ways
- Identify nonnegotiable legal and agency requirements
- Affirm client rights
- Reaffirm choices and negotiable options

The social worker should never use authority to impose a personal standard of conduct, but only to exercise the precise level of authority delegated by the sanctioning body.

Described next is an interviewing style that can be helpful in engaging reactant clients.

Motivational Interviewing

Motivational interviewing is a client-centered, directive method for enhancing motivation to change by exploring and resolving the client's ambivalence (Miller & Rollnick, 2002). It has become quite popular in the past 25 years as a means of engaging clients who are at least initially unmotivated to address problems that are considered serious by significant others. Initially developed for the treatment of substance abuse, motivational interviewing is now applied to many types of problems such as eating disorders, behavioral problems of adolescence, general health care issues, diabetes, HIV high-risk behavior, family preservation, sex offenses, and pain management (Moyers & Rollnick, 2002). Motivational interviewing "sidesteps" denial and instead emphasizes listening reflectively to clients' concerns and selectively emphasizing "change talk." Typically a brief intervention (four sessions or less), motivational interviewing has been employed both as a stand-alone treatment and as an initial step toward engaging clients in other intervention approaches (Walitzer, Dermen, & Conners, 1999).

Major Concepts of Motivational Interviewing.   A major influence on motivational interviewing is the Transtheoretical Stages of Change (TSOC) model, developed to recognize and address the reluctance of many people with substance use disorders to change their behaviors (Connors, Donovan, & DiClemente, 2001; Prochaska & Norcross, 1994). In this model, the following six stages of change have been formulated:

1. Pre-contemplation—the person does not believe he or she has a problem and is unwilling to change.
2. Contemplation—the person is contemplating change (for example, an alcohol-dependent person sees that there are significant benefits to be gained by stopping his alcohol use even as he continues to drink).
3. Preparation—the person is poised to change in the next month and works on a strategy to do so.
4. Action—the person begins to take action (for example, attending AA meetings).

5. Maintenance—sustained change has occurred for six months.

6. Relapse—in the event that the person slips back into old behaviors, the steps are revisited.

Within the TSOC model, motivational interviewing is designed to work with those who are either in *pre-contemplation,* denying that change is needed, or those in *contemplation* who believe there might be a problem but are only considering change. The perspectives of motivational interviewing can be summarized as follows:

- Motivation to change is elicited from the client, not imposed from the outside.

- A client's motivation for enacting change relative to some problem behavior is often impeded by ambivalence.

- It is the client's task to articulate and resolve his or her ambivalence.

- Readiness to change is a product of interpersonal interaction.

- Direct persuasion is not an effective method for resolving ambivalence.

- Practitioner directives are useful, however, in examining ambivalence.

While the major concepts of motivational interviewing (motivation, ambivalence, and stages of change) have been described, several merit additional discussion. The first is *ambivalence* toward change, which is viewed as a natural process in many people (Killick & Allen, 1997). Few decisions that people make, major and minor, are completely free of conflicted thoughts. We might experience agonizing ambivalence when deciding whether to accept a particular job offer, but this sense of uncertainty may also be present as we decide whether to accept an invitation to a party with people we don't know well. Motivational interviewing works with the ambivalence of the client, in which the advantages and disadvantages of the problem behavior, as well as the advantages and disadvantages of changing, are openly considered. The social worker selectively reflects and affirms change talk and asks the client to elaborate on statements about change. Another major focus of motivational interviewing involves a client's *confidence* that he or she can succeed at change efforts. The practitioner assesses not only a client's willingness to change, but also the confidence that he or she can make changes if desired (Miller & Rollnick, 2002).

In motivational interviewing, the initial intervention goal is to build clients' motivation when they are not willing to change, rather than focusing on actual behavior change. A client's perception of the (alleged) problem is thus the focus of the early part of the social worker's contacts. As the work moves into the action stage of the TSOC model, actual client behavior becomes a target for intervention (Treasure & Ward, 1997).

The Social Worker–Client Relationship.   Motivation is not a stable, internal quality of an individual but is affected by the interaction between the social worker and client (Killick & Allen, 1997). The context of the helping relationship is therefore emphasized. The social worker seeks to understand the client's frame of reference about the presenting issue with reflective listening. He or she affirms the validity of the client's perspective and the client's freedom of choice in dealing with the situation. The practitioner then elicits and selectively reinforces the client's own self-motivational statements about the problem issue. The motivational interviewer seeks to engage clients "where they are at" in the stages of change model to build their motivation and enlarge upon the concerns and strengths they demonstrate. Reactance is a problem of the practitioner rather than the client, signifying that the practitioner needs to adjust change strategies to match the client's position toward change. The responsibility for *how* behavior change occurs is left to the client.

Several intervention principles underlie motivational interviewing (Miller & Rollnick, 2002; Killick & Allen, 1997; Treasure & Ward, 1997). The following guidelines can help the social worker to enact these principles:

Begin where the client is. Do not assume that the client is ready to engage in change, or that the client is "totally resistant."

Explore the client's problem behaviors and reflect the client's perceptions. Listen with empathy to the client's concerns to accurately assess his or her relationship to the process of change.

Reinforce client statements about wanting to change. Attend selectively to client expressions about change. Also, seek to create a discrepancy between the client's values and goals, such as long-term health, and how the problem stands in the way.

Affirm the client's statements about his or her ability to change. In this way, confidence is built and the individual feels empowered to take the first steps toward change.

Specific techniques of motivational interviewing include eliciting self-motivational statements, strategies to handle resistance, the decisional balance, and building self-efficacy (Miller & Rollnick, 2002).

Eliciting Self-Motivational Statements.   Self-motivational statements by clients are those that indicate a desire to begin *acting* to bring about a desired change. They emerge from the client's decision to change but also his or her sense of competence, confidence, and awareness of resources that will support change efforts. The social worker elicits self-motivational statements by posing questions that the client might answer in a way that favors change. The conversation will lead into exploring the disadvantages of the status quo situation through:

Problem recognition questions. "What things make you think that this is a problem? In what ways do you think you or other people have been harmed?"

Concern questions. "What worries you about your behavior? What can you imagine happening to you? What do you think will happen if you don't make a change?"

Questions about extremes. "What concerns you the most about this in the long run? How much do you know about what can happen if you continue with this behavior even if you don't see this happening to you?"

Other types of questions encourage the client to explore the advantages of changing. These questions involve:

Intention to change. "The fact that you're here indicates that at least a part of you thinks it's time to do something. What are the reasons you see for making a change? What would you like your life to be like five years from now?"

Optimism about change. "What makes you think that if you decided to make a change, you could do it? What do you think would work for you, if you decided to change? When else in your life have you made a significant change like this? How did you do it? What personal strengths do you have that will help you succeed? Who could offer you support in making this change?"

Questions about extremes. "What might be the best results you could imagine if you make a change? If you were completely successful in making the changes you want, how would things be different?"

These types of questions provoke the individual to consider change by examining and contrasting views of the future (with and without the problem), the functions the behavior serves, and its harmful consequences. The social worker then asks the client to elaborate further on his or her comments that favor change.

Handling Reactance. As discussed earlier, signs of reactance, such as the client's arguing, interrupting, denying, and ignoring alert the social worker of the need to switch intervention strategies. The new strategies should involve reflective responses that diffuse potential power struggles and mobilize the side of the client's ambivalence that is geared toward change (Moyers & Rollnick, 2002). Strategies to achieve this are summarized next.

Simple reflection is acknowledging a client's feeling, thought, or opinion so that the client continues to explore the presenting problem rather than become defensive. ("You have a lot of stress going on in your life right now. Do you think this may not be the best time to change your behavior?") The client, given the freedom to decide where to go with the topic, might respond, "I don't know. Maybe it's not a good time, but I'm not sure" (Carroll, 1998).

Amplified reflection goes beyond simple reflection in that the client's statement is acknowledged, but in an extreme fashion. An amplified reflection, such as the statement, "You say that you're fine the way you are, so maybe there is nothing that you should change," typically has the effect of getting the client to back down from an entrenched position and allow for the possibility of negotiation about change. Sometimes clients who have been entrenched in a negative position regarding change will start to argue from the other side of their ambivalence, the part that wants to change, when the practitioner joins with their position. (For example, "Well, I don't want to say there's *nothing* I can do to make my life better.")

Double-sided reflection taps into both aspects of the client's ambivalence. It acknowledges that when people are exploring the possibility of change, they are divided between wanting to change and also wanting to hold onto the behavior that has become problematic (Carroll, 1998). Examples of this kind of comment are: "You're not sure your drinking is a big deal, and at the same time your girlfriend left you because of how you acted when you were drinking," and "Your relationship was very important to you, and your alcohol use caused problems in the relationship." Double-sided reflection can pull the client's attention to the inconsistency between the problem behavior and his or her major life goals.

Shifting focus is the social worker's moving the client's attention from a potential impasse. When the client begins to argue against what the practitioner might feel is the best course of action, the practitioner should immediately shift his or her position and redirect the focus. ("I think you're jumping ahead here. We're not talking at this point about you quitting drinking for the rest of your life. Let's talk some more about what the best goal is for you right now and how to go about making it happen.") The social worker first defuses the initial concern and then direct attention to a more workable issue.

Agreement with a twist involves agreeing with some of the client's message, but in a way that orients the client in another direction. ("I agree there's no need for you to say you're an alcoholic. I am hearing that there are certain aspects of drinking that you enjoy, and that it's also causing you some problems.")

Reframing involves taking arguments that clients use against change and altering the meaning of the information to instead promote change. A common example involves the tendency of drinkers to consume large quantities without experiencing ill effects. This tendency is sometimes used as an excuse for why the drinking is not a problem. This excuse can be reframed by the social worker as tolerance of alcohol, which is symptomatic of problem drinking. ("You're right, you don't notice any effects from the alcohol. But that's because you've been drinking so long your body is used to it. The alcohol is affecting your body but not your mind.")

Clarifying free choice involves communicating to the client that it is up to him or her whether to make a change, rather than getting into a debate about what the client should do. ("You can decide to take this on now or wait until another time.") This is a useful intervention because when people perceive that their freedom of choice is being threatened, they tend to react by asserting their liberty. A good antidote for this reaction is to assure the client that in the end it is he or she who determines what happens.

Decisional Balancing.   This technique involves weighing the costs and benefits of the client's problem behavior and the costs and benefits of change. The advantages and disadvantages of change are formally gathered together in a "balance sheet" with the social worker and client's participation. The client can perceive in a visual and concrete way the reasons that underpin the problem and those aspects that are pushing him or her to make the change.

Supporting Self-Efficacy and Developing a Change Plan.   Techniques involved in building self-efficacy include:

- *Evocative questions.* "How might you go about making this change? What would be a good first step? What obstacles do you foresee, and how might you deal with them?"
- *Ruler assessment.* "How confident are you that you could stop your purging behavior? On a scale from 0 to 10, where 0 is not at all confident and 10 is extremely confident, where would you say you are? Why are you at two and not zero? What would it take for you to go from two to [a higher number]?"
- *Reviewing past successes.* "When in your life have you made up your mind to do something challenging, and did it? It might be something new you learned, or a habit that you quit, or some other significant change that you made. What did you do that worked?"
- *Discussing personal strengths and supports.* "What is there about you, what strong points do you have that could help you succeed in making this change? What sources of social support do you have? Are there others you could call for support?"
- *Asking questions about hypothetical change.* "Suppose that you did succeed in stopping your drug use and are looking back now on how that happened. What most likely is it that worked? How did it happen? Suppose that this one big obstacle weren't there. If that obstacle were removed, then how might you go about making this change?"
- *Brainstorming.* Freely generating as many ideas as possible for how a change might be accomplished, and as a result perceiving one or two ideas that might work.
- *Giving information and advice.* Social workers should be reluctant to give advice to clients, because doing so takes responsibility for behavior away from the client. Whenever advice is given it should be done reluctantly, tentatively, and on matters that are not likely to have negative consequences. For example, if a client had success with maintaining sobriety in the past because of involvement with Alcoholics Anonymous, a social worker may suggest that the client consider resuming that program as one part of his desire to resume sobriety.

Many of the techniques of motivational interviewing are utilized in the example that follows.

Case Illustration: The School Brawler.   This intervention took place in a school setting where the social worker saw a 12-year-old African American girl named Bettina who had been in trouble for frequent fighting. Following a few minutes of introductions the social worker began with setting a brief agenda: "Bettina, you've been sent to me to talk about some problems at school and what we can do about those, but we can also talk about whatever else you think is important." In this way the social worker directed the focus of the meeting but allowed for flexibility so that any or all of the client's concerns could be given attention. Still, Bettina chose to focus on the presenting problem.

The social worker listened with empathy as she tried to elicit statements about change from the client. She asked Bettina, "What are some of the good things about fighting?" and, "What are some of the not-so-good things about fighting?" Like many clients, Bettina was surprised at the first question. The social worker explained that, "There must be some good things about it, otherwise you wouldn't keep doing it, right?"

As Bettina responded, the social worker probed for more information and selectively reinforced the client's statements about change. On the side of why she liked to fight, Bettina said that it made her feel proud when she won. It also ensured that her peers "respected" her. On the other side, Bettina said she didn't want to get expelled from school or end up in juvenile hall. She was also afraid of the hurt she might cause people. For instance, she found herself during one fight pounding another girl's head against the sidewalk, and she didn't want to do that kind of thing. The social worker, rather than just allowing Bettina to list these reasons for not fighting, explored with her the disadvantages of the status quo. For instance, the social worker asked, "What worries you about getting expelled for fighting?" and, "How will getting expelled for fighting stop you from doing what you want in life?" Thus the social worker helped the client talk herself into changing rather than using direct persuasion.

The social worker avoided challenging the client's statements because direct confrontation was likely to escalate resistance rather than reduce it. Any resistance to change was sidestepped. For instance, when Bettina said, "If I don't fight, I'll get disrespected," the social worker used the technique of amplified reflection: "So the only way to get people's respect is to fight them." Amplified reflection often results in verbal backpedaling from the client, who attempts to soften the extreme position reflected by the social worker. In this case, Bettina said, "No, sometimes I just give them a look. I can give some pretty mean looks."

As part of motivational interviewing, the social worker picks up on what the client holds as important in her life. She then works to enlarge the discrepancy between the client's values and her present problem behavior. Bettina valued her friendships at the school, but her fighting was endangering those relationships: "So on one hand, those friends are important to you, and on the other, if you get expelled for fighting and get transferred to another school, you won't be able to see your friends like you do now."

As the conversation continued the social worker focused on instilling in Bettina some optimism about change. For instance, when the social worker asked the question, "What makes you think that if you decided to make a change, you could do it?" Bettina said, "I can do it if I set my mind to it. I only wanted to cut my fighting down a little bit before. But now I want it to stop." The social worker asked, "What personal strengths do you have that will help you succeed?" The client answered, "I can talk. I know how to talk to people so they don't mess with me. I just lay them straight. No need to fight most of the time." The social worker further inquired about who could help Bettina make these changes. She identified her friends as a support system: "I can say to them, 'You all, talk me down because I can't fight no more. I don't want to get kicked out of school.' So when I'm in an argument they'd probably say something like, 'Forget her—she ain't worth it.' And they'd be right—she ain't."

The social worker assessed the client's commitment to change, as well as her confidence that she could make changes. To begin, the social worker used the commitment ruler technique: "If there was a scale to measure your commitment, and it went from 0 to 10, with 10 being totally committed—nothing could make you fight—where would you say you are right now?" Bettina identified herself at a seven, and the social worker asked her to account for this value. Bettina said, "One more fight, and I'm kicked out of school. They already told me that. They might mean it this time."

The social worker then asked Bettina to rate herself on a similar ruler involving her confidence that she could change. Bettina said about her five ranking, "I already changed some. Like last year I got in trouble every day, but this year I don't get in trouble very often. I try to stay away from people I got a problem with. Before I wouldn't think about it, and I would just fight people and not think about what would happen. But now I think about it."

Since Bettina's confidence that she can change was lower than her commitment, the social worker turned to a technique that would enhance the client's self-efficacy—asking evocative questions: "How might you go about continuing to make change? What would be a good first step?" Bettina answered that she would continue to avoid people who bother her. She would also talk to her friends about helping her "calm down."

When asked about possible obstacles, Bettina admitted it could be difficult if someone "got up in her face." The social worker and client began brainstorming about how to handle this obstacle. With some prompting and suggestions, Bettina produced three options: making threats but not necessarily following through; staying in public settings so that other people could intervene; and telling the instigator, over and over again if need be, "You're not worth it."

In motivational interviewing, when the social worker offers information and advice, it is phrased tentatively. (For example, "If it's okay, I'm going to make a suggestion. I don't know if it will work or not for you. It's worked for others who have struggled with the same things you have.") The social worker seeks to avoid getting into a struggle with the client about what she must do. Instead, the social worker strategically applies techniques so that the client's motivation to change is bolstered. In this way, during the course of a single session, Bettina arrived at a place where she was ready to commit to a change plan. She met with the social worker for several more weeks, reporting on her progress in staying out of fights and getting feedback that helped to maintain her positive direction.

The social worker's ability to engage clients in constructive relationships requires empathy, authenticity, and perhaps motivational interviewing skills. Managing interpersonal boundaries requires special attention to aspects of the relationship at the outset, but also over time.

ESTABLISHING AND MAINTAINING BOUNDARIES IN RELATIONSHIPS

In generalist practice the social worker and client may interact in a variety of settings besides the agency such the client's home or job site. The social worker often develops relationships with the client's friends, family members, landlords, employers, and other helping professionals. The scope and intensity of intervention often challenges the social worker's ability to develop appropriate working relationships with clients. Considering relationship issues from the perspective of boundaries provides an important source of guidance for the social worker. Attention to boundary issues can help social workers negotiate clear and consistent relationships with clients, their significant others, and also members of inter-professional teams.

Boundaries are the assumed, generally unspoken rules that people internalize about the physical and emotional limits of their relationships with other people (Walsh, 2000b). They protect privacy and reflect one's individuality. Boundaries are differentially constructed to facilitate one's desire to be close to, or separate from, others. The nature of generalist practice, with the social worker providing services in the client's territories, ensures that boundary dilemmas will frequently develop. Social workers need to be careful in developing interpersonal boundaries and deciding when they can be crossed. Mutually understood boundaries provide for both clients and social workers an appropriate sense of control, power, protection, and self-determination. Any social worker actions perceived by clients to be boundary transgressions might have negative consequences for the intervention. Clients may feel exploited, angry, and lose their trust in the worker (Gutheil & Gabbard, 1998).

Boundaries include rules about the following aspects of relationships:

Contact time. How much time is appropriate to spend in the client's company? Will this vary depending on whether that time is spent face to face, on the phone, online, or otherwise? On the time of day or day of the week? The purpose of the contact?

Types of information to be shared. What is the appropriate range of topics to discuss with the person? What about politics, religion, and sex? How much depth should the social worker be willing to provide about these topics?

Physical closeness when together. What are expectations about personal space when in the person's company? How closely will the social worker and client sit? Can they touch? What range of nonverbal communications is appropriate?

Territoriality. To which of the social worker's environmental spaces does this person have access? Is he or she restricted from others? Will interactions be limited to the office, or extended to community settings?

Emotional space. To what extent is the social worker willing to share feelings about sensitive topics with the client? Are there limits to topics about which he or she will share feelings?

Boundary establishment is important to the professional survival of social workers. Caring for clients may foster strong emotions in professionals, and clear boundaries provide protection from overextending themselves (Farber, Novack, & O'Brient, 1997). When clients violate boundaries about which they are unclear, social workers may feel angry, manipulated, and lose objectivity about the client's needs. This can interfere with the quality of the intervention as well as lead to burnout. Clear boundaries help the social worker–client relationship by providing the following benefits for *clients:*

- A relationship in which the client feels affirmed and respected
- A safe environment in which the client can feel comfortable sharing personal information
- A stronger sense of individuality that derives from having control over boundaries
- A basis from which to determine whether and when the social worker can cross certain boundaries

Boundary crossing implies appropriate efforts to adjust boundaries toward greater intimacy, while boundary violations are inappropriate entries into a person's privacy and space (Hermansson, 1997). Clear boundaries provide the following benefits for the *social worker:*

- Role clarity regarding the range and limits of intervention activities
- A basis from which to make decisions about how and when to cross boundaries
- A means of preventing burnout by avoiding role overload
- Reminders about legal issues that may emerge if certain boundaries are violated
- Physical safety, when territorial boundaries are maintained (Kanter, 1999)

Crossing Boundaries

The discussion thus far has focused on boundaries as limits, but the concept also has implications for bridging, access, and integration (Petronio, Ellemers, Giles, & Gallois, 1998). People experience natural tensions to remain apart from and to join with others, and this tension underscores the importance of flexibility, permeability, and balance in boundaries. In most of our relationships that persist over time, boundaries change. We test the boundaries of others to determine who they are, how we should behave toward them, and if and when we can move closer. If we attempt to cross a boundary about which another person is not comfortable, he or she may choose to withdraw, and perhaps erect new, tighter boundaries in response.

Boundaries and Power

Boundary awareness is particularly important in social worker–client relationships because a power differential exists between the two parties (Backlar, 1996). A client will loosen a boundary when he or she perceives some benefit to doing so. The client needs to trust the worker and feel confident that the relationship will be enriched as a result of realigning a boundary. Despite the prescriptions of client empowerment and partnership in recent literature (for example, Saleebey, 2002), social workers have more formal power in those relationships. The lack of equal power in the relationship may compromise the client's ability to defend himself or herself with regard to privacy issues. The client will not necessarily articulate any negative reactions to ambiguous boundaries, however, as he or she may be unclear about what appropriate professional boundaries should be. Some workers fail to see how their power may stir the client's resentment in times of conflict.

Boundaries and Professional Groups

The social worker's ability to successfully coordinate interventions for clients also necessitates the existence of clear boundaries with other professionals. As with social workers and clients, members of professional groups maintain boundaries between themselves and other such groups, marked by different bodies of knowledge, language, values, histories, and intervention preferences. Issues of power among the professions have consequences for the quality of client care (Teram, 1999). For physicians, psychologists, social workers, and nurses, boundaries set conditions for group identity and demark realms of expertise. Professionals tend to assert that the problems relating to their specialty should be kept within their domain. This presents challenges to generalist social workers, who may intervene with clients at several levels. They may be excluded from the activities of other professional groups with more clearly defined areas of specialization.

Warning Signs of Possible Boundary Transgressions

Ten possible boundary transgressions that may emerge in the course of generalist social work are listed next. The first six of these are not necessarily transgressions—whether they are so depends on particular circumstances, which will be considered later.

Dual relationships, or those in which the professional interacts with the client or the client's significant others in more than one role (Reamer, 2003). For example, the client or significant other might be the social worker's mechanic, grocer, neighbor, fellow church member, and so on. These situations create potential conflicts of interest as well as opportunities for confidentiality violations. They are most common in rural settings.

Intrusion into the client's territory. The greater utilization of home visits provides one example of how community care has shifted the balance of power somewhat back to the client. The home is an especially private territory in which people can exercise control and expect that visitors abide by their rules (Bruhn, Levine, & Levine, 1993). Intrusive activity includes visiting the client who does not want to be visited or making unannounced home visits, both of which are commonplace, for example, in child protective services work.

Self-disclosure by the social worker. This practice may be legitimate at times as a means to a therapeutic end, but it may also reflect a sharing of personal information for the worker's benefit. A social worker who shares that he had an argument with his son that morning may be using the client as a resource for venting. This may put the client in the inappropriate position of being a caregiver.

Investigating certain details of a client's personal life (Doreen, 1998). The need to know some personal information about clients does not mean that the social worker has a right to know everything. The social worker's curiosity may be voyeuristic at times (about, for example, a client's sexual practices).

Accepting or giving gifts. This may or may not be appropriate, depending on the client and worker's motivations, the nature of the relationship, and the value of the gift. It may be an important action to help clients practice reciprocity in relationships (expressing gratitude for assistance, for example). Often, agencies have policies that the social worker must follow to establish limits in this area.

Touching or physically comforting the client. While appropriate at times, this needs to be monitored in relation to its purpose and the message it gives the client.

The remaining four examples are *always* boundary transgressions:

Socializing with a client. The boundary between intervention and socialization (talking about or attending to issues that are unrelated to the major purposes of the interaction) is often difficult to distinguish. A social worker may be invited to a client's school graduation ceremony or a party planned by a group of clients. These may be appropriate activities depending on what the social worker communicates in doing so. While socializing is useful for establishing a relationship and building a client's social skills, it may indicate that the social worker is gratifying his or her own needs.

Referring to a client as a friend. Social workers rarely interact with their clients in the same manner as they do with their friends. With friends, people tend to disclose their weaknesses and fears, sacrifice personal time to offer assistance, and loan money. Communicating to a client that he or she is a friend is misleading. It may cause eventual hurt to the client or discourage him or her from developing his or her own friends.

Sharing information about a client with an outside party, particularly for reasons that have nothing to do with coordinating an intervention. This is a violation of the client's right to privacy.

Loaning, trading, or selling items to a client.

Intervening Factors.   The previous list consists of many possible, but not actual, violations. A variety of intervening factors must be considered when assessing the appropriateness of a social worker's boundary conduct (Curtis & Hodge, 1994). These include:

- Consultation with colleagues or a supervisor in assessing the situation
- The client's perceived ability to exercise appropriate judgment
- The client's history in relationships (patterns of behavior and his or her ability to manage conflicts or differences of opinion)
- The history and dynamics of the particular relationship (what patterns of interaction have been established, and whether a boundary-crossing activity by the worker is likely to be growth-enhancing or a setback for the client)
- Cultural norms reflected in the behavior of both the worker and client
- Legal liabilities that the social worker might face

Managing Boundary Dilemmas

Listed next are guidelines that social workers can follow to help them reflect on boundary dilemmas and decide what to do about them.

Set clear boundaries with clients at the beginning of those relationships about what the social worker's roles and activities will and will not include.

Clarify boundaries with the client over time, as they will change. As examples, the social worker and client may decide that home visits, not made before, are now indicated, or that they will address a broader or narrower scope of the client's issues than was done initially.

Consider the *preservation of the client's privacy to be a major guiding value.* The social worker should always reflect on how much he or she needs to know about a client, and what the purposes are of acquiring certain information.

Be aware of your own emotional and physical needs as much as possible, and be wary of obtaining too much personal gratification at the expense of a client.

Secure the client's informed consent for all service activities. This may involve written consent for some activities but may otherwise involve explaining the rationales for all interventions, and providing clients with choices about services.

Be educated about the client's cultural and community standards of behavior to understand what boundaries are reasonable in those contexts (Herlihy & Corey, 1997).

Use peer consolation and formal supervision routinely. Most experienced practitioners are sensitive to the difficulty of managing interpersonal boundaries, and thus supervisors are likely to be receptive to processing such situations with supervisees. If the social worker does not have a positive relationship with a supervisor for some reason, trusted peers can also perform this function.

We now move to another important topic in the relationship literature: the social worker's emotional reactions to the client systems with whom he or she works.

PERSONAL REACTIONS OF SOCIAL WORKERS
TO THEIR CLIENTS

The complex problems and challenges faced by clients tend to evoke a range of personal reactions from their social workers (Brody & Farber, 1996). Acknowledging and processing these feelings with supervisors or trusted colleagues can help the social worker maintain a focus on client-centered goals, rather than focusing (perhaps unconsciously) on his or her own feelings about and wishes for the client.

The concepts of transference and countertransference emerged within psychodynamic theory during the early 1900s (Gabbard, 1995). The terms carry a negative connotation with some practitioners who believe that psychodynamic ideas are irrelevant to social work practice in the 21st century. Still, they call attention to subtle aspects of the social worker–client relationship and their effects on the intervention process. *Transference* was initially defined as a client's projection of feelings, thoughts, and wishes onto the social worker, who comes to represent a person from the client's past, such as a parent, sibling, or teacher (Jacobs, 1999). The concept has been expanded to refer to all client reactions, conscious and unconscious, to the practitioner. These include reactions based on interactions with similar types of people in the client's past and on here-and-now characteristics of the social worker. Positive transferences are those in which the client is attracted to the practitioner, which can facilitate the clinical engagement process. Negative transferences, characterized by such feelings as anger, distrust, or fear, can impede the client's participation in the intervention.

Countertransference was initially defined as a clinical worker's unconscious reactions to the client's transference (Jacobs, 1999; Kocan, 1988). Contemporary definitions, however, assume that many of the practitioner's reactions exist independently of the client's feelings. Today the countertransference concept incorporates several meanings, two of which are (Kocan, 1988):

- The effects of the social worker's needs and wishes, based on personal history, on his or her understanding of the client

- The generally conscious attitudes that a social worker has about a range of clients (such as being drawn to working with children or having an aversion to older adults)

Positive countertransference reflects a social worker's attraction to the client, but this can be problematic as well as facilitative of the intervention if the social worker loses the ability to maintain an appropriate sense of detachment from the client's situation. Negative countertransference is almost always a problem, however, as it implies that the social worker is emotionally repelled from the client for some reason.

The interpersonal processes inherent in generalist practice are such that a practitioner should expect to experience mixed emotions with many clients (Tyrell, Dozier, Teague, & Fallot, 1999). Reflecting on these emotional reactions helps the social worker better understand the rationales behind his or her actions, and thus make better clinical decisions.

Common Social Worker Reactions to Clients

Sources of potentially problematic countertransferences include (Basham, 2004; Kocan, 1988; Schoenwolf, 1993):

The need to be needed. If this need is not met in everyday life, the social worker may look to clients for fulfillment.

The need to be liked. The social worker may try too hard to please a client, be hurt by a client's criticisms, or have negative reactions to clients who are not emotionally forthcoming.

The need to feel like an expert, to an extent that a client's ideas are devalued.

The need to be in control. The social worker may tend to keep clients dependent and discourage a client's initiatives or assertive behaviors.

The tendency to be too curious about the details of a client's life.

Discomfort with certain types of emotional expression (for example, anger or tenderness) and thus discouraging those feelings in clients.

Overidentifying with clients whose problems are similar to one's own. The social worker in these situations may be blinded to the part that clients play in sustaining the social worker's problems.

Idealizing clients due to strong positive feelings, and possibly setting unrealistic goals for them.

What follows next are a range of common social worker reactions to specific clients (Abbott, 2003; Kanter, 1996; Schoenwolf, 1993):

Dreading or eagerly anticipating a client. The social worker may dread meeting with an intimidating or demanding client, or look forward to seeing an interesting or attractive client.

Differing responsiveness to clients' phone messages or failure to keep an appointment. The social worker may call back a cooperative client immediately, but wait several days or even weeks to get in touch with a client perceived as unpleasant.

Thinking excessively about a client during and after-agency hours. There are many possible reasons for such a preoccupation, including fear or attraction.

Having trouble understanding a client's conflicts. A social worker who, for example, uses alcohol may have trouble seeing that a client's alcohol abuse is problematic, particularly if the worker is in denial about his own level of use.

Boredom with a client. This may reflect a need to see change occur at a faster pace than a client is capable of.

Feeling angry with a client for nonspecific reasons. As one example, a young social worker may project onto a client his own need to break away from his family of origin. If the client does not do so, the social worker may feel anger but be unaware of its source.

Being unduly impressed with a client. The worker who is a frustrated musician may be extremely impressed with the musical accomplishments of a client. This might result in an idealization that impedes the social worker's ability to help the client achieve more basic goals.

Feeling defensive or hurt by a client's criticisms. This may be related to a social worker's general need to be liked or needed.

Doing tasks for clients that they are capable of doing for themselves. Social workers may be inclined to assist favored clients with activities of daily living. A social worker may enable dependent behavior by assuming responsibility to locate housing for a client who is capable of doing so without assistance.

Feeling uncomfortable about discussing certain topics with a client. A social worker may steer a client away from topics such as sex education and safe sex.

When the social worker develops strong positive or negative feelings about particular clients, or types of clients, the process should be recognized as normal rather than a personal limitation. Personal reactions to clients can only become problematic when they are ignored. These feelings can be best managed when the social worker *expects* a range of emotional reactions to clients, and pursues discussions of them with colleagues and supervisors so that they can be appropriately channeled.

The following example demonstrates how the intervention can be favorably influenced by the worker's personal reactions to the client.

Case Illustration: The Quiet Woman

Robyn was a 28-year-old single female with schizophrenia who lived with her younger sister. She was marginally functional, having been hospitalized with psychotic symptoms three times in the past two years. Were it not for her father's material and emotional support she might have spent even more time in psychiatric hospitals. Robyn did not bathe, wash her clothes, or eat properly. She rarely initiated conversation, seeming lost in her thoughts. She sometimes said, in tears, "Life is too hard for me." At home Robyn did little but watch television. She went out every few days to shop or take walks.

John was assigned to provide Robyn with case management services. Most of John's colleagues thought Robyn was limited in her potential for growth, but he liked her immensely, more so than the other helpers who came to know her. He was fascinated by the extent of her reality detachment and was encouraged by her tolerance of his company. John admitted liking people who were "strange" because he led such a conventional life. Because of his own interpersonal insecurities, John felt good when he perceived that clients needed his help. John presented Robyn with a modest intervention plan that she accepted. They met every two weeks at her condominium and either took a walk or went to lunch. John did not attempt to persuade her to accept medication or attend rehabilitation programs, although he hoped that she eventually would. John thought that she needed a relationship of acceptance above all else.

A positive relationship developed between them, evidenced by Robyn's ongoing willingness to meet with John. Still, for several months they had little verbal interaction. John initiated conversations, avoiding topics that she might perceive as threatening, and Robyn's responses were limited to a few sentences. Robyn still did not bathe or wash her clothes. She claimed to be eating well, but looked pale and thin. John assumed that her sister and father were attending to her material needs (she did not give him permission to talk with them). Eventually, Robyn began to talk vaguely about her anxieties. Over time John learned that she was terrified of death, abandonment by her family, physical injury, and the possibility of living in a hospital for the rest of her life. She was overwhelmed with anxiety and resented professionals who were eager for her to make changes. Robyn wanted to feel calmer, be rid of suicidal thoughts, and have friends. She did not want a job or to be linked with social activities.

John and his supervisor discussed the fact that Robyn needed to experience a safe climate before risking changes. John needed to accept her world rather than expect her to invest energy in his. Had John initially pushed harder for Robyn to enter into formal programs, he may have lost her trust. While John felt good about his work with Robyn, his supervisor suggested after four months that John should encourage the client to take more responsibility for her self-care.

The supervisor recognized that John was reluctant to do this, fearing that Robyn might react negatively to directives and stop working with him. His supervisor realized that John needed to maintain a delicate balance of supportive and more directive behaviors, and that part of John's reluctance was due to his positive feelings about Robyn. John's total acceptance of Robyn had been a great strength of his work for those first three months, but now it was preventing him from helping the client move forward.

John was able to reflect on his supervisor's observations and to present his client with more concrete goal-focused plans. After six months, the extent of Robyn's changes included her bathing weekly, occasionally washing her clothes, accepting medications from the agency psychiatrist (which had modest benefits), and allowing John to talk with her father. She worked toward her goal of making friends by practicing scripted conversations with store clerks, whom she viewed as nonthreatening. While these may appear to be small gains, they were remarkable in the context of her functional limitations. She was not rehospitalized. Robyn was able to accept John's directives because of the strength of their relationship.

Thus far the chapter has focused on processes of developing and maintaining relationships with clients. It is also important to consider how to appropriately end those relationships.

ENDING RELATIONSHIPS WITH CLIENTS

Most social workers are aware of the importance of the ending stage of intervention with clients. Still it should be emphasized that whether or not an ending is managed well can make the difference between successful and unsuccessful outcomes for the client. If intervention gains are not consolidated and the worker–client relationship is not resolved, the client may not sustain his or her growth.

The termination process should begin during the first meeting with a client system. If the social worker utilizes a time-limited intervention strategy, it should be relatively easy to orient the client to the process from its beginning to the anticipated end. If the social worker will use open-ended practice models, he or she should still provide an orientation to the total process, including a review of the indicators for ending the intervention. Students in field agencies always know when their experience will end, and should make sure that clients are aware of this ending date from the beginning.

Types of Endings

In an unplanned ending, the client unexpectedly "drops out" of the intervention. Although the client never shares the reasons for this decision with the social worker, it may occur because the client feels that he or she has made adequate gains but is reluctant to request an end to the intervention, the client is dissatisfied with the absence of perceived gains, the client is uncomfortable with the practitioner or intervention methods, or the client is taking advantage of a perceived opportunity to drop out during involuntary treatment.

The practitioner may initiate endings intentionally, despite a client's failure to achieve his or her stated goals. This may occur in situations where the client will not adhere to an intervention plan deemed reasonable by the practitioner, abuses boundaries in the clinical relationship, engages in unacceptable behavior, or demonstrates a lack of expected progress without the perceived potential to make future progress.

Practitioners prefer planned endings, of course—those that both parties can look ahead to and process. These occur in situations where there is mutual agreement that the client has achieved his or her goals, the professional must observe externally imposed time limitations, the professional utilizes time-limited intervention modalities, the practitioner departs from the setting (often necessitating a transfer), the client fires the practitioner, or the expected death of the client (as in hospice work) (Walsh, 2007).

It is not often articulated that administrators should play a major role in some client–social worker endings (Harrigan, Fauri, & Netting, 1998). Administrators are responsible for maintaining continuity and service satisfaction for clients and staff when personnel changes occur. Policies and procedures should be in place to ensure that staff turnover does not place undue hardships on clients who need to be transferred. Closer to day-to-day operations, however, managers (in addition to supervisors) must oversee particular employee transitions and work to maintain agency morale. These tasks can be difficult when a program is downsized and staff must be laid off. Not only will the well, being of the clients of those particular staff be at risk, but if morale problems affect other clinical staff their clients can be adversely affected as well (Walsh, 2007).

Tasks for Ending

When intervention is organized with attention to ending criteria, the social worker is more likely to conduct a focused intervention process and plan ahead for that ending. Listed next are ending tasks for the social worker to consider (Walsh, 2007):

- Decide when to actively implement the process
- Time the announcement of one's leaving
- Anticipate the client's and one's own reactions
- Appropriately space the remaining sessions
- Review intervention gains
- Generalize intervention gains
- Plan for goal maintenance
- Address the client's remaining needs
- Link the client with social supports (or another practitioner)

- Formally evaluate the intervention (process and outcomes)
- Set conditions and limits on future contact

The social worker must be sensitive to the fact that the ending experience might feel differently to the client than it does to the worker. For many social workers, leaving the field placement is one part of a celebratory process that includes college graduation, summer break, and perhaps the beginning of a paid social work position. This might be an exciting time of transition for the social worker. For the client, the experience might only be a sad one, as a significant relationship is ending. The social worker must be sure that his or her experience does not impair the ability to attend to the needs of the client.

Ending Rituals

Rituals provide effective ending experiences for many clients. A ritual is any formal activity that endows events with a sense of being special. It symbolizes continuity, stability, and the significance of personal bonds while helping people accept change. The structure of rituals provides a safe framework for social workers and their clients to express feelings about the transition. They affirm the importance of closure and imply that gains from the intervention can continue. The social worker may celebrate a client's rite of passage in various ways (Walsh & Meyersohn, 2001).

Formal service evaluations provide a simple ritual that can facilitate the processing of an ending. Looking at and filling out a form "objectifies" for the client a review of the intervention and relationship. It provides the client with a sense of detachment that can paradoxically facilitate expressions of feeling. It gives the client permission to respond to such questions in as much depth as he or she wishes about what it felt like to ask for help, what he or she liked most and least about the process, and how the client is planning for the future.

Expressive tasks promote communication through art forms such as painting, drawing, music, poems, and stories. These tend to lower anxiety and stimulate emotional processing. Themes on which the social worker might focus such an ending activity include "good-bye to the old and hello to the new," best and worst memories, what the client will miss most and least, how the transition is being experienced, and expectations about what lies ahead. Sharing picture books that contain messages about the importance of relationships can be effective with children.

Whether or not it is appropriate for the social worker to accept gifts from clients is an issue that is much discussed and difficult to resolve. Some agencies have policies on this matter but others do not, preferring that the issue be handled on a case-by-case basis. Some practitioners feel that clients should be permitted to express their gratitude and that gift giving may be the client's preferred means of doing so. Denying a client that opportunity may thus be disrespectful. Other practitioners feel that accepting gifts violates professional boundaries between the two parties, and that any expressions of gratitude can be made verbally. Even if the social worker does accept a gift from a client, it should be of modest material value, well within the client's means. There is a significant difference between a handmade card and a new briefcase!

What follows is an example of a positive ending ritual, reported by a student social worker about her field placements.

Case Illustration: The Runaway Shelter

Bethany works at a runaway youth shelter. There are always 40 to 50 older adolescents who live there while staff work to find them permanent housing and healthy community supports. Most of the kids are in the program for at least three months and some stay for up to five months. Staff and residents can get very attached to one another in the intimate environment. It is always a special occasion when a resident completes the program and leaves on good terms. It is certainly a positive event, but the staff and residents have mixed feelings when a person leaves. The staff hopes that the adolescent will succeed as his or her peer support diminishes. Some residents experience the loss of a friend, and others may feel sad to see a peer move on while they remain dependent on the shelter.

According to Bethany, staff celebrate a resident's leaving in the form of a "going-away luncheon." Everyone is invited, and usually 20 or more residents will attend the event along with a number of staff. During lunch, staff say a few words to the shelter community about the departing resident's achievements while at the shelter, his or her contributions to the life of the community, and the challenges that lie ahead. All members of the community are invited to share their thoughts and feelings with the group as well. Staff then present the departing resident with some gifts, usually functional items to help with his or her move, such as apartment supplies. The resident is encouraged to stay in contact with the shelter community and to come back for dinner whenever he or she wishes. Usually, the adolescent visits often during the first few months away, if he or she is living in the area. A final aspect of the ending traditions is that some staff and residents physically assist the person in moving into the new residence. Bethany states that with these practices the adolescents are supported through their transition away from our community, and they are made to feel welcome to remain a part of it.

SUMMARY

Communication and relationship-building skills are essential for social workers to engage clients and their significant others in a productive problem-solving process. These skills are also necessary for coordinating services with other human service providers. The purpose of this chapter has been to review skills that merit ongoing refinement throughout the generalist practitioner's career. Social workers can integrate these ideas with their personal styles of interaction to develop interpersonal practices that serve them well.

TOPICS FOR DISCUSSION

1. Discuss the difficulties you have had in "engaging" particular clients, and the reasons for those difficulties. In retrospect what might you have done differently to be more successful in engaging those clients in an intervention process?

2. Organize role-plays with classmates, including reactant/ambivalent clients of various types; students in the social worker roles should practice motivational interviewing strategies to help the clients resolve their ambivalence.

3. Discuss experiences you have had with difficult endings, with clients or significant others. What were the reasons for the difficulty, and what strategies might have worked better toward a more constructive ending?

4. Discuss problematic boundary issues that you have experienced with clients. How did they develop? Were they satisfactorily resolved? How? If not, why?

5. Regarding countertransference, do you think social workers have a professional responsibility to work with all types of clients, regardless of their personal reactions to the client?

ASSIGNMENT IDEAS

Write papers based on field placement experiences about any of the following topics:

1. The process of engaging a particularly challenging client in a comfortable, trusting relationship

2. The process of engaging a reactant/ambivalent client in a working relationship

3. The process of appropriately crossing boundaries with a client toward the goals of greater trust and client disclosure

Chapter 4

The "Person" of the Social Worker

The purpose of this chapter is to "step back" from the focus on the social work profession and address the needs of social workers in their professional lives. Put another way, this chapter concerns the social worker's interventions into the self, toward the goal of preserving and enhancing one's career.

For many students, the profession of social work represents a vocation. Because of their life experiences, family value systems, desire to make a difference, religious upbringing, and other reasons, students are drawn to the social work major. From the vantage point of a college instructor, it is remarkable to witness this professional development. I have had the good fortune over the years to see many impressive young (and not so young) students passionately work toward developing knowledge and skills for practice, and hear them talk excitedly about their professional plans. Many students overcome personal hardships and endure much personal sacrifice to earn their BSW degrees. While I have had a long career in social work practice I am humbled to observe that many students' dedication to the profession exceeds my own.

After graduation, most BSW students either go on to graduate school or get started on their careers (perhaps after a well-deserved break). While they have had field placement experiences, students often learn more clearly after graduation about the "ups and downs" of social work practice. They hopefully receive intrinsic rewards from their work, and learn over time the kind of practice that suits them best (for me it was direct practice with people who have mental illnesses). They also experience inevitable frustrations such as agency restrictions on their scope of practice, clients who do not seem to benefit from their efforts, and aspects of their jobs that seem to have little to do with client welfare (such as paperwork and some administrative demands).

Generalist practitioners may notice as the years go by that there is a cumulative stress that seems to go with the territory of social work practice. Working with and on behalf of people can be draining as practitioners struggle to help client systems acquire the resources they need. Public social welfare agencies, given their modest positions in the range of government legislative priorities, rarely "overflow" with operating resources. In the past 30 years agencies have tended to experience increased limitations on funding, with a consequent need for staff to "do more with less." Numbers of professional staff, opportunities for professional development, and material supports for clients are rarely adequate to facilitate the comprehensive interventions that generalist practitioners are trained to provide. In short, as rewarding as it might be, social work is a tough job! Many social workers get frustrated with their jobs over time, which may lead to their leaving the profession or burning out (which will be discussed later in this chapter).

Despite these realities I do not think that generalist practitioners must necessarily lose enthusiasm for their work over time. This possibility does exist, however, which is why preventive measures by social workers should be routinely incorporated into their agency and personal lives. With proper self-care, the generalist practitioner's chances of enjoying a long career will be enhanced. Self-care can be achieved through personal means or by the employing agency's efforts. In the case of the latter, it represents a form of agency-based intervention. What follows are descriptions of issues that have relevance to the social worker's attitudes about his or her career, along with a variety of strategies to prevent or manage problems when they occur. It should go without saying (but I'll say it anyway) that clients will always benefit from social workers' positive feelings about their work. The energized, motivated social worker will provide better services to clients than the emotionally drained practitioner.

SELF-AWARENESS

Self-awareness is a process in which social workers continuously monitor how they are thinking, feeling, and behaving in the workplace, and how those activities are related to their lives in general (Yan & Wong, 2005). In another sense, self-awareness is a process in which social workers develop a realistic understanding of what they *can* and *cannot* do well in the course of their work. Self-aware social workers try to be alert to the many factors at work and in their personal lives that affect their attitudes about their jobs, for better and for worse. It is likely that, over time, their attitudes about their careers, and their feelings about the quality of work they provide, will change, sometimes unexpectedly, in response to job and life circumstances.

While an active social worker is continuously *learning,* he or she is not necessarily *improving*. That is, while one's skills probably improve over time, his or her effectiveness may fall in response to stressful life factors. For example, when a social worker is satisfied with her personal life outside the agency, she will have less of a need to find personal affirmation from coworkers and clients. She will be able to maintain appropriate professional boundaries with clients and help them develop good resolutions to their challenges. But when a social worker is having personal problems, perhaps being rejected or feeling unappreciated by close friends and family, work may be the only place where she receives personal affirmation and a sense of being valued. The social worker in this case might rely too much on her clients to be liked or respected. She might be more demanding of her clients than is in their best interest. The social worker might tend to get angry with clients when in fact she is angry with someone in her personal life.

That one's personal life may have an effect on her professional life is inevitable, nothing to be denied or to feel ashamed about. But it is one reason that self-awareness, when exercised properly, can help a social worker maintain appropriate attention on clients. Here are two examples of how this might be attended to.

Nick was experiencing marital problems. His wife left him, taking their 6-year-old daughter with her. Nick had wanted the marriage to continue and was devastated. At the agency he often worked with families in conflict, so during this most stressful period of his personal crisis he approached his supervisor and asked not to be assigned any clients who were seeking help for family-related problems, especially related to couples conflict. Nick was aware that, while he could work with most other types of clients, he would not be able to be "objective" with partner conflicts. He knew that he would tend to take sides based on his own situation. The supervisor honored Nick's request. Several months later Nick resumed seeing families, having dealt with his personal challenges well enough to contain his emotions.

A young social worker named Nancy fell into a depression related to long-standing problems within her family related to sexual abuse. Nancy was committed to her job and tried to keep up with her work, but her supervisor could see that she was struggling and not able to concentrate on her clients. She was understandably preoccupied with her own vulnerable emotional state. Her supervisor suggested that Nancy take a leave of absence until she got her personal issues under control. Nancy negotiated a part-time "leave" and one month later resumed her work at the agency, where she was considered to be an excellent childcare worker. Later that year Nancy left to take a job in the adult criminal justice system, realizing that based on her history she should probably not work around children so much.

The previous examples demonstrate how self-awareness (as well as caring and alert supervisors) helps social workers know when they should exercise caution with, or step away from, certain aspects of their work. This may be difficult because social workers sometimes have a tendency to demand too much of themselves. As noted earlier, they usually work in agencies with limited resources, which promotes a general atmosphere of needing to "do more with less," and pressing on. But self-awareness is not only about avoiding situations that affect us negatively. It is also about helping us develop an awareness of the types of work situations that stimulate and "charge" us—that help us maintain enthusiasm about what we do. One of my supervisors was helpful to me in sorting out the kinds of clients I tended to enjoy and be effective with (people with serious mental illnesses). He helped me to understand how these clients fit with my general personality style, and how I could use my personal qualities to the advantage of these clients.

So how does one develop self-awareness? There is no formula. One principle, however, is that if a person *tries* to be self-aware, he or she probably *will be self-aware*. That is, if a social worker recognizes the importance of self-awareness, he or she will routinely try to monitor how personal situations affect his or her work, positively and negatively. Some people develop self-awareness through a pursuit of interests that have nothing to do with social work, such as writing, journaling, painting, and listening to music. Others do so through personal reflection and perhaps spiritual activities. Another principle of self-awareness is that the social worker should be willing to *ask* for help from trusted others (family, friends, coworkers, or supervisors) about how personal issues seem to affect their work.

What follows is a set of questions for personal reflection, and possibly discussion with others, that can help to enhance self-awareness. These questions attempt to help social workers get at the core of why they became social workers, how it helps and perhaps can be harmful at times to their well-being, and what aspects of relationships they value most. These reflections may help the social worker feel anchored when he or she begins to experience professional stress and self-doubt.

Being a Social Worker

Why did you decide to become a social worker? What was it about the idea of social work practice that was appealing?

At what point in your life did you begin to act as a helper for others? How did helping others serve to help yourself? Did you pay a price for helping others (such as focusing too little on your own needs)?

How does helping others continue to help you now? Do you continue to pay a price for helping others, in your work and personal life? Can you organize your life so that the price you pay for helping others does not significantly harm you?

Recall an adult who helped you in your early (pre-college) life. Of the following factors, which contributed *most* to your being helped? Which was *least* important? Was it the personal characteristics of the helper (respect, awareness, compassion), your own characteristics (motivation, openness, developmental readiness), or the technique the helper used (reflective listening, confrontation, advice, and so on)?

Which of the three factors described do you currently value the most? Why? How is that evident in your work? Are you able to recognize that others may respond to different helping factors than you do?

Cognitive, Physical, and Emotional Development

Social workers need to develop their cognitive, physical, affective, spiritual, and social dimensions to be able to assess and intervene most effectively with diverse client populations. *Cognitive* development incorporates our *beliefs* about self and others, our problem-solving and decision-making capacities, and our utilization of various forms of intelligence. Issues from the *physical* dimension relevant to practice include our perceptions of the connection of the mind to the body, our trust or distrust of internal perceptions (gut feelings), how we accept and manage personal attraction toward clients, and how we model physical self-care for clients. (The other dimensions are defined later.)

Which of your developmental dimensions do you value the most, and why?

Which of the five dimensions were most emphasized during your upbringing? How have those experiences affected your development?

Which dimensions do you rely on when under stress? Do you rely on the same dimensions when working with clients?

What forms of intelligence—linguistic, analytic, musical, physical, spatial, interpersonal, and intrapersonal (Gardner, 1999)—do you value the most? Why?

How could you learn to develop greater intellectual diversity?

What emotions in yourself are you most aware of? What emotions are you least aware of? Why is that?

What emotions in yourself do you accept the most easily? What are the most difficult for you to accept? Why?

What emotions are the hardest for you to accept in others? Why? How could you learn to better accept diversity of emotion?

Think about a person in your life who was compassionate with you. What did it feel like to be with that person? How was he or she able to be so compassionate?

Think of a time when you felt unusually compassionate toward someone else. Why were you able to be that way with him or her?

Think of a time when you felt unusually *unable* to be compassionate. Why was that? How might you overcome whatever obstacles to compassion you identify?

Spiritual Development

Spirituality is a broad term, and refers to each person's search for, or adherence to, ultimate meanings, purposes, and commitments that guide their lives (Frankl, 1988). It may refer to religious beliefs (which include adherence to specific and shared dogmas) or more generally to individual quests.

What aspects of spirituality are most important in your personal life? How were they instilled, or how did they arise, in you?

How does your spiritual life compare with that of others? Are you tolerant of, or interested in, the spiritual systems of others?

Are your personal values the same ones that underlie your social work practice?

Are you still open to revising your values, or your spiritual dimension?

What values or types of spirituality of others are the hardest for you to tolerate? How can you learn to better accept diversity in this way?

Social Development

This refers to our patterns of relating to family, friends, coworkers, and supervisors. Social development has implications for self-discipline, and our ability to relax, communicate, be assertive, and express emotions.

How comfortable do you feel around other people in general? Do you tend to see people as welcoming or threatening?

Are you energized or exhausted by social interaction? Why is that?

How does your general interpersonal style affect your interactions with peers, supervisors, and clients?

What interpersonal traits are the hardest for you to tolerate in other people? Why?

How can you become more accepting of this diversity?

How safe do you feel in the workplace or classroom? Can you examine your strengths and limitations with others there? Are the obstacles to safety internal or external?

Self-awareness is a process; it is never complete. And because we change over time, we will continue to discover new aspects of ourselves in relation to our social work practice. Self-awareness has an important preservative function, but despite our best intentions it is possible to wear out over time—to lose enthusiasm for our work. We now turn to a discussion of burnout and compassion fatigue, two similar conditions in which enthusiasm and energy wane to a degree that our professional commitment may come into question.

BURNOUT AND COMPASSION FATIGUE

Burnout is a condition that is characterized by a social worker's loss of emotional responsiveness to clients, often accompanied by a negative attitude about his or her job, that results from experiencing increasing amounts of job stress (Lloyd, King, & Chenowith, 2002). Burnout can result from work environment factors that add to stress in the absence of factors alleviating it, a lack of clarity about job roles and expectations, administrative demands of workers (the agency system requires more energy than clients do), and a lack of supportive coworkers and supervisors. A social worker who is burned out will have less energy to invest in clients and coworkers, will respond to clients in detached, dehumanizing ways, and will experience a reduced sense of personal accomplishment in his or her work. Ironically it may be an agency's best employees who are at risk for burnout, because they put so much of themselves into their jobs.

Stress events are neutral, as described in the Chapter 10 discussion of crisis intervention. For example, the social worker who sees the stress of working with difficult clients as a challenge will feel motivated and energized about the task. The social worker who interprets the stress of working with such clients as negative will feel overwhelmed, irritable, and worried. It follows that while job stress is unavoidable, burnout can be prevented or ameliorated by adjusting the work environment so that it is perceived as supportive.

Compassion fatigue is a related but slightly different negative outcome of professional practice. It is a term often used interchangeably with burnout, but more specifically it refers to a physical and emotional fatigue that causes a gradual decline in a social worker's ability to feel and care for others (Collins & Long, 2003b). The social worker devotes a great deal of energy to others over a period of time, but doesn't get enough back from other agency employees (or clients) to feel reassured that the work is relevant. As one example, the social worker who sees, day after day, children who have been molested will probably begin to suffer emotionally over time. The suffering that these children experience is quite tragic and visible to the social worker, who thus experiences the pain to at least some extent. Compassion fatigue develops over time, taking months or years to surface. Clearly, seeing clients recover or make progress is one antidote to this fatigue (Collins & Long, 2003a).

In the remainder of this section we will consider the possible effects of burnout or compassion fatigue on social workers, as well as interventions that can help to prevent or remove those phenomena. The possible effects on the social worker of burnout and compassion fatigue include (Netting, Kettner, & McMurtry, 2004):

- Passive capitulation (going through the motions of one's job without much emotional investment)

- Finding a comfortable niche (a job or work schedule that is tolerable or comfortable, but does not demand much spontaneity or intensity of effort)

- Withdrawal (similar to the previous response, but characterized more by interpersonal avoidance, such as the social worker who keeps to himself and stops participating in team projects at the agency)

- Overidentification with disempowered clients (siding with clients as oppressed people in a way that is not productive, such as joining with their complaints merely as a means of venting)

- Advocating for changes that will help to reduce and prevent burnout

Notice that only the final response is a constructive one in the context of professional growth. In that spirit we now turn to strategies for reducing and preventing burnout and compassion fatigue.

GOOD SOCIAL WORKER CARE:
AGENCY STRATEGIES

What follows is a list of strategies that agencies may implement to address staff burnout issues (Collins & Long, 2003b; Figley, 2002; Keidel, 2002; Lloyd, King, & Chenowith, 2002).

Policies and procedures about employee activities that include "latitude," so the agency can be responsive to the particular needs of social workers for different types of work experiences. An agency may, for example, allow interested direct practitioners to assume some managerial roles.

Clarity of job descriptions and worker tasks. Social workers function best when they know the range of activities that comprise, and do not comprise, their jobs. For example, community-based case managers often provide a wide range of services for their clients. This can be exciting work, but some case managers may not develop an appropriate sense of limits and become exhausted in trying to respond to the seemingly endless material and interpersonal needs of clients.

The incorporation of variety into caseloads and other work assignments. One of my directors had a policy that direct practice staff needed to work with at least one client from each agency program (older adults, adolescents, shoplifters, people from the psychiatric hospital, and so on) so that they would not become, in her words, "bored" or "boring."

Staff development programs, especially those including staff input. Learning new practices that may enhance their work is stimulating for social workers, and these programs are also a break from the agency routine.

Promoting peer camaraderie through formal and informal agency support systems. Examples include social work departmental meetings and Friday lunch outings.

Formal and regularly scheduled supervision (individually or in groups).

A shallow agency hierarchy (functionally if not officially) so that social workers (and others) feel they have easy access to agency administration when they have ideas or concerns.

Staff participation in decision making, to the extent that this is feasible within the agency. This can be accomplished through departmental meetings in which social workers can set some policies, and also by having the department represented in a meaningful way on the agency's administrative team.

Differential and varied rewards for good work and commitment to the agency. If all staff tend to get the same annual salary adjustments due to agency policies, for example, other rewards could be implemented for good performance such as time off, opportunities to supervise, participation in program development, and so on.

These strategies are for implementation by agency administrators. What follows next are strategies for social workers to address individually toward their professional self-care.

SOCIAL WORKER SELF-CARE

Several years ago, two psychologists compiled a therapist's self-care "checklist" (Guy & Norcross, 1998). Items on their list were drawn from a literature review of articles about therapist self-care. While generalist social workers do not function in the same manner as psychologists or psychotherapists, most of the items from their list are applicable to social workers and are reviewed here.

Appreciate the Rewards of Social Work Practice

Let your style of practice capitalize on your natural helping characteristics. Never lose sight of the ways in which you interact most comfortably with clients. When we learn how to work with new client populations, or learn a new intervention technique, we sometimes try to act in ways that are contrary to our natural, caring selves. We should always integrate that real part of ourselves into our work. In doing so we will feel most alive and connected with others. For example, there may be a client population with which you need to be more confrontational than is natural for you. You can learn this skill without sacrificing your natural helping style.

Focus on those occasional but exciting life-changing practice experiences in which you had the good fortune to participate. When I get frustrated with my work, and begin to ponder how often I fail to make a difference, I think about the clients whom I have helped, especially in situations where it didn't seem likely that my intervention would be successful. Those were thrilling moments and they sustain me through times of frustration. I can look forward to having experiences like that in the future, and the thought helps me to keep my day-to-day work in a larger perspective.

Clinical practice won't make you rich, but it is a fascinating way to make a living. When I have dinner with relatives, most of whom are businesspeople with high incomes, and we talk about our jobs, I rarely become jealous (well, sometimes I do). This is because as I hear other people talk about their job routines I appreciate how exciting it is to spend my workdays interacting with such interesting people. The clients I encounter may be funny, frightening, courageous, intimidating, marginal, and colorful, but they are always interesting. The variety of personalities I meet is a built-in barrier to the relative monotony of some other types of work I hear about.

Attend to your ongoing professional growth. Practitioners may always be at-risk for burnout and compassion fatigue, so they have a responsibility to keep themselves interested, most significantly by learning and growing. At one of my agencies the social work staff decided to offer workshops to professionals in the region. The director assigned a support staff person as a "marketer," and staff selected topic areas for presentation in which they were experienced or interested. Presenting social workers were given one day off to research the topic. The continuing education series was offered annually for three years. Now, some social workers may groan at the idea of "adding" work as an antidote to burnout, but this worked for us. It had a side benefit of increasing staff camaraderie.

Do Not Deny or Minimize the Stresses Inherent in Social Work Practice

Accept the universality of the stresses social workers experience. Rather than feel that they should be able to resist, or rise above stressful experiences with clients and perhaps coworkers, social workers should realize that these are normal aspects of professional practice. Social work is stressful much of the time, and it may help practitioners manage that stress if they accept and "roll with," rather than deny, its inevitability. Part of this acceptance is the awareness that other practitioners feel the same emotions, which may help us to process them with others. For example, one practitioner in my program felt guilty, immature, and incompetent because he developed a crush on one of his same-age clients. He carried these feelings around for weeks. While this is admittedly a difficult subject to process with anyone, the social worker was eventually able to open up to a peer and was relieved to learn that there was nothing uncommon about his feelings. It is the social worker's response to these feelings, rather than the feelings themselves, that determined whether there were ethical problems.

Invite friends and family to point out when you become too "professional" in your everyday life. Social workers, particularly when they are new to an exciting job, sometimes forget that their friends and family may not be interested in hearing them analyze troubled people and social problems in their daily lives. I was at a party one evening with a dozen or so young social workers. In a humorous act of defiance, their dates banded together and walked out after listening to their partners sit in a circle to (anonymously) discuss their challenging new clients. The tone of the conversation was reminiscent of a staff meeting. After the partners walked out, the social workers got the point, and the party resumed with a happier outcome. Social workers should be particularly careful not to casually apply their intervention skills to family and friends. This may create an artificial distance in those relationships.

Refuse to believe either your most idealizing or devaluing clients. Nothing feels more gratifying than having a client express gratitude for work we have provided. We should accept these thanks and take them to heart. However, this should never go to our heads. If it does, we are likely to be equally impressed in a negative way by the client who tells us we are the worst, least mature, most judgmental, most bored human service professional he has ever known (I have been called all of those things). As one of my supervisors said, "If you don't take the praise too seriously, you won't take the criticism so seriously either, and you'll live longer [as a social worker]."

Pursue unrelated interests in your personal life. As dedicated as a person may be to his or her career, one's life always needs balance. Social workers will feel more energetic and refreshed, and maintain a more objective perspective on their careers, if they can truly get away from the work, mentally and physically. I personally believe that the more different those interests are from social work practice, the more balanced that life will be. For example, if one looks for balance by volunteering as a tutor at the local middle school, the school and its students might benefit. The social worker, however, may feel drained at times as he moves from the job to the school, experiencing similar pressures in both places. My friend the beekeeper seems to have a more refreshing diversion.

Get your paperwork done right away. It won't be any easier tomorrow. Actually it will be more difficult, because you will begin to forget important details. Few aspects of human services practice seem to deaden one's enthusiasm more so than paperwork—but it has to be done! I've always been pretty good at keeping up with paperwork. I consider the first 10 minutes after the end of a meeting as a part of that meeting. I can't take a coffee or bathroom break until my note is written. I won't say this is pleasurable, but I've never been reprimanded at the end of the month when administration does its charting reviews.

Nurture Relationships Inside and Outside the Office

Social worker–client relationships are not intended to be reciprocal, so in order to get our interpersonal needs met, it is important to cultivate and maintain our connections with other people. We can take care of this need in the following ways.

Make sure you get good supervisory support. The importance of having empathic, available, and confidential mentors was described earlier in this chapter. We want to feel safe with some people at work, safe enough to express our self-doubts, and that is part of what a good supervisor can provide.

Create opportunities for contact with other supportive practitioners, either at the office or from other agencies. This support network can keep us updated on issues in practice and provide us with people to listen when we face certain stresses. These connections can also provide an outlet for fun. For example, at one agency I played first base for two years on the softball team (combined record: won 8, lost 10).

Define your relationships with colleagues and staff with care. Don't become obstacles to each other, or expect too much in the way of help and availability. My good friend Kathy was very good at this. As much as she enjoyed our working together, if I ever needed consultation on a client, I needed to make an appointment to talk with her. On the other hand, it was perfectly fine if I stopped into her office to say hello and chat about the weekend.

Spend some time every day with those people at the office who make you feel comfortable (including support staff). I enjoy spending time with nonprofessional staff, as well as with my colleagues, not because I like them more, but because their routines and perspectives are different than mine and I find them refreshing.

Break up your workday with short contacts with friends and family. Phone calls, e-mails, and lunch contacts can bring freshness to one's day. I once worked near a mall (who doesn't, in cities, anyway). My friend Ken, who worked at a school, used to meet me at a music store once every week and browse for compact discs. I was always in a good mood when I returned to the office, and the afternoon passed quickly.

Establish an identity apart from your role as a clinician (even at the agency). Assert your individuality at the agency by letting your personality show. Are you a good writer? Musician? Painter? Comedian? Stock market analyst? All people have their talents, and it is often fun for you and your coworkers to let these surface in the context of agency life. My friends and I developed an exotic coffee club at one agency, introducing a new brew each week for our subscribing members. It was legitimate but all in fun, too. The only problem is that it encouraged caffeine addictions among some staff!

Use trusted family and friends to "reality test" regarding your professional concerns. When you become concerned with issues at the office regarding your job, it is helpful to bounce your thinking off friends and family who are detached from the situation and may be able to offer an unbiased perspective. This is different than the earlier point about bringing one's work home, because it pertains to seeking out the help of friends and family rather than simply venting about clients.

Set Clear Boundaries with Clients

Avoiding burnout and compassion fatigue requires that we not get overly involved with our clients. This will be discussed in Chapter 8. The following are additional strategies for maintaining boundaries.

Be clear with clients about how your practice is organized. Make sure your clients know what they can and cannot expect from you. For example, clearly delineate with clients your policies about extra time, extra meetings, late appointments, and telephone availability. This will help you feel less "pulled" into additional work.

Always remember that your clients are not there to meet your needs. Client–social worker relationships are not reciprocal. We became social workers because we find gratification in helping others, and it is well and good that we do this. But we cannot count on our clients to meet our personal needs for companionship and intimacy. My friend Shanza, who was about 35 years old, became overly involved with her adolescent clients because she always wanted children but had none. At one agency, where I was the least experienced practitioner, I became overly involved with my clients with schizophrenia because I was trying to prove to my colleagues that I could be as effective as they were.

Schedule variety into your workday. Don't see clients all day every day (unless you find that energizing). Organize your day in a way that both builds in variety and also capitalizes on your strengths. I have most of my energy in the morning, so I like to schedule clients from 9:00 until about 2:00. After that I spend time alone in my office, recharging and getting paperwork done. I'd end the day with a home visit.

When you end relationships with clients, be clear about the conditions under which they might return. It is not unusual for clients to call back for additional meetings following a termination. They may want permission to check in or remain friends. While we might (or might not) enjoy contact by former clients, we will be able to function better, and let go, if there has been closure to the work.

Create a Facilitative Physical Work Environment for Yourself

Enhance your physical work environment. I have never worked in an agency that was materially attractive in a conventional sense, or that offered much in the way of office decor. In fact, I have worked in some jobs where I didn't have an office at all. I may have shared an office with other staff or worked in a cubicle. And I have always been lazy about decorating whatever space I have with furnishings of my own. On the other hand, I have watched coworkers take time to bring in wall hangings, comfortable furniture, pictures, posters, decorations, books, and incense, among other items, to make their surroundings comfortable. I think this is important, again as a way of feeling good while at work. Sitting in a gloomy office has never helped my mood. I need to get better at this!

Cultivate a Sense of Mission

The following items ask us to step back from our day-to-day work and reflect on our place in the big picture, the social work profession itself.

Reflect on your sources of optimism about human nature. We became social workers for a variety of reasons, but one commonality is that we believe (though we may doubt ourselves at times) that all people in need deserve help, can respond to offers of help, and can change and grow. At those times when we question ourselves or the profession it is helpful to remember where our basic beliefs came from. Again, they may derive from personal example, religious faith, a sense of spirituality, or a desire to connect with others. Getting in touch with our basic faiths in human nature can help us to maintain a positive stance in our work.

Try to identify a personal mission or purpose in your clinical career. This involves taking a long view of one's work, and placing day-to-day episodes (both ups and downs) and perhaps longer-term issues related to frustrating job experiences into a broader perspective. That is, what are we working toward, professionally? What accounts for that direction, and that evolution? Many of the questions presented in the previous section can be considered here.

Develop a sense of connection with the social workers that have come before you. You learned in your first social work course that the profession has been active in the United States since the late 1800s. I am personally fascinated to learn what the early social workers achieved. They were determined men and (mostly) women, driven by a desire to make contributions to society in an era when their work was not widely respected. They are the people who account for where social work is today, for how far it has moved in becoming a respected profession and area of academic study. The historical perspective may not be everyone's cup of tea, and it may only become interesting as a social worker becomes older and can see professional evolution even in his or her own career.

SUMMARY

The material in this chapter has been intended to underscore the importance of self-care in one's professional career. I close the chapter with a reflection on the importance of each social worker's contribution to the future of the profession. Generalist practitioners are immersed in the raw material of the social work profession every day, and trying to bring about change always prods the self-aware practitioner to question and improve ideas and practices. Once the social worker achieves a certain level of expertise in school, the main source of useful new knowledge becomes his or her clients. As the social worker graduates and goes to work, he or she should become willing to take risks and forge new interventions on behalf of clients.

Through your devotion to personal and professional growth, as well as your client's well-being, the future of generalist practice is in your hands!

TOPICS FOR DISCUSSION

1. Reflect on and discuss several of the questions listed in this chapter on the topics of:

- Being a social worker
- Your physical, cognitive, emotional, spiritual, and/or social development

ASSIGNMENT IDEAS

1. Maintain a journal in which you reflect on your typical life stressors and how you might take better care of yourself with regard to them. Include thoughts on how such stressors might negatively or positively affect your practice as a social worker.
2. Interview a direct practice social worker and a social work administrator about some common issues in their agencies related to burnout and compassion fatigue. Ask how they have made efforts to deal with those issues, if they exist.
3. Select any one or several of the self-care strategies described in this chapter and describe how you might apply it to yourself in a social work job, student placement, volunteer experience, or any other type of current or recent employment.

PART II

Intervention Theories and Applications

Chapter 5

Behavior Theory

In this and the following chapter we will focus on the behavioral and cognitive practice theories, representing a broad class of interventions with a shared focus on changing *behavior,* changing *cognition* (thoughts, beliefs, and assumptions about the world), and building clients' *coping skills.* The behavior and cognitive theories emerged from different perspectives on human behavior, but they can be integrated into a comprehensive approach to working with individuals, families, and groups. We will focus on this integration in the next chapter. Cognitive theory itself focuses on the rationality of one's thinking patterns (the degree to which conclusions about the self and the world are based on external evidence) and the connections among behaviors, thoughts, and feelings. Behavior theory is not concerned with internal mental processes but rather how human behavior, whether adaptive or problematic, is developed, sustained, or eliminated through *reinforcement* and *punishment.* Both theories have many practical applications for generalist interventions with individuals, families, and groups. This chapter will trace behavior theory with a focus on its applications for change.

Behaviorism has been prominent in the social sciences since the first half of the 20th century, and it became a popular theory among social workers and other clinical practitioners in the 1960s. Among its pioneers were Pavlov (1927), Watson (1924), and Skinner (1953). In social work, Thyer and Wodarski (2007) and Wodarski and Bagarozzi (1979) are respected behaviorists. The rise of behaviorism reflected a new emphasis in the social sciences on empiricism (observable evidence) in evaluating the outcomes of intervention. Behavioral interventions can be helpful for clients of all types, but they are especially effective with clients who have cognitive deficits (people with autism and mental retardation), clients whose cognitive capacity has not developed sufficiently for them to engage in abstract thinking (such as children and young adolescents), and clients who are not by nature reflective. Verbal interventions are in fact generally limited in effectiveness prior to adolescence. Today's service delivery environment, with its focus on concrete outcome indicators, owes a great debt to the behaviorists, who remain the most diligent group of practitioners in measuring intervention outcomes (Granvold, 1994).

BASIC ASSUMPTIONS OF BEHAVIOR THEORY

The basic principles and assumptions of behavior theory are as follows (Leahy, 1996; Wilson, 2000; Wodarski & Bagarozzi, 1979):

Behavior is what a person does, thinks, or feels that can be observed. Inferences about a person's mental activity should be minimized because it cannot be directly observed. Assessment should focus on observable events with a minimum of interpretation.

People are motivated by nature to seek pleasure and avoid pain. They are likely to behave in ways that produce encouraging responses, or positive reinforcement.

People behave based on their learning. They learn through direct environmental feedback and also by watching others behave and interact.

Behavior is amenable to change. A prerequisite for change is that the behavior of concern must be defined in terms of measurable indicators.

Intervention should focus on influencing reinforcements or punishments for client behaviors.

Consistent and immediate reinforcement produces change most rapidly.

Thoughts and feelings are also behaviors and are subject to reinforcement principles.

The simplest explanations for behavior are always preferred. Social workers should avoid reification (giving life to esoteric concepts such as the "ego") and the search for ultimate causes of behavior.

Behaviorists do not work from any particular theories of human development. They do acknowledge, however, that genetic and biological influences are relevant to a person's physical and trait development. That is, a person's ability to learn, and sensitivity to certain environmental cues, will influence his or her response to potential reinforcers and punishments.

THE NATURE OF PROBLEMS AND CHANGE

All behavior is influenced by the same principles of learning, which include classical conditioning, operant conditioning, and modeling (from social learning theory). These are described next. In short, a person's behaviors change when the reinforcements in his or her environment change. *Reinforcement* can be understood as any environmental feedback that encourages the continuation of a behavior, and *punishment* is feedback that discourages the continuation of a behavior. Intervention always involves changing a client's reinforcers so that more desirable or functional behaviors will result.

Classical Conditioning

Conditioning is a process of developing patterns of behavior through responding to environmental stimuli or specific behavioral consequences. The earliest behavioral research involved *classical* conditioning in which an initially neutral stimulus comes to produce a conditioned response after being paired repeatedly with a conditioned stimulus. In Pavlov's famous research, food (the conditioned stimulus) naturally produced salivation (a nonvoluntary response) in dogs. A bell (the unconditioned stimulus) initially failed to evoke salivation. However, after the bell was paired with the food over time, the dogs started to salivate when presented with the bell by itself. The bell at this point attained the status of a conditioned stimulus since it was capable of producing a response.

Classical conditioning plays a role in many behavioral problems that clients experience. For example, previously neutral cues, such as certain places (restaurants or bars), people, or feeling states (such as boredom) may become associated with problem behaviors such as overeating or substance abuse. Many anxiety-related disorders are also classically conditioned. For instance, a bite by a dog might generalize to a fear of all dogs. A series of stressful classroom presentations in grade school might generalize to a person's long-standing fear of public speaking.

During social work intervention the principles of classical conditioning are reversed. For example, consider a client struggling with a drug problem who has urges to use when experiencing boredom. The conditional pairing between boredom and drug use could eventually lose its association over time if the person abstained from using drugs to counteract boredom and instead developed new ways to cope with that feeling. As another example, fear-laden situations such as those involving confronting an authority figure (such as a boss) may be rank-ordered by a client and social worker according to the level of fear they invoke. The client may isolate the steps of preparing his message, rehearsing the message, walking into the workplace, entering the boss' room, and looking at the person. The client may even first perform these steps with mental images before doing so in actuality. The client then learns to face each event or item on the list, starting with the least anxiety provoking, by learning to pair relaxation exercises with the event rather than anxiety. In this process of *systematic desensitization,* clients work their way through the rank ordering of fears until they are no longer plagued by the anxiety.

Operant Conditioning

The main premise of *operant* conditioning is that future behavior is determined by the consequences of present behavior. A student's good study habits may reflect her desire to make the honor roll (a future consequence). The social worker's attention is also paid to the *antecedent,* or prior, conditions that may trigger the behavior. Two types of reinforcement are postulated in this model—positive and negative. Keep in mind that both positive and negative reinforcement encourage the continuation of a behavior. *Positive* reinforcement encourages the continuation of a behavior preceding it. For instance, alcohol use is positively reinforced by the resultant feelings of well-being and pleasant social interaction with others. *Negative* reinforcement is the process by which an aversive event is terminated by the individual's behavior and, therefore, the behavior is reinforced. Alcohol use, for example, is negatively reinforcing if it leads to escape from negative feelings. Compulsive behaviors, such as overeating or substance abuse, are reinforced positively by the feelings of well-being that are created and the social interaction with others involving the food or substance. In practice clients are helped to seek out behaviors that can offer alternative reinforcements, that is, other activities such as relationships, work, or hobbies, so they will not be as prone to indulging in the problem behavior.

Social Learning

Social learning theory emphasizes that learning takes place through observation, practice, and interaction between the person and others in the environment. Not only does desirable behavior increase with the use of positive consequences, but a supportive social context contributes to motivation, retaining information, and generalizing knowledge across situations. Social learning theory relies to a great extent on principles of conditioning, which assert that behavior is shaped by its reinforcing or punishing consequences (operant conditioning) and antecedents (classical conditioning). Albert Bandura (1977) added the principle of vicarious learning, or *modeling,* which asserts that people often acquire behavior by witnessing how the actions of others are reinforced. Social learning theorists also emphasize that thinking takes place between the occurrence of a stimulus and our response, and they call this process *cognitive mediation.* The unique patterns people learn for evaluating environmental stimuli explain why they may adopt very different behaviors in response to the same stimuli. In social work intervention from this perspective, there is a focus on creating support for client learning and building on the social context in which their learning takes place.

Modeling, or watching others engage in and be reinforced for behavior, is a pervasive means of learning for children and adolescents. For instance, children may learn to act appropriately in school by seeing classmates praised for listening to the teacher and criticized for talking while the teacher is lecturing. People may begin using alcohol or acting aggressively because they see their parents and other relatives acting this way. Modeling is one of the chief methods of behavioral change. By modeling, the social worker shows the client how to enact a new behavior for which the client is likely to be rewarded. The client then practices the new behavior (called behavioral rehearsal), receiving supportive feedback and suggestions for its refinement.

Role-playing, a component of modeling, involves the social worker first modeling a skill followed by the client's rehearsing the new behavior. The practitioner's use of modeling offers a number of advantages as an intervention tool. First, the social worker demonstrates new skills for the client, which usually is a more powerful way of conveying information than simple instruction. The second advantage is that by playing the client, the social worker tends to gain a fuller appreciation of the challenges the client faces (Hepworth, Rooney, Rooney, Strom-Gottfried, & Larsen, 2006). At the same time, the client's taking on the perspective of the other person (family member, boss, friend) allows the client to more easily understand this other person's position. Taking on other roles also introduces a note of playfulness and humor to a situation that may have been previously viewed with grim seriousness. These new perspectives sometimes encourage clients to try out alternative behaviors. After modeling, it is helpful for the social worker to share the difficulties he or she experienced in the process so that the client receives validation for the problem.

In summary, all situations in which people find themselves (except for truly novel ones) cue or prompt behaviors based on principles of classical conditioning (paired associations with certain aspects of the setting), operant conditioning (prior experiences in similar situations), or modeling (watching others behave and receive feedback). During the first day of class during a new academic year at a new school, for example, a student may be inclined to socialize with others based in part on conditioned positive associations of the classroom setting with other peer situations. She may respond eagerly to the instructor's questions due to her anticipation of positive reinforcement. Finally, she will watch how students behave in this new school to learn what other classroom behaviors are reinforced by other students and the instructor.

GOALS OF INTERVENTION

The goals of behavioral intervention are to help the client achieve new, desirable behaviors by manipulating the environment to change reinforcement patterns. For example, returning to the previous scenario, if a child behaves in school in ways that are disruptive to the classroom process (from the perspective of the teacher), the social worker can devise a plan in which those negative behaviors are extinguished and new, more acceptable classroom behaviors are reinforced. One of the challenges in behavior intervention, however, is to identify the *specific* responses that are reinforcing to the client among the many responses that he or she receives. A teacher's displeasure with acting out behaviors might serve as punishment to some students but as reinforcement to others (who may be more focused on peer reactions).

BEHAVIOR ASSESSMENT

The generalist practitioner can perform a comprehensive behavioral assessment through *functional analysis*, a process in which the client's problem behavior is broken down into its specific manifestations, the conditions (cues) that produce it, and the consequences that follow. The practitioner asks questions of the client

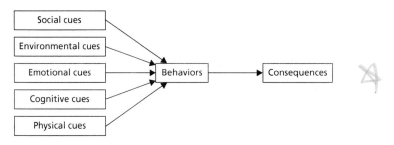

FIGURE 5.1   Functional Behavioral Analysis

about environmental cues in each of five areas that may be related to the problem situation, as noted in Figure 5.1 (Carroll, 1995).

The following are examples of assessment questions (Bertolino & O'Hanlon, 2002):

- When do you experience the behavior?
- Where do you experience the behavior?
- How long does the problem typically last?
- What happens immediately after the behavior occurs? That is, what do you do?
- What bodily reactions do you experience?
- How long do these reactions last?
- How often does the problem typically happen (once an hour, once a day, once a week)?
- What is the typical timing of the problem (time of day, week, month, year)?
- What do the people around you usually do when the problem is happening?

The social worker attempts to discover the specific antecedents and reinforcers of the problem behavior. Table 5.1 includes a list of cues, behaviors, and consequences to investigate in each of the five domains.

From this functional analysis, the reinforcers and triggers that are maintaining the client's problem are determined. This leads to a process in which the social worker and client construct concrete target behaviors that attend to the antecedent conditions and consequences required to bring about the desired new behaviors. Homework assignments for the client in which these conditions are applied are critical for the success of behavior intervention. Learning and putting behavioral principles into operation are the only way it can work.

To review the quality of the assessment, the social worker can ask himself or herself the following questions:

- Is the client's problem stated specifically?
- Can the problem be translated into concrete behaviors?
- Is the client motivated to actively work on the problem?

TABLE 5.1   The Five Domains of Behavioral Analysis

Domain	Antecedents (Triggers, Cues)	Consequences (Reinforcers)
Social	With whom does the client spend most of his time? Does he have relationships with people who do not have the problem? Does he live with someone who is involved in the problem?	Has the client's social network changed since the problem began or escalated? How have his relationships been affected?
Environmental	What people, places, and things act as cues for the problem? What is the level of the client's day-to-day exposure to these cues? Can some of these cues be easily avoided?	What people, places, and things have been affected by the problem? Has the client's environment changed as a result of the problem?
Emotional	What feeling states precede the occurrence of the problem?	How does the client feel afterward? How does he feel about himself?
Cognitive	What thoughts run through the client's mind, or what beliefs does he have about the problem?	What is he thinking afterward? What does he say to himself?
Physical	What uncomfortable physical states precede the problem occurrence?	How does the client feel physically afterward? What is the state of his physical health as a result?

- What reinforcers tend to be most influential in the client's life?
- Who is available to assist the client in problem resolution?
- What resources can the client mobilize to resolve the problem?
- How can the client's behaviors be measured over time?

GOAL SETTING AND INTERVENTION PRINCIPLES

The process of goal setting and intervention in behavior theory is quite systematic, and includes the following steps:

- The client's problems are stated in behavioral terms. Measurable objectives related to problem reduction are developed.
- The social worker and client gather baseline data (its current frequency and intensity of occurrence) on the problem through *observations* of client

behavior, any *records* that might be available, *tests or scales,* or client *self-report* (although the last of these does not match well with observations).

- The steps required to reach problem resolution are specified.

- The client's personal and environmental resources (including client system strengths) for making changes are specified. Any other people who will participate in the intervention are identified and sought out for consultation.

- Possible obstacles to goal achievement are identified in advance, and plans are made to minimize them.

- An appropriate intervention strategy is chosen with the participation of the client and with an emphasis on behavioral reinforcement rather than punishment.

- The social worker, client, or others collect data and document the client's behavior changes on a regular basis with graphs, charts, or other records. Intervention and baseline measures are compared to determine the extent of change.

- When change has taken effect, reinforcement is applied more intermittently. Clients are helped to reward themselves for success.

- Intervention ends after the client achieves his or her goals with the likelihood of goal maintenance.

Intervention in behavior theory is ended through a process of *fading*. That is, after an intervention has been underway for some length of time and the client has acquired the desired new behaviors, any artificial supports (including the social worker and the reinforcement schedule) are gradually eliminated (or faded). This includes reducing the frequency of meetings between the client and social worker.

There are many behavioral interventions that the social worker may select, depending on the presenting problem, the client's preferences, and the time and resources available to the practitioner. Described next are two extended examples of behavioral interventions. Other approaches will be introduced in later chapters of this book.

PARENTING EDUCATION

A model of operant behavioral intervention has been developed around teaching parents to apply the principles of reinforcement to their children's behavior. Called *parenting education,* it is a process in which parents are helped to reinforce desirable behaviors in their children and ignore or punish negative behavior. The intervention model can be provided in individual, family, or group formats. The components of successful parenting education involve the following steps:

- Parents select a priority goal around the child's behavior.

- Goals are broken down into their smaller, observable components called *tasks.*

- Goals and tasks are formulated to encourage a presence of positive behavior rather than the absence of negative behavior.
- A behavior baseline is determined.
- A target behavioral goal is established.

As an example, Ms. Cheng elected to participate in parenting education because her son Johnny would not do his homework. He also engaged in disruptive behaviors at bedtime. This was almost a crisis for Ms. Cheng, because as an Asian American woman she assumed primary responsibility in the family for caregiving and the children's education. In order to determine a reasonable target for the desired behaviors, *the baseline,* or current occurrence of the behaviors, must be determined. Its occurrence can be measured in different ways—through its frequency (Ms. Cheng says that Johnny never does his homework, so his baseline would be zero) or its duration (Ms. Cheng says that Johnny shows "appropriate homework behaviors" for only two minutes at a time).

The behavioral term *shaping* means that successive approximations of a desired behavior are reinforced to eventually meet a goal that is initially out-of-reach for a client. The child must receive clear messages in order to understand the parent's specific behavior expectations. In parent training the social worker may provide parents with a handout on command-giving, which includes the following points (Webster-Stratton, 2001):

> *Only use commands that are necessary.* Giving too many commands may stifle the child, lead to negative interactions, or lead to parental commands being ignored.
>
> *Issue only one command at a time.*
>
> *Issue clear and specific commands* ("Stay at the desk during your homework time") *rather than vague warnings* ("You better get that homework done").
>
> *Issue statements* ("Be in bed by 9:30") rather than questions ("Why don't you get ready for bed?") or "Let's" commands ("Let's go upstairs and put our pajamas on") unless the parent plans on being part of the effort.
>
> *Phrase commands as to what the child should do* ("Do your homework in the dining room rather than the TV room") rather than on what the child should not do ("Don't go into the TV room after 7:00").
>
> *Keep commands brief* (rather than lecturing).
>
> *Praise compliance to a command* ("You're all ready for bed! Good boy!").

Reinforcement systems should include high–probability behaviors, social reinforcement, and token economies. *High-probability behaviors* are those in which children frequently engage, such as playing outside, talking on the phone, using the Internet, playing video games, and watching television. Because the child values the activities, he or she will be motivated to maintain them. *Social reinforcements* include interpersonal rewards such as praise, hugs, pats on the shoulder, a smile, a wink, or a thumbs-up sign. *Token economies* are systems in which a parent gives the child points or tokens for desirable behaviors. As they accumulate, the tokens can be traded in for an agreed-upon reward (Barkley, 2000). A token economy involves the use of tangible reinforcers, such as chips, coins, tickets, stars, points, stickers, or check marks, for desirable behaviors that are then traded in for a reward that might include money, movie tickets, magazines, compact discs, or anything else that the child values.

With Ms. Cheng, the social worker provided education on the benefits of praising her child. They went down a list of "do's" and "don'ts" that demonstrated how Ms. Cheng could enact the principles of praise with Johnny. The list of "do's" included the following:

- Labeling praise, or describing specifically what Johnny does to deserve praise ("I'm happy that you got your math homework done tonight.")
- Coupling verbal praise with eye contact, a smile, and/or physical affection
- Praising effort and progress rather than just achievement ("You were 10 minutes late getting to bed tonight, but that's better than you did over the weekend. That's good, Johnny. I can see you are trying.")
- Praising immediately after the behavior is performed

The list of "don'ts" included:

- Using unlabeled praise (global statements about the child: "What a good boy you are!")
- Coupling praise and criticism ("Okay, you did your homework, but you whined so much about it!")
- Waiting too long after the behavior to praise (in this case, until the next day)
- Taking feelings of awkwardness (for example, when giving hugs, if these are not characteristic of the relationship) as a sign to stop praising

Extinction is a process of no longer reinforcing a negative behavior, which if successful results in a decrease of the behavior or its eradication. When applying extinction to a particular behavior, one must first examine the function of the behavior. In Ms. Cheng's situation, Johnny engaged in disruptive behavior at bedtime to prolong his time awake and to get special attention from his mother. Ms. Cheng was told about the importance of being consistent, ignoring Johnny's behaviors every time they occurred. She was also encouraged to make sure Johnny got sufficient attention for positive behaviors so that he may not feel a need to misbehave at bedtime. Ms. Cheng was asked to practice in the session after watching the social worker model appropriate behaviors during a tantrum such as looking away, maintaining a neutral facial expression, and avoiding any verbal or physical contact.

Punishment involves the presentation of negative events (for example, physical discipline, harsh words, criticism) or the removal of positive events (for example, privileges) that decrease the occurrence of a response (Kazdin, 2000). These strategies can be effective, although parent training experts recommend that positive reinforcements be provided at three times the ratio of punishments. This is because punishment tends to be demoralizing for people of all ages.

Time out is a form of punishment that involves physically removing the child from the source of reinforcement for a brief period. The time out should be structured around a certain amount of time, observing the general guideline of one minute per year of the child's age. Its purposes are to extinguish the negative behavior, help the child calm down, and help the child understand why the behavior is unacceptable. The location for time out should be free from reinforcement, meaning there should be no activities available, and the child is to do nothing. Ms. Cheng said she could move a stool for Johnny to the front hallway of their home for a time out, although he could see other family members in the living room from there and might call out to them. The social worker instructed Ms. Cheng that Johnny's attempts to engage family members in annoying behaviors should be ignored. If Johnny's disruptive behaviors escalated there, the time-out period would only resume after he got his behavior under control. The time out should end with the child's being reminded why he was punished. This final step is critical in that the child can learn the reasons for his or her punishment and also reconnect with the parent.

Parents have to be warned that they will initially experience an increase in the undesirable behavior when they begin employing extinction techniques. Ms. Cheng was told to take the inevitable "extinction burst" as a sign that the technique was working. She was assured that Johnny's behavior would improve and that gains would last if she consistently ignored any recurrence of the undesirable behaviors. Ms. Cheng was also reminded to pair her extinction behaviors with positive reinforcement for appropriate behaviors (Kazdin, 2000). She worried that ignoring bad behavior seemed to implicitly encourage it. The social worker emphasized that refusing to give in to the behaviors would help Johnny learn over time that they had no effect. If reinforcement of desirable behaviors and ignoring undesirable behaviors failed to stamp out the problems, then they would consider implementing punishments.

For young children the technique of pairing distraction with ignoring negative behaviors can be effective (Webster-Stratton, 2001). For instance, if a young child cries because he wants to play with the remote control, the parent could take the remote control away and divert his attention to a brightly colored ball: "Here's something else you can play with. See if you can catch it!" Distraction helps to avoid arguments about a parental command.

The example of parenting education incorporates a number of operant behavior intervention principles, as well as the social worker's modeling. The following example of intervention with an older adult also includes attention to issues related to classical conditioning.

SYSTEMATIC DESENSITIZATION

Systematic desensitization was described earlier as a process by which a client gradually overcomes his or her anxieties by working through a rank ordering of fears, from less to more incapacitating. This behavioral intervention technique was helpful to Mr. Tucker, an older adult who had developed panic disorder with agoraphobia. This is a condition in which the person experiences overwhelming anxiety when in certain public places. Mr. Tucker was a 72-year-old Caucasian widower, living alone in a small house he had shared with his wife for more than 40 years prior to her death three years ago. His son, living in a nearby city, had become concerned about the well-being of Mr. Tucker, noticing that he was isolating at home and not tending to his physical health. The previously robust man appeared to be malnourished and physically weak, and his diabetes was going unattended. His son had initially thought that Mr. Tucker's condition was related to grieving the death of his wife, but his father had by now achieved a stable mood even as his avoidance behaviors were increasing.

A social worker who agreed to make home visits assessed Mr. Tucker as having a serious problem with anxiety—that through a process of classical conditioning he had become fearful of being outside the house. Mr. Tucker had been a healthy working man most of his adult life, keeping long hours at a printing company while leaving most domestic responsibilities to his wife. Mrs. Tucker developed breast cancer in her mid-60s and experienced a slow decline until her death four years later. Mr. Tucker dutifully cared for his wife during the illness, assuming such responsibilities as grocery shopping and escorting his wife to her doctor's appointments.

As his wife's condition worsened, Mr. Tucker understandably became more upset. Through a process of classical conditioning he came to associate his relatively new activities of going to the doctor's office and shopping with feelings of fear. After his wife's death, and as he adjusted to living alone, Mr. Tucker continued to associate common activities of daily living outside the home with those anxiety states. Mr. Tucker gradually stopped going outside except when absolutely necessary to purchase household supplies. He welcomed friends and family into his home and was clear-headed and personable there. But because he was an aging man who would not attend to his physical needs, his health was suffering greatly.

The social worker's functional analysis of Mr. Tucker's anxiety (see Table 5.1) revealed that his problematic behavioral responses were primarily related to environmental cues, and those responses featured physical symptoms such as nausea, dizziness, and mild hand tremor. Following the social worker's education of Mr. Tucker about the rationale underlying the technique, Mr. Tucker agreed to work toward overcoming his anxiety through desensitization. It should be emphasized that Mr. Tucker's isolation was also being reinforced through operant conditioning, as his family and friends indulged his requests to visit him at his home rather than expect him to venture outdoors more often. Still, the desensitization strategy to work against his classically conditioned anxiety was identified as having a strong potential for success.

The social worker invited Mr. Tucker to select specific goal activities as a focus of the desensitization process. He chose grocery shopping and going to the doctor's office for checkups, and he chose the former activity as a starting point, feeling that he would have a better chance of success. Mr. Tucker articulated a goal of being able to independently go shopping for all of his needed groceries once per week. He and the social worker constructed a complete list of tasks associated with grocery shopping. The tasks included making a shopping list, searching the day's newspaper for coupons, getting into the car and driving onto the road, driving to the outskirts of the neighborhood, driving past the grocery store, driving into the lot and parking, walking from the car to the store, selecting a pushcart and walking through the store, selecting items for purchase, and making payment at the cash register. Mr. Tucker opted to address the tasks in sequence. The social worker suggested that Mr. Tucker select a time of day when he felt most able to tolerate these tasks. The client chose early morning when there would be fewer crowds on the road and in the store. The social worker also suggested that Mr. Tucker consider asking his son to go to the store with him during his first attempts. The client agreed that this would be helpful.

Before Mr. Tucker addressed the first task on the list, the social worker taught him a relaxation technique and rehearsed it with him at some length. A client needs to feel calm when approaching a stressful activity, and he needs to be able to relax himself *during* the activity if his anxiety escalates. If this process is successful, the client will begin to dissociate the task from the anxiety and fear that was once paired with it. The client will associate the task instead with calm feelings and a sense of mastery. The social worker helped Mr. Tucker master a basic natural breathing technique that includes the following steps (Davis, Eshelman, & McKay, 2000):

- Sit comfortably and close the eyes
- Breathe through the nose
- At a pace that is slow but comfortable, gradually inhale, concentrating internally on how the lower third, middle third, and upper third of the lungs are filling with air
- When inhalation is complete, hold the breath for a few seconds
- Exhale slowly, pulling in the abdomen as the air leaves the lungs
- Relax the abdomen and chest
- Repeat the technique up to five times

It is crucial that the client achieves confidence with the relaxation technique, and is able to utilize it in abbreviated form in public situations, prior to confronting anxiety-provoking situations.

As final steps in the preparation process, the social worker reminds the client not to expect complete success on his first attempt at task completion. Confronting one's fears is never easy, and this message helps prevent the client from becoming demoralized if he experiences difficulty. The social worker assures the client that he can terminate an activity at any time if it seems overwhelming. If the client is unable to successfully complete a task, the social worker takes responsibility for the failure (perhaps for initiating a step prematurely) and then moves to an easier task for the client. Finally, the client is helped to identify rewards for successful task completion. This builds operant reinforcement into the process. Mr. Tucker, an avid music listener, decided to treat himself to a compact disc from his mail-order record club following his successful completion of two repetitions of a task.

Systematic desensitization interventions often work relatively quickly (Thyer & Bursinger, 1994). Positive results often occur by the third or fourth session. The social worker is intensively involved during the early stages, in person or perhaps by phone, to coach the client through the process and revise steps as necessary. Mr. Tucker was able to achieve his goal of weekly shopping trips within three weeks. He had the most trouble with the step of walking into the store and selecting a pushcart. His son accompanied him to the grocery store three times before Mr. Tucker was able to follow through with that step. The social worker reviewed the client's physiological reactions that accompanied those failures and helped Mr. Tucker practice the relaxation technique until he felt relief from those reactions. Mr. Tucker's son was also present for the client's first two successful shopping trips before removing himself from the process.

Mr. Tucker accomplished his second goal of keeping doctor's appointments more quickly, his confidence bolstered by the earlier success. The social worker then faded from Mr. Tucker's life, gradually reducing the frequency of his visits, and finally keeping contact with occasional phone calls until the client was able to maintain his behaviors independently. The social worker felt that Mr. Tucker's achievements would generalize to other areas of his life outside the house.

There are other behavioral interventions that a social worker might use in working with individuals, families, and groups. All of them, however, are based on the principles of conditioning, reinforcement, and punishment. The strategies introduced here may thus be generalized to many other practice situations.

PROFESSIONAL VALUE PRINCIPLE: COMPETENCE

This is the first chapter in which specific intervention strategies have been introduced for use with individuals, families, and groups. For that reason it is important to reflect on the ethical responsibility of social workers to strive for competence when implementing these and any other practice interventions. There are many interventions that social workers may select for their practice—many more than are described in this book. Further, there are no particular strategies that all social workers *should* adopt, as they all have strengths and limitations in different circumstances. It is not possible for a social worker to become familiar with *all* intervention theories and strategies. But in the words of one of my former professors, the professional value of competence mandates that, "whatever you do, do well." The NASW Code of Ethics (1999, p. 6) addresses this issue:

> Ethical Principle: Social workers practice within their areas of competence and develop and enhance their professional expertise.
>
> Social workers continually strive to increase their professional knowledge and skills and apply them in practice. Social workers should aspire to contribute to the knowledge base of the profession.

It is not assumed that a social worker will become a true expert in any practice technique. Social workers serve many types of challenging clients from different social and cultural backgrounds, with different personal characteristics. No social worker will feel comfortable making intervention decisions in all practice situations, because every situation is unique and requires creative and flexible thinking. It is expected, however, that social workers will always be thoughtful in planning interventions, seek supervision or consultation in making difficult practice decisions, and develop the ability to evaluate their interventions. It is also the social worker's responsibility to acquire and maintain the necessary knowledge and skills to consult the professional literature for information about effective intervention for various presenting situations. These processes can be attended to formally and informally as well, through consultation with peers and reading professional literature.

The NASW Code of Ethics (1999) contains several specific references to the issue of competence in addition to the one just described. With regard to *responsibilities to clients,* social workers should provide services within the bounds of their ability and credentials; provide new interventions only after engaging in appropriate study, training, and supervision; and use care when selecting interventions that are not yet extensively explored in the literature or are not familiar to a supervisor. Social workers should develop competence in working with members of other cultures and social, racial, economic, and oppressed groups through personal study, education, and supervision (p. 9). Regarding *responsibility to colleagues,* social workers should consult with colleagues about issues of observed incompetence and, if this is not effective, process the issue through established agency channels. Regarding *responsibilities as professionals,* social workers should accept employment in agencies where they have or can achieve competence, keep current with emerging professional knowledge, and intervene with recognized standards of knowledge, including empirically based knowledge (p. 22).

Students sometimes feel intimidated when considering the value principle of competence, fearing that they cannot practice responsibly until they achieve facility with an intervention technique. This is certainly not the intention of this value principle. Achieving competence is a career-long process, and social workers can gain expertise only through practice, which involves trial and error and a willingness to take some risks. For example, an inexperienced social worker might effectively apply the parent training and systematic desensitization strategies described in this chapter through adequate preparation characterized by reading, talking with more experienced peers, and consulting with a supervisor. The social worker would improve his or her skills in these areas with experience, of course.

Good supervision is certainly a key to developing professional competence. Over the years I have surveyed my students about what they consider to be the characteristics of good supervision. Their responses, based on field placement experiences, are as follows:

- Uninterrupted supervision time is structured into the work week.

- The student is encouraged to seek additional time for consultation from the supervisor or other staff as needed.

- The student is expected to bring issues for discussion—that is, an agenda is not preset but emerges from the student's perspective or from mutually articulated topics.

- The supervisor acknowledges and appreciates the power differential in the relationship.

- The supervisor promotes an atmosphere conducive to risk-taking.

- Any criticisms of student performance are presented constructively; the supervisor also affirms what the student does well.

- The supervisor does not act as the student's therapist.

- The supervisor maintains appropriate interpersonal boundaries.

- The supervisor models ethical behavior.

- The supervisor assumes a teaching role, applying particular client issues to a broader context of theory and intervention.

- The supervisory process is mutually evaluated on occasion.

- The student does not feel blamed as the cause of all problems (if any develop) within the supervisory relationship.

When considering a job a social worker should always evaluate an agency's policies regarding supervision so that he or she will be assured not only of achieving competence, but also of ongoing professional growth.

SUMMARY

Interventions associated with behavior theory are suitable for generalist social work practice with many types of individuals, families, and groups. In this chapter we reviewed the principles of behavioral theory including factors influencing its development, its perspectives on the nature of learning, problems, and change, and the associated processes of assessment, goal setting, and intervention. Two detailed examples of behavioral intervention, one with a child and one with an older adult, were described. Finally, the professional value of competence was presented in the context of the social worker's becoming able to utilize these and any other interventions effectively. Behavioral interventions are consistent with the problem-solving approach described in Chapter 2. Next we will consider cognitive theory, another related approach that adds to the practitioner's range of interventions for generalist practice.

TOPICS FOR DISCUSSION

1. Do you think that behavioral theory represents an antihumanistic approach to working with people? Why or why not?

2. Develop a list of examples of how client problems can develop through the processes of classical conditioning, operant conditioning, and modeling.

3. Describe clients with whom you have worked or are otherwise familiar. Consider how the clients' presenting problems were represented in the five domains of functional assessment.

4. Whether or not you adhere to the philosophy of behavioral intervention, it is possible that you have used behavioral training principles with some clients in combination with other interventions. Give some examples of these circumstances. What kinds of problems seemed appropriate for this type of intervention?

5. In what situations might it be appropriate for a social worker to suggest to a supervisor that he or she is not competent to work with a particular client? In what situations should the social worker attempt to work with a client even though he or she may lack confidence in addressing the presenting issue? What are the differences in these two circumstances?

ASSIGNMENT IDEAS

1. Write a paper about a real or hypothetical client who demonstrates problems that may be appropriate for behavioral intervention. Focus on how he or she did (or would) decide what behaviors to target. What are (or were) some other possible targets of intervention?

2. Read and study a case illustration provided by your instructor that includes presenting problems, relevant background information, and the client's general goals. From this information develop measurable goals and interventions for the client. Consider various ways this challenging part of the planning process can be addressed.

3. Devise an intervention (the previous illustration could be used for this purpose) that includes either behavioral training of some type or systematic desensitization. Pay careful attention to the process of developing evaluation criteria for the intervention.

Chapter 6

Cognitive Theory

B ehavior theory, which originated in the first half of the 20th century, is concerned with *overt* actions that can be observed and measured. The importance of a person's *covert* operations, or thoughts, was later identified as significant to human services intervention and fully developed as a theory for practice in the 1960s. Cognitive theory emerged in part in response to learning theories in education that de-emphasized the role of unconscious mental processes. From the perspective of cognitive theory it is a person's *conscious thoughts* that are the primary determinants of feelings and behavior, as illustrated in Figure 6.1 (Berlin, 2002; Lantz, 1996; Leahy, 1996).

Thoughts, or cognitions, include a person's beliefs, assumptions, expectations, attitudes, and perceptions. Our thoughts can reflect what is happening in the external world, but they can also be distorted to a degree that we misperceive what is happening around us. If a person carries negative attitudes about authority figures, for example, he will misperceive some actions of his boss as malevolent. Many problems in living are the result of cognitive misperceptions, or beliefs that are not supported by external evidence. Cognitive interventions help clients to gain awareness of the self-defeating thoughts and misconceptions that contribute to their problems, and replace them with beliefs and behaviors that lead to enhanced functioning.

The purpose of this chapter is to review the principles of cognitive theory for generalist practice and demonstrate several of its uses. Keep in mind, however, that social workers should never assume that a client's difficulties are rooted entirely in

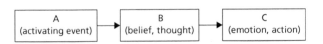

FIGURE 6.1 The Nature of Emotions in Cognitive Theory

cognitive misperceptions. Doing so would amount to "blaming the client" in many situations. Cognitive theory helps clients develop more flexibility in their thinking, but problems in living are usually related to real mismatches between people and their environments, as will be described in the next chapter.

COGNITIVE DEVELOPMENT

Within cognitive theory we become inclined to act in certain ways through habits of thinking, and these tendencies can be adjusted by acquiring new information. Our capacity to effectively adapt to the social world unfolds over time with the biological maturation of cognitive capacities. Piaget's work is a well-known account of the process by which we gradually develop the capacity for abstract reasoning from childhood through adolescence and early adulthood (Maier, 1978). Natural, healthy changes in physical and neurological development are necessary for a person's cognitive development to unfold successfully.

The habits of thinking referred to earlier are known in cognitive theory as *schemas,* or systematic patterns of thinking, acting, and solving problems (Corcoran, 2006). Schemas are based on core beliefs about the self and the world that are acquired in childhood. These habits of thinking are natural and functional. We would be overwhelmed if we experienced every situation in life as unique! In order for us to adapt to new situations, however, our schemas must also be flexible, or capable of making adjustments in novel situations. The way in which schemas develop is illustrated in Figure 6.2.

As a part of the schema, *causal attributions* refer to three sets of assumptions that people carry about the sources of influence in their lives. First, we might assume that life situations are *more* or *less* changeable. Second, we may believe that, if change is possible, the source of power to make such changes exists either *within* or *outside* the self. Finally, we might assume that the implications of our experiences are limited to the *specific situation,* or that they are *global.* For example, a woman who is unable to provide for her family during a period of temporary unemployment might, in a negative sense, assume that she is a thoroughly incapable parent all the time.

So long as a person's cognitive style promotes his or her goal achievement, it is considered positively adaptive. Such rational thinking can be understood as thinking that:

- Is based on external evidence
- Is life preserving
- Keeps one directed toward personal goals
- Decreases internal conflicts

One's thinking patterns can, however, feature distortions in thought processing—cognitive biases that dismiss the relevance of certain environmental information. These may lead to maladaptive emotional and behavioral responses.

Relevant Early Life Experience
For example: negative comparison of self with siblings

Core Beliefs/Schemas (pervasive and rigid, but changeable)
Fundamental assumptions about the *self*, *others*, the *world*, the *future*;
when problematic these involve themes of *helplessness* or *unlovability*:
"I don't have qualities that can attract other people."
"I'm not capable of being successful."

Coping Assumptions
May be constructive or destructive:
"If I work hard, I can do well."
"If I don't do well, then I am a failure."

Coping Strategies
For example: high standards, hard work, correcting shortcomings (positive);
over-preparation, manipulation, avoiding seeking help (negative)

Specific Situations
For example: performance in graduate school

Thoughts and their Meanings
May be constructive or destructive:
"I can get through this if I go to every class and do all the reading."
"I can't do all this work. I don't have the energy."

Emotions
Pride, excitement,
depression, guilt

Behaviors
Organizing a study schedule,
cheating, quitting

F I G U R E 6.2   The Influence of Core Beliefs

Cognitive interventions are applicable to clients over the age of approximately 12 years because the person must be able to engage in abstract thought. To benefit from these approaches clients must also be able to follow through with directions, demonstrate stability in some life activities, and not be in an active crisis.

THE NATURE OF PROBLEMS AND CHANGE

Many problems in living result from misconceptions—conclusions that are based too much on habits of thought rather than external evidence—that people have about themselves, other people, and their life situations (Beck, 1967). These misconceptions may develop for any of three reasons. The first is the simplest—the person has not acquired the information necessary to manage a new situation. This is often evident in the lives of children and adolescents. They face many situations at school, at play, and with their families that they have not experienced before, and they are understandably not sure how to respond. This lack of information is known as a cognitive *deficit* and, when it creates problems, can be remedied with education. A child who has trouble getting along with other children may not have learned age-appropriate social skills, and the social worker's teaching that child about social skills may resolve the problem.

The other two sources of misconceptions are more complex and are rooted in rigid personal schemas. The first is related to *problematic causal attributions*. The person may function with one or more of the following premises: life situations are not changeable, all power to make changes lies outside the self, and any personal shortcomings indicate general incompetence. A person who develops these attributions may have been given negative messages by significant others during childhood, or perhaps had genuinely negative experiences that conveyed those messages. Still, the attributions may not necessarily reflect one's potential to manage life challenges.

The other source of misperceptions is *cognitive distortions* of reality. Because of our tendency to develop thinking habits, we often interpret new situations in biased ways. All of us develop such patterns, and they are generally functional because many situations we face are similar to previous ones, and can be efficiently managed with patterned responses. These habits become a source of difficulty only when they are too rigid to allow for the input of new information. For example, a low-income community resident may believe that he lacks the ability to advocate for certain basic resources and, as a result, continues to live without those resources. This belief may be rooted in a cognitive distortion of personal worthlessness and the sense that other people will never respect him. The client may have had real difficulties over the years with failure and discrimination, but his belief that this will happen in all circumstances in the future is arbitrary. Table 6.1 includes some widely held cognitive distortions, as identified by Beck (1967).

With reference to these points regarding problem development, people can change in three ways. They can *acquire new information, adjust cognitive assumptions* (beliefs and expectations), or *change habits of thinking* (which includes giving up cognitive distortions). Even when some of a person's beliefs are distorted, the potential to correct those beliefs in light of contradictory evidence is great.

COGNITIVE ASSESSMENT

In assessment, the practitioner accepts the client's perspective as valid and gathers information about the presenting problem (Beck, 1995). The social worker next asks questions to examine the client's assumptions about the self and the outside world, identify thinking patterns, and consider the evidence supporting the

T A B L E 6.1   Common Cognitive Distortions

Distorted Beliefs	Examples
Arbitrary inference: Drawing a conclusion about an event with no evidence, little evidence, or even contradictory evidence	"I'm not going to do well in this course. I have a bad feeling about it." "The staff at this agency seem to have a different practice approach than mine. They aren't going to respect my work."
Selective abstraction: Judging a situation on the basis of one or a few details taken out of a broader context	"Did you see how our supervisor yawned when I was describing my assessment of the client? He must think my work is superficial."
Magnification or *minimization:* Concluding that an event is either far more significant, or far less significant, than the evidence seems to indicate	"I got a B on the first assignment. There is a good chance I will fail this course." "I don't really need to get to work on time every day. My clients don't seem to mind waiting, and the administrative meeting isn't relevant to my work."
Overgeneralization: Drawing the conclusion that all instances of some kind of situation or event will turn out a particular way because one or two such situations did	"My supervisor thinks that my depressed client dropped out because I was too confrontational. I don't have enough empathy to be a decent social worker."
Personalization: Attributing the cause to, or accepting responsibility for, an external event without evidence of a connection	"The instructor didn't say this, but our group presentation got a mediocre evaluation because of my poor delivery."
Dichotomous thinking: Categorizing experiences at one of two extremes— complete success or utter failure (usually the latter)	"I didn't get an A on my final exam. I blew it! I'm not competent to move on to the next course." "I got an A on the midterm. I can coast the rest of the way through this course."

client's conclusions about his or her life situation. When those conclusions seem *valid* (an accurate representation of the situation) the social worker helps the client develop better problem-solving or coping skills, and perhaps helps secure resources for the client. When the conclusions are *distorted,* the social worker utilizes techniques to help the client adjust his or her cognitive processes in ways that will better facilitate goal attainment. As the client's thinking changes, so do emotions and behaviors with respect to the problem situation.

The rationality of a client's thinking is assessed through a process of Socratic questioning (Carey & Mullan, 2004). The social worker assesses the validity of a client's assumptions associated with a problem issue through detailed, focused questioning to examine the evidence for and against problem-related beliefs, attitudes, and assumptions. The social worker then steers the client to a conclusion about the rationality of his or her thought patterns, and examines his or her willingness to consider alternative perspectives. The following types of questions guide the social worker's assessment:

- What is the logic behind the client's beliefs?
- What is the evidence to support the client's views?
- What other explanations for the client's perceptions are possible?
- How do particular beliefs influence the client's attachment of significance to specific events? To emotions? To behaviors?
- How strongly does the client believe that approval from others is necessary to feel good about himself or herself?

Following are some additional questions to use when assessing the validity of a client's thoughts:

> *What is the evidence?* These questions involve analyzing faulty logic and providing information to dispel unrealistic fears. "Might there be any exceptions to your conclusions about what is happening here?" "What are the most likely outcomes of this situation?" "Are there any experiences from your past that could lead to another outcome?" "What are the real odds that what you fear will happen?" "Does anything from your past lead you to expect even a possibly better outcome than the one you fear?" "Of all the times you've done or felt this in the past, how many times did the catastrophe occur?" "What has usually happened during similar circumstances in the past?"

> *Are there other ways for you to manage the situation?* These questions provide alternative perspectives on the client's options for coping. "How could you use your social skills or problem-solving skills to handle this situation?" "Could you create a plan to change the situation?" "Is there someone you know who might deal with this differently? What would that person do?" "How long is this experience likely to last? How might you cope with it for that period of time?"

> *What is the worst thing that can happen to you here?* These questions examine how the client can cope even if the worst fear comes true. "So what if it does happen? Will you be ruined?" "You're not going to die, are you?"

In order to help a client adjust his or her beliefs about a challenging situation, three steps can be followed. The first is to help the person identify the thoughts preceding and accompanying the distressing emotions and nonproductive action ("What was going through your mind . . . ?"). Some clients may require tangible ways to grasp their thinking patterns. For example, participating in a reenactment of a problem situation can help clients retrieve the thought patterns maintaining the problem.

The second step is to assess the client's willingness to consider alternative thoughts in response to the problem situation. This can be done through dialogue or with the paper and pen technique known as the ABC review (described later in this chapter).

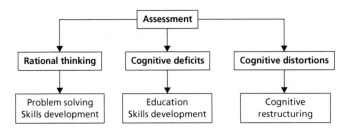

F I G U R E 6.3   Deciding on an Intervention Strategy in Cognitive Theory

The third step is to challenge the client's distorted beliefs by designing natural experiments, or tasks that he or she can carry out in daily life to test their validity. For instance, if a college student believes that if she speaks out in class everyone will laugh at her, she might be asked to volunteer an answer to find out what the reactions of others would be. By changing clients' actions, cognitions and emotions are also indirectly modified. That is, the actions clients perform provide data to refute their illogical beliefs.

In summary, the steps in cognitive restructuring are as follows:

- Educate the client in the logic of cognitive theory.

- Assess the client's cognitive assumptions, and identify any misperceptions that may contribute to problem persistence.

- Identify situations that trigger misconceptions.

- Determine how misperceptions can be most efficiently adjusted or replaced with new thinking patterns.

- Implement corrective tasks.

- Evaluate the efficacy of the strategies.

Following assessment, then, the social worker can decide on intervention strategies based on whether the client's thinking is accurate or characterized by cognitive distortions or deficits, as illustrated in Figure 6.3.

INTERVENTIONS

Cognitive interventions focus on present rather than past behavior. The past is important for discovering the origins of a client's thinking patterns, but it is present thinking that motivates behavior. The nature of the social worker–client relationship is important for successful intervention, as it must encourage the difficult process of the client's questioning some of his or her basic assumptions. The social worker must demonstrate positive regard for the client while alternately functioning as a model, collaborator, and trusted representative of objective thinking. The social worker is active, participating with the client in discussions and the mutual development of change strategies.

There are many particular strategies for cognitive intervention, but they fit into two general categories (Leahy, 1996). The first of these is *cognitive restructuring*. These are used when the client's thinking patterns are distorted and contribute to problem development and persistence. Through a series of discussions and exercises the social worker helps the client to experiment with alternative ways of approaching challenges that will promote goal attainment. Some strategies that can be used toward this end include:

Education (providing information to the client). This is particularly effective with children and adolescents who experience cognitive deficits.

Attribution development. Helping the client understand that his or her potential for goal attainment may be more related to arbitrary attitudes and thought patterns than external conditions than previously assumed.

The ABC review. This is a reflective "paper and pencil" technique in which the client learns to differentiate thoughts about challenging situations from their emotional and behavioral consequences, and then considers alternative ways of appraising those situations.

Point–counterpoint. Reviewing with the client the relative evidence for and against a certain belief, and also the costs and benefits to the client for maintaining certain attitudes.

Several of these interventions will be described in detail in this chapter, and others will appear elsewhere in the book.

The second category of cognitive interventions is *cognitive coping*. The practitioner helps the client learn and practice new or more effective ways of dealing with stress and negative moods. All of these involve step-by-step procedures for the client to master new skills. Some techniques include:

Self-instruction. Helping clients develop "internal speech," or internal cognitive frameworks, for instructing themselves in how to cope effectively with a challenge. This also provides a method for combating the confusion that often plagues clients in the midst of a difficult situation.

Problem solving. A structured means of helping clients to become better problem solvers by learning to generate and evaluate many possible solutions.

Communication skills development. Helping clients to become more direct, and thus more effective, verbal and nonverbal communicators. This is based on the premise that many problems result from distorted communication.

Other types of social skills development (such as interpersonal and assertion skills). Helping clients learn and practice new ways of interacting with others through step-by-step methods.

Relaxation skills development, such as deep breathing. These are behavioral components to cognitive intervention and include strategies to help clients maintain a sense of control as they experiment with new ways of thinking about problem situations.

As with behavioral interventions, cognitive interventions require clients to be active in resolving their problems, and they need to practice solution strategies first with the social worker and then in their natural settings.

Cognitive Restructuring

Cognitive restructuring is the main technique by which people identify and change maladaptive thinking patterns. Cognitive restructuring was formulated from two different schools of cognitive therapy—rational-emotive therapy (Ellis, 1962) and cognitive therapy (Beck, 1976). Both schools share the assumption that problematic feelings and behaviors result from interpretations of situations that are often negative or illogical (as described in Table 5.1).

The ABC model of cognitive restructuring is useful to share with clients. As illustrated in Figure 6.1, the social worker summarizes the steps of cognitive processing in which A is an activating effect, B is a person's belief about the event, and C is the consequence of A and B for the person (emotion and action). For example, if A is an event that occurs (a rainy day) and C, the consequence, is the person's emotion of depression, then B (the belief) might be "Everything's gray and ugly. Nothing can go well on a day like this." If the same activating event (rain) occurs, and the resultant emotion (C) is contentment, the belief might be, "Today I can stay home and read. It'll be really cozy." Clients often make the assumption that "A" directly causes "C," but except in certain reflexive actions (such as placing a finger on a hot stove and then abruptly pulling it back) there is always a cognitive event, "B," that intervenes between the two.

The ABC Review.   This cognitive intervention technique requires that the client fill out a form over a specified period of time. Its purpose is to help the client become more aware of automatic thoughts and subsequently work toward modifying them so that the emotional and behavioral experiences can become more productive (Beck, 1995). The social worker prepares a sheet of paper with four columns (see Table 6.2). The first column is headed "situations that produce stress" (the "A" component of the cognition process). The client is instructed to write down during the course of a day the specific situations that produce the negative emotions or behaviors for which he or she is seeking help. The next column is headed "automatic thoughts" (the "B" component), where the client records the thoughts that accompany the situation. This step takes practice for many clients who tend to overlook the relevance of cognitive reactions that

T A B L E 6.2   The Thought Record

A Situations that produce stress	B Automatic thoughts	C Emotional responses to the thoughts	(For later) Alternative thoughts
1. _____	_____	_____	_____
2. _____	_____	_____	_____

intervene between situations and emotional and behavioral responses. Sometimes clients record emotions rather than thoughts in this column. As they meet during the course of the intervention, the social worker can help the client learn to distinguish between thoughts and feelings. Next, the client is asked to think about and record the assumptions that underlie the automatic thoughts. For example, a client who is rejected as a job applicant (the situation) may think that he will never get a good job (automatic thought) because "I am worthless in general" (the underlying assumption). Finally, the client is asked to record the emotional response to each automatic thought, such as depression or panic (the "C" component).

The social worker may ask the client to fill out the form each day between appointments, when they can review it together. The social worker continuously helps the client clarify his or her automatic thoughts and understand which of them are arbitrary. The client is encouraged to consider and experiment with alternative thoughts about problem situations that might be more constructive, and at some point the client is encouraged to enter these in the fourth column. Over time the client and social worker process how the client's feelings and behaviors might have changed as the alternative thoughts are implemented.

What follows is an example of a client who benefited from a social worker's cognitive interventions.

Cognitive Restructuring and the Single Parent.   Suzanne was a 26-year-old single Caucasian parent who was faced with the responsibility of raising her 4-year-old son while attending college to get a degree in business. Suzanne maintained an apartment with money acquired from a computer programming job she kept during school breaks. Her parents, both of whom lived in town and were divorced, helped Suzanne with occasional money and babysitting assistance. Her son attended a day care center while Suzanne went to school. She had many friends, most of whom did not have children.

Suzanne sought help from a social services agency because, overwhelmed with stress, she had begun to physically strike her child. Her mother had demanded that she seek help as a condition of not being formally reported for abuse. Suzanne readily admitted that she had little time to relax, lived on a tight budget, had an unsatisfying social life, and was a "bad parent" because she was preoccupied with school and often lost her temper. She could not sleep, was always irritable, and could not concentrate on schoolwork. Despite her goals of being a businesswoman she wondered if the material and emotional costs were worthwhile. The social worker acknowledged that this was a difficult time in Suzanne's life, but pointed out that she demonstrated many personal strengths such as persistence, resilience, and love for her child. The social worker educated Suzanne about several community agencies that might provide material assistance to her household, and made formal referrals for Suzanne to some of them.

Suzanne was a suitable candidate for coping skills development, which will be discussed later in this chapter. Still, much of her difficulty was rooted in her *causal attributions* and *cognitive distortions*. The social worker concluded after the assessment that Suzanne had a basic sense of powerlessness to change any aspect of her life situation. Further, Suzanne had a tendency to engage in *overgeneraliza-tion,* believing that any failures on her part implied that she was completely incompetent. She also *personalized* negative episodes in her life, believing that anything negative that happened was due to her own inadequacies, ignoring the part that other people or circumstances might play in those situations.

The social worker organized an intervention with Suzanne that included *attribution training* and *cognitive questioning.* The social worker initially educated Suzanne in the ABC sequence of cognitive operations, helping her see that her appraisal of life situations, based on core beliefs that may or may not be consistent with external evidence presented by the event of concern, had a role in producing her negative emotions. Like many clients, Suzanne was able to understand this point after some discussion and reflection. She could see, for example, that her father's high expectations of her as a child and adolescent resulted in her belief that she should be competent in every aspect of her life.

It was more difficult for Suzanne to see that she might have the power to change some of her problem situations. The social worker eventually helped Suzanne see that there were some areas of life where she could be proactive in making adjustments. As one example, Suzanne had become reluctant to ask her grandparents to sit with her son on weekends, feeling that they resented the intrusion on their time. Suzanne reported at other times, however, that the grandparents loved her son and seemed to be feeling lonely as they aged. The social worker explored these contradictory statements with Suzanne and helped her work out a flexible schedule of family babysitting requests so that she would call on her mother, father, and grandparents every few weeks in rotation for that purpose. This worked out well, providing Suzanne with more predictable time for study and even a few hours for working. The process also taught Suzanne that she could have impact on her environment.

In the *cognitive questioning* process, the social worker and client reviewed specific situations in Suzanne's life that made her feel sad or upset and looked at alternative interpretations of those situations. It is important to understand in cognitive therapy that some negative emotional responses to situations reflect a client's accurate appraisals. For example, Suzanne discussed with the social worker her frustrations with several professors that appeared to accurately reflect their insensitivity to her learning needs. On the other hand, the issue of Suzanne's anger at her friends for their alleged unwillingness to understand her limited social availability seemed to the practitioner to reflect an oversensitivity to rejection. Suzanne believed that her friends did not want to spend time with her anymore, and thus she tended not to seek them out. Through questioning the social worker helped Suzanne to see that there was limited external evidence for Suzanne's assumption. The practitioner suggested as one alternative that Suzanne's friends were aware of her busy schedule and that calling less often might be a sign of their caring. As a result of this process Suzanne changed her thinking about her friends' behaviors and did resume more comfortable relationships with several of them.

The second category of cognitive interventions is cognitive coping, to which we now turn.

Cognitive Coping

In contrast to cognitive restructuring, which involves helping clients to alter their negative and distorted thoughts, cognitive coping involves skills development that targets thinking processes with the goal of helping clients more effectively manage their challenges (Berlin, 2002). Clients can modify their cognitive distortions by successfully enacting new coping skills, because improved capabilities can change one's assumptions about the world. Further, if people have good coping skills they will more successfully elicit reinforcement from the environment. A list of coping skills that can be taught in cognitive intervention was provided earlier. Several of these will now be described in detail.

Self-Instruction. When people find themselves in difficult situations that evoke tension or other negative emotions, their thinking may become confused, and their ability to cope diminishes. Skills in self-instruction give clients an internal framework for coping with problem situations (Meichenbaum, 1999). It is based in part on the premise that many people routinely engage in internal speech, giving themselves pep talks to prepare for certain challenges. Some clients may have a lack of positive cues in their self-dialogue. Having a prepared internal or written script for those situations can help a client recall and implement a coping strategy. Self-instruction has mainly been studied in relation to children and school task completion, but it can also be used with adults.

When using this technique, the social worker assesses the client's behavior and its relationship to deficits in subvocal dialogue. The client and social worker develop a step-by-step self-instruction script following their completion of a plan for confronting a problem, including overt self-directed speech to guide new behavior. Such a script may be written down or memorized by the client. The social worker and client then visualize and walk through the problem situation together as a means of rehearsal. The client then uses the script in his or her natural environment, either before or during an assigned task. The client gradually moves from overt self-dialogue to covert self-talk (which is how many people "think").

As an example, Suzanne (who was introduced earlier) felt guilty dropping her young son off at the day care center every morning on her way to classes, feeling that she was a poor mother for indulging herself at the expense of time with her son. This negative feeling stayed with her much of the day. She developed a self-instruction script with the social worker that included the following statements: "My son will be well cared for. Many good parents take their children to day care when they go to work every day. I spend every evening and every weekend with my son. When I get my degree I will be a better provider for my son and myself. It is good for my son to learn to interact with people other than me. He has a chance to play with other children while there. I will be a better parent if I take care of myself as well as my son." Suzanne had written down these and other statements but quickly memorized them. She spoke them aloud every morning before she left the apartment with her son.

Problem-Solving Skills Development.   Problem solving was discussed in detail in Chapter 2 as an organizing framework for generalist social work practice. There is a different but related problem-solving *skill* that clients may develop for learning to cope more effectively with life challenges. Problem-solving skills development is a structured, five-step method for helping clients who do not experience distortions but nevertheless struggle with managing problems. Clients learn how to produce a variety of potentially effective responses to their problems (McClam & Woodside, 1994).

The first step in problem solving is *defining the problem* that the client wishes to overcome. Solutions are understandably easier to formulate when problems are clearly delineated. Only one problem should be targeted at a time. The next step involves the client and social worker's *brainstorming* to generate as many possible solutions for a presenting problem as they can imagine. At this point, evaluative comments are not allowed so that spontaneity and creativity is encouraged. Many possibilities are written down, even those that seem impossible or silly. Some supposedly ridiculous ideas may contain useful elements on closer examination. It is important in this step for the social worker to encourage additional responses after clients decide they are finished. Members often stop participating when a list contains as few as five alternatives, but when pressed they can usually suggest more.

The third stage of the problem-solving process involves *evaluating the alternatives*. Any patently irrelevant or impossible items are crossed out. Each viable alternative is then discussed as to its advantages and disadvantages. More information about the situation may need to be gathered as a result of the work in this stage. For instance, information might be gathered about other agencies and resources (including other people in the client's life) that can assist in making some of the choices more viable.

Choosing and implementing an alternative involves selecting a strategy for problem resolution that appears to maximize benefits over costs. While the outcome of any alternative is always uncertain, the client is praised for exercising good judgment in the process thus far and is reminded that making any effort to address the problem is the most significant aspect of this step. The social worker should remind the client that there is no guarantee that the alternative will succeed, and that other alternatives are available if needed.

During the following session, the social worker helps the client to *evaluate the implemented option*. If successful, the process is complete except for the important discussion about how to generalize problem solving to other situations in the client's life. The exploration of any "failures" must be examined closely for elements that went well in addition to those still needing work. If a strategy has not been successful, it can be attempted again with adjustments or the social worker and client can go back to the fourth step and select another option from the list.

The following vignette provides an example of how the problem-solving process can be effectively used to guide a group intervention.

Case Illustration: The Adolescent Girls Group.   Ridgedale High School was located in a lower-class section of a large city and served neighborhoods that experienced much criminal activity. Most of the residents were of African

American or Latino cultural heritage. Drug dealing, prostitution, grand and petty theft, and burglaries occurred in its vicinity at a high rate. As one preventive measure, the school offered a number of coping groups for students who were considered at-risk for developing delinquent behaviors. One such group was of-fered to female adolescents who demonstrated chronic school truancy. The eight-week time-limited group, like others at the school, was led by a social worker. This "academic and personal success" group used the problem-solving model as a basis for intervention.

The social worker devoted the first meeting to the girls getting acquainted with each other and generating topics for discussion. Subsequent meetings in-cluded structured discussions among the girls about ways to problem solve with regard to the topic for that day. During one group experience the girls selected the topic of safe sex. The girls agreed that they did not want to become pregnant and some were opposed to the idea of having sex at all. All of them had faced difficulties with boys who were sexually aggressive.

The social worker's responsibilities each week included reviewing the problem-solving model and encouraging its use as an effective way to address a variety of problems in living. She believed that engaging in this practice, while productive with individual clients, was even more effective when done in groups, which offered the benefit of immediate input from peers. In the first part of this meeting the girls were asked to specify a problem related to the gen-eral topic of safe sex. They eventually agreed that they wanted to learn how to reject the advances of boys who tried to talk them into sex. The practitioner asked the girls to role-play several scenarios to get a clearer idea of the situations they had in mind. This was helpful in clarifying the topic and also provided the girls with some amusement as they acted out the parts.

Next the girls brainstormed possible solutions to the challenge. Because all ideas are welcomed and none are censored, this task was also fun for the girls. They could laugh and be outrageous with each other while sharing suggestions about physically protecting themselves, making specific and assertive verbal re-sponses, limiting their dates to certain kinds of settings, avoiding certain topics of conversation with boys, addressing their preferences before a date began, and many others. It was important during this step for the social worker to encourage additional responses after the group members decided they were finished. Often it is only after a list of standard alternatives is presented that creative thinking begins. The social worker asked the students to think harder, and they were able to suggest many more ideas.

In the group setting, unlike individual or family settings, it was not necessary that each member agreed on one item from their list for implementation. Each girl was expected to select her own solution, and these were supported by the social worker so long as the member could articulate reasons for the choice. At the end of the meeting the social worker asked the girls to make a commitment to implement their solution if and when the problem situation arose. In this par-ticular instance, the girls agreed that greater assertiveness would help them main-tain control of the situation when alone with a boyfriend. The girls could not all implement their strategy in the context of a date situation during the next week, but they could practice assertiveness skills in a variety of other contexts with boys.

The following week the girls shared their experiences with exercising assertive behavior with boys either at school or over the weekend, and whether they considered these episodes to be successes or failures. Of the eight girls in the group, two had not exercised assertive behavior. One did not feel that she had been in an appropriate situation. The social worker and the other girls discussed her account to see whether she might have failed to identify any appropriate opportunities to use assertiveness. The girl agreed to try again during the coming week. The second girl had simply not followed through with the task. Her peers gave her negative feedback about this oversight and in doing so impressed upon her the importance of task follow-though. Several of the remaining girls had been on dates or with boys in other private situations. One had specifically experienced the problem of aggressive behavior with a boy and described how she had responded assertively with success. The girls helped each other evaluate their task implementation and were again, with the social worker's example, constructive in their comments. As a final stage of their problem solving, the girls helped each other refine their approaches to assertiveness and consider new strategies for the coming weeks.

Communication Skills Development.   Communication skills cover a wide spectrum of interventions that includes attention to clients' social, assertiveness, and negotiation skills. Positive communication builds relationships and closeness with others, which in turn helps improve mood (Lewinsohn, Clarke, Rohde, & Hops, 2001). Social support provides not only a source of positive reinforcement, but it also buffers individuals from stressful life events. In addition, processing the effects of problems with other people may broaden one's perspective on problematic events. When a person can openly state his or her feelings about a situation, other people involved can provide more thorough feedback.

Communication skills development includes the client's using "I" messages, using reflective and empathic listening, and making clear behavior change requests. "I" messages are those in which a person talks about his or her own position and feelings in a situation, rather than making accusatory comments toward another person. The basic format for giving "I" messages is: I feel (the reaction) to what happened (a specific activating event). For example: "I feel angry when you break curfew on Saturday night. I also worry about you." This is a clearer communication, and also includes content about caring, than saying "How dare you stay out so late!" which makes the other person feel defensive.

Listening skills include both reflective listening and validation of the other person's intent. The purpose of reflective listening is to ensure that one understands the speaker's perspective. It decreases the tendency of people to draw premature conclusions about the intentions and meaning of another's statement (Cordova & Scott, 2001). Reflective listening involves paraphrasing back the feelings and content of the speaker's message with the format: "What I hear you saying is . . ." or "You seem to feel [feeling word] when . . . ." Beyond reflection, validation is an advanced skill and involves conveying a message that, given the other person's perspectives, his or her experiences are legitimate and understandable ("I can see that if you were thinking I had done that, you would feel that way").

A third component of communication skill development involves teaching people to make clear behavior requests of others. Such requests should always be *specific* ("Pick up your toys") versus global ("Clean up this room"), *measurable* ("I would like you to call me once per day"), and *stated as the presence of positive behaviors* rather than the absence of negative behaviors ("Give me a chance to change and look over the mail when I come home" rather than "Stop bothering me with your questions"). The following is an example of an application of these concepts.

Case Illustration: Managing Family Friction with Communication Skills. Nita, a married mother of two sons and a daughter, sought assistance because of family conflicts. Her sons, ages 22 and 20, had each gotten married within the past year and moved their new wives into the house. Nita's daughter, age 8, was feeling neglected by her parents and brothers because of these changes. Nita reported that her husband, who had refused to see the social worker, was angry about the lack of responsible behavior among his sons, and at Nita for unclear reasons. Nita felt anxious, depressed, and hopeless. She wanted to feel more allied with her husband and to be able to work outside the home. She also wanted her sons to move into their own homes.

Nita and her husband had moved to the city from a rural Appalachian community, where women were expected to be the family caregivers, and often to quietly tolerate absences from their husbands, whose lives typically involved much more social interaction. The social worker asked Nita to invite the other family members to the next session, and her sons, their wives, and Nita's daughter all came. Her husband again refused. The practitioner observed the family's interactions for a period of time and noted that they exhibited poor communication patterns. Their conversations quickly became contentious, they constantly interrupted each other, and they accused each other of behaving irresponsibly in many situations. The family's interactions were negatively charged and lacked a shared process of problem solving. The social worker decided that an important starting point for intervention should be communication skills development. He explained his rationale for this strategy and the family agreed to participate.

The social worker was active in the skills development process, which was the focus of four sessions. He took control of a chaotic situation and modeled the skills he was trying to teach. He assured all family members that they would have the opportunity each week to make their thoughts and feelings known. The practitioner set a ground rule that no one could be interrupted when expressing a thought or feeling. The practitioner did, however, give himself the right to intervene if he perceived that communication was breaking down. Even this much intervention made a difference in family dynamics during the sessions, reducing tension in the room.

The social worker next taught listening skills by asking each person to always repeat back what someone had said to him or her, to make sure he or she had received the message accurately. The members felt awkward following this directive because it felt unnatural, but they were amazed to learn how often they were misunderstood. The practitioner pointed out that this represented a learned family pattern. The receiver of a message began to defensively formulate a response for the sender before the sender had completed the message.

When the family had made some progress in these ways, the social worker taught the use of "I" messages. For example, Nita, instead of angrily saying to her son, "You need to get a job and get out of the house," was asked to formulate the message as "I feel angry when you are not working because a husband should provide for his wife." Her son was instructed to say, even though Nita would not agree, "Sometimes I feel uncomfortable living here when I'm not working, but I think parents should support their kids." These messages resulted in a clearer articulation of core family conflicts. The family had difficulty getting into the habit of communicating in these ways, and the social worker gave homework assignments for them to practice using "I" messages. At subsequent sessions the family members were expected to report on how consistently they adhered to the practice and whether it seemed to make a difference.

As a final component of this process, family members were asked to role-play a variety of conflicted interactions that occurred in the household. Members usually portrayed themselves in these role-plays, and other members were asked to comment afterward on the quality of the communication and problem solving, and to make suggestions for more effective ways to interact and negotiate. The social worker organized reverse role-plays at times so members could better understand the thoughts and feelings of the other party. During the role-plays members were helped to make clearer and more specific requests of each other. For example, Nita tended to be negative in her interactions when angry, saying, "I get upset because you're so lazy." She was encouraged to give the same message in a more clear and constructive way, saying, "I would not be so upset if I thought you were trying harder. I think you should go out at least two days a week to look for work."

The social worker had mixed success with this family. The level of tension in the household diminished and each member seemed to acquire improved communications skills. Nita gained assertiveness and confronted her husband about his detachment, even though he was not willing to work on their relationship. The sons remained unreliable about working, but Nita decided to get a job, which benefited her both financially and socially.

Combining Cognitive and Behavioral Intervention

Many social workers *combine* intervention approaches from cognitive theory and behavior theory when working with clients. The two theories are compatible because cognitive interventions help clients to develop alternative ways of thinking, and behavioral approaches help reinforce new behaviors based on those thought patterns. Their combination also helps clients set up natural experiments to test the extent to which their beliefs about an event of concern are "rational."

For example, consider Makita, a new university student commuting from a small town who feels depressed because she is not fitting in to the large campus environment. Through arbitrary inference, she concludes that the other university students are not friendly because no one ever approaches her in the student commons. She also concludes that she will continue to be lonely and sad. To help adjust her thoughts a social worker might help Makita learn to evaluate her external environment differently. The client can be helped to change some of her beliefs and expectations about how to make friends in an environment more impersonal than she is used to. Makita's thinking might be adjusted through the techniques of education and the ABC review. She might conclude that the commons is not an appropriate place to meet people, because it is crowded and students tend to be hurrying through lunch and off to classes. She might also learn that she needs to be more assertive in making friends.

In addition to assessing and adjusting Makita's thought patterns, a behavioral component to the social worker's intervention would help to adjust Makita's present set of reinforcers. Through desensitization and behavioral rehearsal, for example, Makita and her social worker could design and practice a series of steps whereby Makita learns to approach a small group of students at a lunch table and asks to join them. Her positive reinforcers might include success experiences and a new sense of efficacy through improved anxiety management.

Makita's story, though brief, describes several aspects of a cognitive–behavioral approach known as *social skills development* (Foster & Crain, 2002), which includes the following components:

Improving cognitive capacity. Providing knowledge about relationships (what they are, why they are important, how they develop, social norms); enhancing perceptual skills (how the client interprets the social world around him or her); improving decision-making skills about when and how to approach others; and improving the client's assessment skills (how to consider a variety of possible explanations for the observed behavior of others).

Improving behavioral skills. Self-presentation (to enhance likelihood of positive responses); social initiatives (includes starting conversations); conducting conversations (talking, listening, turn-taking); maintenance of relationships over time; and conflict resolution (handling disagreements, disappointments).

Keep in mind that while cognitive interventions often include task assignments for the client, behavioral interventions require that the social worker takes a systematic approach to organizing any environmental activities, measuring them as carefully as possible. The steps involved in social skills development are described in more detail in Chapter 10.

It should be evident that there are many specific interventions that are based on cognitive theory (and cognitive–behavior theory). More of these will be illustrated in later chapters on intervention with individuals, families, and groups. At this time we step away from practice theory and consider another value principle from the NASW Code of Ethics.

Value Principle: Integrity

The ethical principle underlying the core social work professional value of *integrity* asserts simply that "social workers behave in a trustworthy manner" (NASW, 1999, p. 6). This principle has implications for social workers' behaviors with regard to the mission of the profession, the functioning of individual social workers, and the promotion of ethical practices within employing agencies.

The value principle of integrity is referenced throughout the NASW Code of Ethics. It pertains to social workers' ethical responsibility to intervene in response to the perceived emotional impairment, incompetence, or unethical conduct of colleagues. This does not necessarily pertain to situations of overt misconduct. It may be appropriate, for example, to suggest that a colleague who is grieving the loss of a family member be excused for a period of time from working with clients who are dealing with the same kind of loss. Likewise, social workers are mandated to monitor their own capacity to provide quality services to client systems.

This value principle also pertains to social workers' ethical responsibilities to their employing agencies. They must adhere to commitments made to employers, improve agency policies and procedures when appropriate, support ethical behavior within the organization, and use agency resources diligently. An example of advocating for agency change was featured in Chapter 1 with regard to the "separate but equal" waiting rooms. Adhering to agency commitments may include giving adequate notice when changing jobs (which has an impact on clients) or going through formal agency channels when advocating for clients within the community. Their integrity requires social workers to always represent the profession well, and to differentiate their actions as private individuals and members of the profession when appropriate. Finally, with regard to the profession at large, social workers must promote high standards of practice, uphold the principles of the profession, and use their expertise to contribute to the development of the profession and its knowledge base. This responsibility may be addressed by educating members of other professions within one's agency about the social work perspective on client intervention.

Related to the topic of this chapter, the principle of integrity mandates that when social workers provide cognitive (or any other) intervention with a client system, they must secure informed consent. Social workers must "use clear and understandable language to inform clients" of the purposes, risks, limits, costs of, and reasonable alternatives to a proposed intervention (NASW, 1999, p. 8). Clients must be informed of their right to refuse or withdraw consent to the intervention, and the time frame covered by their consent. The code points out that there are several limits to informed consent, but the main point here is that clients need to understand as completely as possible the social worker's rationale for an intervention technique and how that process will unfold. Interestingly, this point is supported by cross-cultural studies, in which human service clients are shown to benefit most from services when they have been fully oriented to the intervention procedures (Frank & Frank, 1993).

SUMMARY

Cognitive theory is highly compatible with generalist social work practice. With its focus on conscious thinking and a client's potential to develop a rational, problem-solving perspective on issues of concern, it provides the practitioner with many intervention options. In conclusion we provide some additional points about the social worker's use of these interventions.

Social workers can minimize their own possible cognitive biases when working with clients by generating a variety of hypotheses about problem situations, using several sources of feedback (peers and supervisors) about the working hypothesis, and utilizing concrete measures of client change. To maximize the reliability of clients' self-reports, the social worker should inquire about cognitive events of concern as soon as possible after the event and minimize probing, as this may influence a client's ability to reflect objectively on thoughts and feelings. A client's potential to generalize learning can be facilitated by intervening in the natural environment or simulating real-life situations as much as possible. Positive outcomes are also enhanced by using homework activities to practice alternative thoughts and behaviors, promoting rehearsal, working with a client's significant others when appropriate (for support development), and focusing on lifelong rather than situational change.

We will consider other opportunities for social workers to use behavioral and cognitive strategies with clients later in the book, but now we turn our attention again to the larger systems level of generalist practice. The approaches described in the last two chapters can be effective for individuals, families, and groups, but they must always be utilized in a context of a client's environment. In fact, many interventions should be primarily directed toward that environment.

TOPICS FOR DISCUSSION

1. Do you accept the premise in cognitive theory that thoughts precede feelings? If so, are there any important exceptions to this assumption?

2. List a variety of stresses that people experience in their everyday lives that may feature cognitive distortions. Try to identify examples of all six cognitive distortions described in this chapter.

3. Cognitive errors are said to be common among children and adolescents. Try to identify examples of problems of adults that may be related to cognitive deficits. How would interventions tend to be designed to help the adult clients overcome those deficits?

4. Discuss types of clients for whom any of the interventions described in this chapter would be appropriate *or* not appropriate. What are the differences in these types of clients?

5. What are some ethical problems that may arise during the process of the social worker's assessing the "clarity" of a client's thought processes?

ASSIGNMENT IDEAS

1. Select and write about a client who, for you, represents a *special population* (based on age, race, gender, sexual orientation, or socioeconomic status). Describe any cognitive patterns of the client that might be different from your own, but that may not represent distortions. Some research into cultural differences will help you to minimize the possibility of seeing cultural differences as representing distortions.

2. Cognitive theory emphasizes the influence of cognitive distortions and deficits on clients' lives. Devise an assessment and intervention strategy for an otherwise well-adjusted client who is being discharged after spending three days in a hospital after a first heart attack.

3. Write a group intervention proposal on some topic of interest to you that includes both cognitive *and* behavioral interventions. Explain how the presence of numerous clients might facilitate *and* possibly limit the effectiveness of the intervention.

Chapter 7

Community and Social Support Theory

P eople are by nature social beings. Collective effort is superior to individual effort in achieving many group and individual needs and aspirations. However, defining the term "community," that place where people come together, is not easy. A century ago, most Americans would probably define their communities in terms of the geographic areas where they lived. They might refer to their neighborhood, church, and work communities. All of these incorporate the idea of a community with physical boundaries. As populations have become more transient and communication is based less often on face-to-face interactions, however, the concept has become more elusive. Communities are not necessarily bound by limited territories, but can span the country and even the world. Some people, for example, might identify their most important community as including people they interact with only on the computer.

The profession of social work was founded in the late 19th century as a means of helping people to build more facilitative, supportive communities. It sometimes seems that generalist practitioners, however, due to the diversity of professional roles and the "fracturing" of modern community life, do not routinely have opportunities to work at the large-systems level (Johnson, 2004). The purpose of this chapter is to discuss the concept of *community* so that social workers can assess the nature of their clients' communities (all types) and plan useful interventions when indicated. Another major topic in this chapter is *social support theory,* which provides the social worker with guidance in understanding how people come to feel connected to their environments.

DEFINITIONS OF COMMUNITY

Hutchison (2008) defines community as people bound together by geography or network links, sharing common ties, and interacting with one another. Further, the *sense* of community is the feeling that members matter to one another and to the group, and a shared faith that their needs will be met through a commitment to be together. The essential elements of community include membership, the possibility of influence, the integration and fulfillment of needs, and a shared emotional connection.

A community may be *territorial,* based on geographic characteristics, or *relational,* based on interactions that might take place outside a geographic context. These two facets of community may, of course, coexist. A major change in community life over the past three decades has been the rise in relational communities, and the subsequent decline in the strength of geographic communities (Garreau, 1991). Consider, for example, that a person may attend school, belong to discussion groups and clubs, and have long-term relationships with other people without having to physically move beyond the area of a computer terminal. That same person may live in a densely populated suburban neighborhood and have few interactions with her neighbors. Still, many potential client populations rely primarily on territorial communities. These include children and their caregivers, people who are elderly, people in poverty, and people with a variety of disabilities. Many members of these groups are geographically bound because of circumstances that restrict their physical mobility and access to electronic communications. Still, it should be noted that some members of these populations may also belong to cultural communities (for example, older adults in communities of seniors, people in poverty who are African American or Latino, and deaf people who participate in deaf culture).

Two theories of human behavior development that incorporate themes central to community life have relevance to generalist practice. *Social learning theory* and *social exchange theory* provide perspectives that can help social workers organize cognitive and behavioral interventions at the group level as well as larger-scale interventions. The two theories are described next and will be developed throughout this chapter.

Social Learning Theory

As presented in Chapter 2, learning occurs by reinforcement but also by modeling—as people watch the behavior of others and see how it is either rewarded or punished (Thyer & Myers, 1998). People of all ages imitate the behavior of others they want to emulate. Children in a neighborhood might pattern their behaviors on that of the older children—perhaps the bully who gets his way, the older sister who makes friends by being helpful to others, the gang member who is accepted for engaging in delinquent behaviors, or the student who receives honors by studying hard. The person's sense of what is appropriate is established and modified as he or she observes other people and their interactions, and how they are rewarded for their actions.

People who are new to a community may be most responsive to a particular segment of that community. For example, a Russian immigrant in Richmond, Virginia, is likely to model after his Russian peers there more so than members of the majority culture. Linking new immigrants with such a community is an appropriate way to, among many other things, expose them to positive models toward the goal of community adaptation. Based on social learning theory, a social worker's intervention may focus on linking members of social groups with appropriate models to help them feel more secure in their community environments.

Social Exchange Theory

Social exchange theory asserts, in short, that people give so they can get. That is, people interact with and make contributions to their communities to the extent that they are rewarded for doing so (Widegren, 1997). They will participate with others to the extent that there is something to be gained. This notion reflects the concept of *reciprocity*. While this theory is sometimes criticized for portraying people as innately selfish, it does remind the social worker that he or she needs to insure that clients are offered opportunities to contribute to their communities. In other words, while social workers often tend to see clients as service recipients, they should also consider ways for clients to feel that they are contributing members of their communities. The social worker should consider the client as embedded in a community of *reciprocal obligation,* rather than a person who is solely a recipient of assistance. Successful integration into a community involves giving as well as receiving, and the client should be helped to develop relationships in which he or she can be an active contributor—if the client wishes to do so, and in a manner that is agreeable to the client.

When we consider ways to develop community-level interventions, the perspectives of these two sociological theories will be evident.

VALUE PRINCIPLE: IMPORTANCE OF HUMAN RELATIONSHIPS

Probably no activity underscores the importance of human relationships on a broad scale more so than community intervention. The ethical principle that derives from this final principle from the NASW Code of Ethics (1999) states simply that "[s]ocial workers recognize the central importance of human relationships." The nature of relationships between and among people is almost always a target of the social worker's change activities. The social worker profession may in fact be unique in its desire to engage clients as partners in the helping process. Problem solving in communities necessitates constructive interaction with clients as well as other professionals, agencies, and community groups. This value principle should support social workers' positive attitudes about their communities as potentially offering opportunities for client participation in community life. Social workers attempt to strengthen relationships among people to enhance their well-being at all five levels of generalist intervention.

This value principle is inherent in all six ethical standards of the profession. It directly relates to interactions with clients but applies equally to relationships with colleagues. Social workers, and generalist practitioners in particular, should always understand that they can achieve more when working openly and cooperatively with members of other professions and other agencies who have resources to offer their clients. This value should be evident in all of the examples included in this chapter.

THE NATURE OF SOCIAL ORGANIZATION

It is important for social workers to be aware that how they conceptualize community intervention for their clients will be influenced by their own attitudes about community life. Social scientists have produced many theories about the nature of societies during the past century. Two somewhat extreme perspectives are presented here as a starting point for our study of community. One, structural functionalism, a theory developed in the 1940s, conceptualizes societies as a naturally evolving phenomenon in which groups of people work toward consensus. It reflects still-prevalent notions of many people about how society should operate. The second, postmodernism, argues that there is very little social consensus remaining in light of increasing fragmentation, and that efforts to solve social problems on a broad scale are doomed to failure. How the social worker perceives his or her own and the client's society will affect choices for intervention. These strategies may be based on *conflict* or *cooperation* with target groups, and feature an *agency-based* or broad *social action* orientation.

Structural functionalism asserts that social structures (patterns of behavior) in a society or community should be understood in terms of their contribution to the maintenance of the large system (Charon, 1992). This is a *consensus* theory that highlights the importance of shared norms and values among members of a society to meet their common needs. The social system is a relatively self-sufficient collection of people who are motivated toward gratifying their various needs. Social change is an evolutionary process that is ideally slow and orderly. Radical social activism is considered to be disruptive to natural processes.

According to structural functionalism, all societies include four functions. *Goal attainment* functions are played out in the realm of government, which represents the negotiated interests of the members of a society. These goals may include full employment, a certain standard of living, or spiritual fulfillment. *Adaptation to the external environment* includes those activities that help the internal system adjust to changes in surrounding systems. This is represented by the economy and the military. *Integrative functions* insure that deviant members of the society are helped to become more constructively involved with their society. The legal and social welfare systems provide examples of this function. Social workers are a part of the integrative function of society. Finally, *pattern maintenance* functions serve to furnish, maintain, and renew the motivations of members to participate as members of their societies. The cultural system and the family are primarily responsible for this.

The theory also asserts that all societies establish institutions to maintain order through rules and behavior norms. In the United States these include the economic, health care, governmental, religious, educational, social welfare, and family institutions. They provide ready-made patterns of intervention to deal with social problems. They are validated by tradition and experienced as morally right. They serve as the primary basis for social order.

Behavior that is disruptive to the orderly functioning of the social system is classified in structural functionalism as *deviance* (Merton, 1994). These behaviors serve as an indication that the established institutions within the system are not working appropriately. Interventions may be provided by members of a variety of institutions, but they are always in response to, rather than in anticipation of, social problems. This explains why social workers often are hired to provide small-scale, residual interventions rather than large-scale systems change.

Critics of structural functionalism have argued that it exaggerates the degree to which consensus and shared social goals guide human actions. Still, many people believe that a society should work for consensus regarding social goals.

Postmodernism, though not associated with a particular theory, holds that there has been a radical rupture in industrial societies during the past 30 years (Cooper, 2002). Societies have become less cohesive and more fragmented, comprised of subgroups that have little interaction or commonality with one another. Because of these changes it is no longer possible to find rational solutions to any identified social problems, or even to get broad agreement on what qualifies as a social problem. This postmodern society has developed as capitalism's emphasis has gradually changed from people as producers of goods to people as consumers of goods. Consumerism is said to promote superficiality, a waning of emotional experience, a loss of historical context, and a dominance of "reproductive" technologies such as the television and computer. People become increasingly passive and apathetic.

What follows are some characteristics of the postmodern society shared by a number of prominent theorists:

- A rejection of "inclusive" theories of communities, and a greater interest in local and personal narratives as sources of knowledge

- Social and cultural pluralism, and the lack of a basis for social, national, and ethnic unity

- Skepticism of notions of progress; a rise in anti-technology thinking

- Personal fragmentation, with people having multiple, conflicting identities

- A rise in alternative family units, marriage models, partnering, and child raising

- A loss of effectiveness in centralized social controls

- A rising dominance of popular culture

- Personal identification with smaller groups
- A sense of indeterminacy of what "causes" social phenomena

The challenge of postmodernist thought for social workers is that it tends to reject the value of large-scale interventions. If these postmodern ideas are valid, even in part, it follows that the community practitioner may have difficulty bringing groups together for cooperative change activities.

We next consider four perspectives on community that a person may hold, each of which includes assumptions for the social worker to consider in deciding how to intervene. To provide a context for this discussion, the range of intervention strategies for the generalist practitioner include neighborhood and community organizing, program development, and political and social action (Long, Tice, & Morrison, 2006). These strategies will be more fully developed in Chapter 12. The roles that a generalist practitioner may fill in providing these interventions include (from Chapter 1) service accessibility advocate, environmental practitioner, agency program and policy developer, community resource developer and advocate, and outcome evaluator.

FOUR PERSPECTIVES ON COMMUNITY

Thus far the concept of community has been described rather generally. Now we will consider four perspectives clients might hold about their communities, both positive and negative, that have relevance to the social worker's interventions (Hutchison, 2008). The social worker needs to assess the ways in which the client is motivated to develop and maintain supports within his or her identified community prior to initiating any interventions.

Community as Spatial Relations

A client may view community primarily as a set of *spatial arrangements*. This reflects the earlier point about the territorial perspective, but with the additional consideration of the physical arrangement of that territory. In assessing a community's spatial arrangements on behalf of a client, the social worker should consider the location of the client within the neighborhood relative to necessary resources for his or her functioning. It is important to insure that the client population's basic needs can be met. The assessment must go beyond the mere availability of resources, however, to include issues of accessibility. For example, is public transportation available? Are buildings accessible to clients with handicaps? For long-range planning the social worker should also consider population growth patterns in the community, zoning patterns, and relationships between the central city and surrounding suburbs (Wong & Hillier, 2001). Urban areas can change so quickly that patterns of resource availability cannot be assumed to be long-term.

Described next are two examples of client populations that are reliant on the location of resources within their communities.

The Shelter Relocation. In the downtown area of one midsize city there was a shelter facility that served many people in poverty. Because of changes in city zoning laws, the shelter was required to move. A controversy arose between the shelter board of directors and city officials around the issue of where to relocate the shelter, which all parties agreed was an essential city resource. Some decision makers wanted the shelter moved several miles outside the downtown area, so that the inner-city business revitalization efforts could proceed. The business leaders were concerned about the possible problem of vagrancy. This was opposed by many client advocates, including social workers, who argued that the majority of social services utilized by shelter residents (such as employment programs, health and mental health agencies, housing agencies, and the social security administration) were located downtown. Clients would no longer have access to these basic resources.

Shelter advocates argued that clients would not be able to make the two-mile trip into town for these support services. Many clients would likely drop out of the shelter program altogether and resume living on the streets. In the end, the shelter advocates prevailed and the facility remained in the downtown area. All parties eventually acknowledged that the proposed move would disrupt the spatial relationships of support services within the city so drastically that many clients might not survive. Still, it was anticipated that the issue of shelter location would arise again, as trends in city sponsorship of business development would continue.

Because this issue was so important to all interest groups in the city, all four intervention strategies (neighborhood and community organizing, program development, and political action) were utilized by the social workers, most of whom were agency employees or board members. Further, several interest groups (including current and former clients) were challenged to combine their advocacy efforts in order to insure that the needs of the client population were adequately represented.

The Cobblestone Controversy. An urban university embarked on a campus beautification effort that involved, in part, replacing the pedestrian asphalt streets that ran through the campus with new cobblestone streets. This was done during a summer in which relatively few students were present on campus. The university had apparently not considered that these new streets would be problematic for students with certain physical handicaps. When classes resumed in the fall, three incidents occurred during a two-week span in which students with walkers and wheelchairs fell due to the uneven street surfaces. There was an outpouring of concern by the student body that the university was becoming *less* rather than more accessible to people with disabilities. Again, a variety of advocacy groups, including the Social Workers with Disabilities Association, the student government, and the faculty senate, joined forces to petition the university administration to amend their mistake. The university was initially reluctant to make additional changes to the streets because of the financial cost, but a compromise was eventually reached in which brick walkways were installed in the middle of the cobblestone streets.

Community as Conflict

Clients may also view their community as a setting for unceasing *conflict*. This is a negative view of community as characterized by a push and pull among competing interest groups, all of whom desire to protect and expand their privileges without serious concern for the fate of others. Members of marginalized social groups, who are often clients of social workers, may hold this perspective, viewing the community as a place where, as relatively powerless people, they cannot trust that others will act in their best interest. Social workers will readily recognize that many of their clients are members of disadvantaged and disempowered social groups. Social workers themselves may hold the conflict perspective, as they experience frustrations in carrying out linkage and resource development activities with community organizations that do not seem responsive to client groups. The person with chronic mental illness may accurately perceive that relatively few social resources are available to enhance his quality of life. This perspective may also be found among families of client groups who have been frustrated trying to make human service professionals responsive to their needs.

This perspective of community as conflict was initially developed by Marx and his followers, who emphasized the inevitability of class conflicts due to different economic interests (Young, 1999). Neo-Marxists argue that cultural and intellectual forms of domination have replaced mere economic domination in today's society. Some people, interestingly, feel that social conflict has become more common as communities have become multicultural, perceiving that the groups have fundamentally different interests (Burbach, 1998). The two vignettes that follow illustrate this perspective on community.

The Family Support Group.   Several years ago a social worker organized the first-ever family support group in his city of residence. He invited the family members of all clients with mental illnesses from his agency to attend. One parent refused to consider attending and even berated the social worker during their conversation. She had become so angry with professionals, who, in her view, kept crucial information about her son's mental status from her because of confidentiality rules and also stigmatized her as enabling her son's problem behaviors, that she no longer had any faith that they cared about helping clients. She believed that the support group represented an insincere effort by the social worker to give the appearance of reaching out to families while he would probably continue to minimize their concerns. The woman had recently joined another parent organization in the community that focused on advocacy efforts *against* human service workers. She eventually agreed to join the family group and had a positive experience, because the social worker developed a program based on a partnership that featured joint session planning. The leader came to understand, however, that the woman's earlier anger had been based on real experiences of rejection.

It is useful for social workers to think of the contest perspective as a potential product of client and family experiences with organizations and community actors who appear to discount the client's welfare in their process of seeking services. If the social worker can enter into partnerships with client and family groups, then the client with a "contest" perspective may come to see that his or her interests can be sincerely represented in a community system.

ADHD School Programs.   The conflict perspective can also be seen in the struggle of some parents with students in public school systems to establish programs for their students with special needs. Educational institutions, like most others, function with limited resources, and schools are not able to implement the range of programs that would meet the needs of all their constituent groups. A high school system, for example, may include a growing number of students with attention deficit/hyperactivity disorder. The actual prevalence of the disorder is unknown but it has been diagnosed increasingly often since the 1990s (Loeber, Green, Lahey, Frick, & McBurnett, 2002). Many of these children do not benefit from standard classroom settings that require the ability to sustain concentration and control behavior, but the school may not have the resources (space, materials, and qualified instructors) to establish special classrooms for the students. The parents of these students may thus organize and establish a campaign to get services for their children. Other student groups, including those without special needs, with other types of special needs, or with special talents may also mobilize to hold on to their resources. The relative power and influence of the various interest groups, as well as the priorities of school administrators, will determine any resulting changes in the school's programs. The ADHD parent advocates may feel that only through sustained conflict with these other groups will they have a chance to realize their goals.

Community as Social System

A third perspective of community is that of a *social system*. This most closely approximates the traditional notion of community as a predictable structure of roles, interactions, and activities, and permanent networks of organizations having clear relationships to one another. Equally important, this assumes the existence of a relatively uniform community culture in which members have a generally shared set of goals, values, and sense of the common good. The person who holds the social system perspective views the community as a positive entity and expects that his or her needs can be fulfilled through processes of reciprocal obligation. This perspective does not deny the possibility of conflict but sees it as a natural process that can be negotiated by opposing parties who, again, share many underlying values and goals.

The Supervised Apartment Program.   A group of social workers from an agency that specialized in services to people with mental retardation developed a supervised apartment program, including 12 two-person units scattered throughout a larger apartment complex. This was based on a perspective of the community as offering support opportunities for members of marginal groups, if resources could be creatively engaged. For the 24 clients who lived there, the complex represented a small social system, supported and supervised by the social workers. Components of the system included structured, client-organized task activities (such as laundry, shopping, and cooking), shared recreational activity planning, and organized problem-solving and support groups. All of these activities encouraged regular interaction and relationship development with peers. One member of this community, Jason, emerged as the social chairman. He loved having friends over to his apartment for cards and listening to music almost every evening. He was less capable as a budgeter of money, and allowed others to take the lead in organizing shopping trips and recreational outings.

The Sibling Support Group.   A mental health organization concluded after a needs assessment that the urban area could benefit from a support group for the siblings of people with mental illnesses. Such a resource would bring together these people from a broad geographic territory who had similar concerns but would otherwise not have a chance to meet. This group, led by a social worker and conducted for one year, was a success and signifies the potential for members of a community system to develop mutual aid resources. It is important to note that social workers and other mental health interest groups in the community had an interactive tradition such that various needs of residents could be cooperatively identified and addressed. That is, the sponsoring agency had worked with neighborhood officials in the past on various initiatives intended to help residents with special needs, such as older adults and juvenile offenders. The agency had built a spirit of goodwill in the area that facilitated its implementation of new programs such as this one.

Community as Social Bond

The final community perspective is related to the social system model, but goes further in identifying community as a *social bond*. This is probably the least shared perspective on community in the United States. It assumes that the collective good may take precedence over individual interests, which opposes the strong ethic of individualism in mainstream American society. The community as a social bonding experience assumes that people are inherently connected with each other, and should always prioritize active cooperation in pursuing ends, motivated by traits of common human nature and universal dignity. This perspective incorporates the assumption that one's sense of self is intimately tied to interactions with significant others. However, there is a "first language" of individualism in the United States, with a relative inability to conceive of the primacy of the common good (Bellah, Madsen, Sullivan, Swindler, & Tipton, 1985). The view of community as a social bond assumes that the primary good is achieved in contributing to the group. From this perspective the social worker should be alert to opportunities for clients to participate in activities that lead to these kinds of fulfilling experiences.

Many people experience the social bond perspective at least occasionally. Few examples are so moving as those involving communities that come together in a united effort to recover after the occurrence of a natural disaster such as a flood or hurricane. It is not unusual to hear the people involved describe how the experience has changed them forever, not because of material loss but because of their renewed sense of fellowship. Step programs represent a social bond for some people. In Alcoholics Anonymous, for example, each member must concede his or her powerlessness over the disease, and rely on other group members and a higher power to maintain sobriety.

Next is an example of a "social bond" phenomenon that in fact is quite negative in its implications for community members. Nevertheless it represents a product of people's desire to transcend the evident limits of their surroundings.

Gangs.   Gangs, organizations of young men or women who participate in socially deviant activities, are generally considered to be a negative phenomenon. However, they do provide a means for otherwise marginalized people to develop an identity and a commitment to something "greater" than themselves. Children and adolescents who reside in low-income urban areas and are faced with oppression, poverty, and restricted social opportunities often find acceptance, meaning, and clear roles in gang activity. Gang members are often expected to subjugate their personal needs to that of the gang, which helps explain why members will risk their lives in activities intended to promote the gang's survival. Social workers find gang participation to be problematic for their clients, but it must be understood that these groups offer a greater sense of purpose than the person would have been able to secure otherwise. A challenge for the social worker is to help client members of organizations such as gangs to find alternative sources of interpersonal and community fulfillment.

Final Thoughts: Dimensions of Community

The four perspectives on community described here are not necessarily exclusive of one another. The social worker can assess the nature of the community in which he or she is working with regard to its relevant variables, as illustrated in Figure 7.1.

A community may be more or less territorial, open, cooperative, voluntary, and multicultural. It may also feature a focus on individuals within the group or the collective. Relationships among community members may or may not be intimate. Assessing these characteristics can help the social worker to decide what types of intervention are more likely to be successful with a client or client system. The social worker must also recognize that he or she may not be a part of the community in which he or she is working. He or she may be considered "alien" and need to establish a means of entry into the setting prior to initiating interventions (this topic is addressed in Chapter 12).

Regardless of his or her particular perspective, the social worker as change agent can conceptualize communities as networks of people, groups, or agencies interacting across space. Interventions can easily incorporate this notion of

Territorial --- Relational
Closed -- Open
Conflicted -- Cooperative
By necessity --- By interest
Single culture --- Multicultural

Focus on:

Basic needs --- Self-actualization
Individual --- Collective

Nature of Relationships:

Instrumental (task oriented) -- Emotional

F I G U R E 7.1   Dimensions of Community

supportive or nonsupportive networks. Thus we now turn to the topic of social
support as a framework for community intervention. In moving to this topic, our
client system shifts from the community at large to individuals, families, and small
groups that reside within those communities.

SOCIAL SUPPORT

Social support can be defined as the interpersonal interactions and relationships
that provide people with actual assistance or feelings of attachment to other people perceived as caring (Hobfoll, Freedy, Lane, & Geller, 1990). People require
support resources in the areas of health, housing, safety, education, personal fulfillment, employment, and legal justice to meet their basic needs. Appropriate
social supports, which are by definition external to people, have been consistently shown to promote their improved physical health, mental health, coping
capability, and community integration (Cohen, Underwood, & Gottlieb, 2000).
Social supports may be delivered by individuals but may also be provided
through families, groups, and organizations.

Three theorists in the 1970s were primarily responsible for generating interest in social support theory. Cassel (1976), an epidemiologist, wrote that psychosocial processes are important for understanding disease etiology, and that social
support plays a role in both the development and treatment of stress-related disorders. His work spurred interest in analyzing how people's interactions with
their social environments affected their vulnerability to disease, and how social
forces could be mobilized to protect one's health. Cobb (1976) defined social
support as information that leads a person to believe that he or she is loved and
cared for, is valued and esteemed, and is part of a network of communication
and reciprocal obligation. This information fulfills two basic human needs including social interaction and protection from the effects of stress. Like Cassel,
Cobb's emphasis was on social support as a buffer against stress.

Caplan (1989, 1990) focused directly on issues of prevention and intervention for human service practitioners. His theory asserts that the experience
of stress creates emotional arousal in the neuroendocrine system that features
an erosion of cognitive functioning; disorders of attention and information

collection; and diminished access to memories that bring focus to perceptions and judgment. Social support serves to compensate for those perceptual deficits; it sustains the person's sense of identity and preserves a self-monitoring capacity. Caplan's 10 characteristics of effective support include:

1. The nurturing of an ordered worldview
2. The promotion of hope
3. The healthy promotion of timely withdrawal and initiative in problem solving
4. The provision of guidance
5. Providing a communication channel with the social world
6. Reminding one of his or her personal identity
7. The provision of material help
8. The containing of distress through reassurance and affirmation
9. The insurance of adequate rest
10. The mobilization of other supports by relatives, friends, and professionals

While recognizing formal and informal systems as two categories of support, Caplan also stressed the distinct support role of religion, which addresses one's spiritual realm.

There are two schools of thought concerning how social support produces beneficial effects (Goldsmith, 2004). The *main effect* model holds that support is related to an overall sense of personal well-being. Social supports provide people with regular positive experiences, and their consistency enables people to enjoy stability, predictability, and recognition of self-worth. The *buffering* model asserts that support is a factor that intervenes between a stressful event and one's reaction by diminishing the stress response. The perception of support availability redefines the potential for harm or reduces the stress reaction. Most research on social support has focused on its buffering effects, in part because these are more accessible to measurement.

Most social support research has been done with general populations. There has not been a clear appreciation of the fact that social supports are organized, perceived, and received differently in client populations. Challenges for the social worker is to learn how client groups use support and then facilitate their development of supportive community environments. Several groups that appear to have particular vulnerability to social support deficits include chronically ill and elderly clients, disabled adults and children, homeless people, people living in rural isolation, culturally isolated people (refugees and immigrants), and abusive and neglectful parents (Cohen, Underwood, & Gottlieb, 2000).

Differences in the support acquisition behavior of subgroups can be seen through example of race. The kin networks of African Americans tend to be larger and more supportive than those of Caucasians. Multigenerational family systems have been a cultural tradition for African Americans since the slavery era (Green, 1999). These systems developed as a means of enhancing economic and emotional security with the inability of African Americans to fully participate in dominant societal institutions. All cultures must meet the sustenance and nutritive needs of its members, and African Americans must function in two separate cultural realms (the minority and the dominant) in order to get each set of needs met. One study of social networks of African Americans found that a primary coping mechanism for many involved the use of extensive social support systems and flexible family roles (Taylor, Chatters, Hardison, & Riley, 2001). Another study of African American, low-income, single-parent families indicated that kinship systems are more helpful than social agencies in meeting a variety of parent support needs (Whitfield & Wiggins, 2002).

Operationalizing Social Support

Social support is an abstract concept and must be operationalized for social work practice. The behaviors and relationships involved in social support have been articulated in various ways. Three examples are described next (there are many others), and then a fourth option will be recommended for the generalist practitioner. Before describing them, however, two important terms must be introduced. A *social network* is an individual's concrete patterns of interaction with those who share some commitment to the relationship (Piselli, 2007). These network relationships can occur in a variety of *clusters,* which are types of people with whom the person interacts in a particular role or activity (Levine & Kurzban, 2006). Clusters can be delineated in various ways but may include (Walsh, 2000a):

- Family of origin
- Extended family
- Family of choice
- Identified friends
- Work or volunteer contacts
- Neighbors
- Informal community relations
- Church or religious groups
- Members of associations
- Recreational partners
- School colleagues

As a general practice it is desirable for clients (and people in general) to have contact with supportive others in a variety of clusters. This provides the person or group with more options for social support acquisition when problems develop in a particular cluster. If a person loses a job, for example, she will have more trouble coping with the loss if all of her personal supports were located there.

Hobfoll and Vaux (1993) operationalize social support to include *social networks* (the number of people available to provide support behaviors), *supportive behaviors* (the number of support behaviors provided to a person in some period of time), and *support appraisals* (the person's assessment of the quality and adequacy of his or her supports). They emphasize social networks as important components of support, as they include information about an individual's potential for support resource acquisition.

Sarason and Sarason (2001) assert in contrast to Hobfoll and Vaux that a client's *perception of support* merits the closest scrutiny in practice. Their research concludes that for many client populations the objective connections revealed by social network analysis are not highly associated with actual received or perceived support. They describe two components of perceived support including *observed external resources* and the *sense of acceptance* by others. The latter of these components is a factor of personality, and the impact of social support thus encompasses situational, interpersonal, and intrapersonal contexts. One example of a psychological assessment of social support is provided by Procidano and Heller (1983) who developed an instrument to measure perceived support from friends and from family.

With this introduction we now turn to the practical matter of how social workers can assess clients' social supports.

ASSESSING SOCIAL SUPPORT

Generalist practitioners can assess and intervene with their clients' support systems with a focus on three variables. These include *material, emotional,* and *instrumental* supports, defined as follows (Walsh & Connelly, 1996).

Material support includes assistance with acquiring items needed to function in the course of daily living. Examples include food, money, household items, clothing, furniture, transportation, and entertainment resources.

Emotional support includes advice with personal problems; time spent with friends, visitors, and other companions; welcome phone calls; kind words; good listening; and religious help. Emotional supports provide people with a sense of positive social attachment.

Instrumental support includes any action that is a means to some end, sometimes of relatively minor significance, and often delivered by a person whom one does not know well. This may include resource information from a layperson or interactions with newspaper and mail deliverers, a person who provides directions on the street, the grocery clerk, and the barber or stylist. Instrumental support does not evoke a strong affective response toward the supporter from many types of people, nor does it typically involve the giving of essential material goods. Still, some client populations, such as people with mental illnesses, rate these supports as extremely important.

Measuring Social Support

Many instruments are available for measuring a client's social support. Most of them fall into the category of perceived support (Cohen, Underwood, & Gottlieb, 2000). Some instruments address social network resources (Fischer, 1982; McFarlane, Neale, Norman, Roy, & Streiner, 1982), and a few measure actual supportive behaviors (Barrera & Ainlay, 1983). The social support assessment form provided here (see Figure 7.2) is a relatively simple form that helps the social worker to learn about a client's social network, support experiences, and perceptions of support, as well as to differentiate material, emotional, and instrumental support. During assessment clients are asked to complete a daily log of incidents of social support. Sources of support to be included are all people, excluding human service professionals, with whom the client has interactions judged to be supportive in any way. For each incident of social support, clients are instructed to write the first name of the person who provided support, the person's relationship to the client, and the specific action or behavior that was supportive. This form taps into network members (columns 1 and 2), supportive behaviors (column 3), and support appraisals (as the social worker discusses with the client how the people and behaviors listed are perceived).

In order to get a complete assessment of their range of supports, clients may be instructed to complete seven daily log sheets over a four-week period, with every calendar day of the week represented during that time span. For each of the four weeks, clients are instructed to complete at least one, but not more than two, response sheets. That is, one week the client may focus on Tuesday and Thursday, and another week the client may focus on Friday and Saturday. The

Name: _____   Date: _____

Person Providing Support	Relationship to You	What the Person Did
1._____	1._____	1._____
2._____	2._____	2._____
3._____	3._____	3._____
4._____	4._____	4._____
5._____	5._____	5._____
6._____	6._____	6._____
7._____	7._____	7._____
8._____	8._____	8._____
9._____	9._____	9._____
10._____	10._____	10._____

choice of particular days is up to the participants. The rationale for this procedure is to achieve as broad a social support profile as possible. If participants do not encounter any support on a scheduled recording day, they should leave the form blank except to note the date. Clients may be assisted in the completion of the forms, if desired, by the social worker or a significant other, who can also monitor the process and respond to the client's questions.

Assessing and Utilizing Community Resources

Following support system assessment, social workers can strengthen a client system's positive ties to current supports, increase numbers of affiliations within existing support systems, and experiment with creating new systems, by addressing the following questions:

- Which network features are associated with certain problems and positive outcomes for this client group?

- What sources of strength can be identified in the client's existing support systems?

- What community resources might offer positive support to the client?

- How can community resources offer more effective support for this person?

- What types of affiliations with people and groups will empower this client system?

- How can educational interventions help this client group understand the nature of their real and ideal network structures?

Case Illustration: Leanora's Odd Lifestyle.   Leanora was a 43-year-old unemployed Caucasian widow who was trying to regain custody of her two adolescent children. She had a mental disorder that featured mild paranoid ideas and idiosyncratic thinking that made it difficult for her to manage structured jobs and social situations. After her husband's death from cancer several years ago, her parents-in-law accused her of being an unfit mother and successfully acquired temporary custody of the children through the children's service bureau. Leanora wanted the children back with her, and after many appeals the children's bureau was preparing to return them. A casual friend suggested to Leanora that getting counseling would further impress the bureau.

During her initial meetings with the social worker, Leanora was suspicious, quiet, and ill at ease. She had no agenda except to get her kids back home. Her affect was constricted and her communications were terse and obscure. Her grooming was haphazard. The social worker learned that Leanora's work involved collecting aluminum cans every day for recycling. Otherwise, she spent her time taking long walks through her town of residence. She had a positive relationship with her mother but no one else. The social worker knew that people with Leanora's diagnosis, and people with major mental illnesses in general, tend to function best with a small number of social contacts spread over a wide number of clusters. This enables them to avoid overstimulation while having supports in a variety of areas of life. He also knew, however, that Leanora's attitude about her community was one of "contest." She did not view her community as a place where help can be found, but rather as a source of opposition. She did not want to get involved in formal community functions.

Leanora was willing to complete the Social Support Assessment Form and seemed to enjoy doing so. The social worker suspected that her range and number of supports would be minimal. While this turned out to be true, Leanora noted many supportive others from the "instrumental" category. That is, she enjoyed her interactions with store clerks, police officers, and the guards at the local swimming pool. She also enjoyed having her children in the apartment, although she preferred limited interactions with them. She enjoyed seeing her mother, but only every few days.

Following the assessment, the social worker can select From the community intervention strategies described earlier. In this case he helped Leanora plan her time more predictably, being home for her children in the mornings as they were waking up, working in the afternoons, taking her walks around the town in the early evenings, and visiting her mother on certain days of the week. Leanora also started attending a community center three times per week where she played basketball with other members. After a few months Leanora's level of social adaptation improved significantly. She looked and felt better, even though her changes were not radical and to her neighbors she probably remained the eccentric lady on the block. The social worker felt that Leanora was able to benefit from intervention because of her range of external connections, especially the children for whom she felt responsible. There were no further complaints filed about her parenting from her extended family or neighbors.

SUMMARY

People may live in a variety of communities, both geographic and relational. The problems they experience in their lives often bear a direct relationship to the nature of community resources and the quality of their participation with those communities. The most effective intervention that a social worker may provide is often at the community level, where he or she addresses the client system's opportunities to meet their material and interpersonal needs. Even when social workers are employed in agencies where interventions are prescribed only at the individual, family, or group levels, he or she should always assess a client system's community functioning and consider how interventions may affect the quality of that functioning. This is, of course, the basis of the profession's person-in-environment perspective.

This chapter concludes Part II of the book, in which several theories and related intervention strategies relevant to generalist practice have been presented. In Part III, many additional intervention strategies will be presented for application at each of the five levels of generalist practice.

TOPICS FOR DISCUSSION

1. About what range of possible communities should a social worker be alert when assessing a client's community involvements?

2. The NASW Code of Ethics emphasizes the importance of human relationships. With computers and other media being so prevalent in American life, do you think there is perhaps less need for human relationships compared to 25, 50, or 100 years ago? If so, what are the implications for social work practice?

3. A variety of examples were included in this chapter of individual and social behaviors, and even programs, that reflect each of the four perspectives on community life. Discuss some additional examples of these four perspectives.

4. If a client system characterizes his or her community as featuring only conflict, should the social worker attempt to adjust the client's perspective? If so, how might this be done?

5. Which theory of social organization (structural functionalism or postmodernism) best approximates your own perspectives on social life? What are the benefits and limitations of each perspective with regard to generalist social work practice?

ASSIGNMENT IDEAS

1. Develop a list of questions that might comprise an assessment tool to determine a client's perspective on his or her community of residence.

2. Complete the Social Support Assessment Form with a client or some other suitable respondent. Following that activity, identify the respondent's strengths and limitations with regard to social support.

3. Compare and contrast the desirable characteristics of one's social support network with regard to any two of the following age groups: children, adolescents, young adults, and older adults. You may add details (about race, ethnicity, urban vs. rural home environment, and any others) as is appropriate to your own community or practice settings.

Intervention Methods for Levels of Practice

Chapter 8

Practice with Individuals

In Parts I and II of this book the nature of generalist practice was described, along with a set of practice theories that social workers can use when working from the generalist perspective. The five chapters in Part III are concerned with specific intervention strategies and techniques for generalist social workers. This chapter focuses on intervention with individuals. We begin with an outline for assessing individual clients, a brief review of problem solving, and then we cover the strategies of task-centered practice, stress management and prevention, social skills development, and crisis intervention. This is not a comprehensive discussion of cognitive–behavioral interventions, but rather a selection of strategies that are useful with social work clients (see Walsh, 2006, for a summary).

The cognitive and behavioral theories for generalist practice were described in Chapters 5 and 6. Several examples of interventions related to those theories that can be used with individual clients were also described in those chapters, including parent education, systematic desensitization, the ABC technique, problem solving, and communication skills education. We will add to our repertoire of intervention techniques here, considering several others that are useful with a variety of client populations. Any of these may be used as a primary intervention or one of a set of interventions with clients. We emphasize that the intervention techniques presented in this and the subsequent chapters in Part III are not necessarily limited in their applicability to one client system. When a technique is transferable to another client system, its flexibility will be noted.

ASSESSING INDIVIDUAL CLIENTS

The first step in the intervention process is, of course, the assessment. This topic was introduced in Chapter 2, but in this and the subsequent four chapters we offer specific intervention protocols for each level of generalist practice. We begin by describing a client who presents with one or more problems relevant for generalist intervention, and then provide an assessment outline that can be used with her as well as any other individual clients.

Case Illustration: The Adolescent Mother

Eva first came to the attention of her school social worker two years ago. At that time she was a 15-year-old African American high school freshman who was frequently truant. Her social worker learned then that Eva was also in trouble with the police for several misdemeanor violations, was a chronic runaway, and was said by her 33-year-old single working mother (Doris) to be incorrigible. Doris, who worked successfully in computer programming, noted that Eva would not abide by basic household rules, had parties when her mother was away, lacked any sense of personal responsibility, and spent her time with a "bad crowd." The school social worker had limited success engaging the young woman in a relationship, but her mother had been interested in working to resolve their problems. The social worker's involvement ended when Eva began attending school more consistently.

Today, Eva is the 17-year-old single mother of a newborn girl. Once pregnant she again developed a truancy problem, and now she is also under the supervision of the county children's services agency. Eva lived at home through her pregnancy, but since the birth of the infant, her mother has become increasingly exasperated with her, and depressed.

Eva shows little apparent concern about meeting the child's basic needs. She expects her mother to take care of the baby while she pursues an active social life. Doris believes that Eva is again in danger of getting into trouble with the law, although she isn't sure how her daughter spends her time. In fact, Doris is so distressed about the situation that she lost her job due to absenteeism and poor performance. She must now survive on public welfare benefits. She tends to stay in bed for much of the day. A member of the family's church who had observed the deteriorating home situation made the referral to the children's services agency.

Despite being concerned about the infant's welfare, Doris lacks the energy to provide proper care for her. Further she has thrown Eva and the infant out of the house four times in the past two months. She believes that mothers need to care for their young children, and she will not provide a setting where Eva can avoid responsibility for her own child. There is an extended family in the neighborhood, and Eva and the baby stay at the homes of her aunts, uncles, cousins, and friends for brief periods. In fact, the neighborhood of small African American families tends to be a cohesive one in the sense that residents know each other and offer help to each other when needed. Doris does eventually allow Eva to return home, but the cycle continues.

Some members of the local church are upset about Doris' failure to consider the infant's safety as a priority. They are pressuring Doris to keep Eva in the home, at least until some other suitable arrangements can be made. Doris remains frustrated with her daughter and cannot in good conscience permit her to stay there continuously.

Doris is willing to participate in the interventions offered by the school and children's services agency, but is less enthusiastic than before because of her depression and the ongoing conflicts with her daughter. Eva shows some willingness to invest more energy in the social workers' interventions, if only to get these agencies out of her life. She continues to rely on her circle of friends and relatives for most of her emotional and material support.

With this brief introduction to Eva and her situation we will look at examples of assessment outlines that a social worker might use at each level of generalist practice.

ASSESSMENT OUTLINE FOR INDIVIDUAL CLIENTS

The referral statement should include the source, reason, and date for the referral or service application; previous client contact with this agency; any other agencies providing social services to the client (past and present); and all sources of data used in the referral statement, as well as the assumed accuracy of that information.

Identifying information includes the client's name and address; date and place of birth; racial or ethnic background; educational level; employment; religious or spiritual orientation; marital or partnership status; legal status (voluntary or involuntary); and present living arrangements.

Problem identification and definition includes a summary of the presenting problem or problems, including precipitating events and current status; contrasting perspectives on the problem held by the client, any significant others, and the social worker; and the history of the problem, including its onset, development over time, and the client's prior attempts at resolving it.

We assume that Eva will not define the problem in the same way as, for example, her mother and the school personnel. Eva might emphasize that her mother and school are both unsupportive of her positive move into parenthood, while Doris might identify her daughter's lack of parenting ability as the major issue. The social worker may also perceive the problem differently than Eva. The social worker should explore all perspectives in an effort to achieve at least partial consensus.

Biological factors and functioning refers to physical appearance, including height, weight, and any distinguishing features; overall physical functioning and health; history of any biological or development problems; and information about any current medical treatments, including medications.

The fact that Eva has recently given birth to a baby clearly calls for an assessment of her current physical health and how well she is physically taking care of herself and the baby.

Psychological factors and functioning refers to cognitive functioning, including intelligence, creativity, and judgment; emotional functioning, including temperament, disposition, and moods; life-cycle stage (such as young adolescent, older adolescent, and so on) and whether the client's role behavior is appropriate to this stage; and results of any psychological testing that may have been done.

Eva gave birth to a child in her mid-adolescence, which puts her out of step with our society's typical adolescent developmental processes. She is being asked to assume many adult responsibilities and does not appear to have the emotional maturity, or the desire, to do so. The social worker may assess Eva's range of moods in different challenging situations and review school records to get a sense of Eva's academic and general learning potential.

Family factors include the composition of the nuclear and extended family and the nature of those relationships, past and present (including members who may be deceased).

Social factors include descriptions of everyday interactions with significant systems, including school, neighborhood, church, other agencies, recreational facilities, employers, and other social networks; interpersonal functioning, including the nature of relationships, ability to trust, management of conflict, and verbal and nonverbal communication skill; income level and sources and employment history; and educational history, including relationships with peers and teachers.

There is much to be explored in the previous two sections related to Eva's problem situation. The social worker needs to understand the nature of her relationship with Doris and also extended family members (including the whereabouts of her father, if he is living) and the many other systems with which she routinely interacts such as the church and school. The social worker will attempt to learn about positive support systems during this process.

Cultural factors and transitions refer to significant cultural factors in the client's life, including matters related to race, religion, ethnicity, age, gender, sexual orientation, and disability; the consistency of the client's behaviors with community norms and values; the consistency with which the client's cultural norms coexist with wider societal norms; and how cultural norms affect the client's attitudes about receiving help.

Eva is an African American adolescent and a member of a lower socioeconomic class. The social worker may wish to explore the demographic composition of the neighborhood and larger community to determine how similar or different Eva is in these ways to other residents. It will be important to assess how her minority status affects Eva's ability to function in mainstream social institutions and what strengths her racial customs may provide her (such as available extended family support).

Substance use information should include use of prescription drugs (type, dosage, and rationale); use of alcohol and other drugs, including frequency of use and circumstances of use (at parties, every day after work, alone versus with friends, and so on); present versus past use; personal, legal, or employment problems related to substance use; prior treatment for substance abuse; and family history of substance abuse problems.

Eva's lifestyle and demographics suggest that she is at risk to use illegal substances. The social worker may also wonder if any patterns of abuse are present in her extended family that may influence her choices.

Resources for problem solving include the client's positive capacities, including skills, successful methods of coping with previous problems, motivation, hope, ability to access external resources, understanding of the current problem, and current problem-solving resources (including formal and informal supports). This is not a separate category of assessment, but the information should emerge as the social worker investigates all aspects of Eva's life.

A *concluding statement* is a summary statement of the problem(s), including the relative influence of strengths and impairments in the client's functioning and the factors that create disequilibrium between the person and situation. The social worker considers all of the information gathered, weighs the problem issues against the client's strengths and potentials for resolution, and concludes with a refined problem statement that will become the focus of intervention activities.

Goals are the results the client wants to achieve. Eva's goals might include keeping her baby, putting her baby up for adoption, cooperating on child care with her mother, finishing high school, getting a job, moving in with relatives, or some combination of these.

A *plan* is a document or shared understanding identifying what will be done to facilitate the change process. It should identify specific intervention strategies, the rationale for their use, and activities of both the client and social worker in the process (see Chapter 1 for a fuller discussion of this activity).

We now turn to a consideration of several practical methods of generalist intervention for use with individuals. It should be evident throughout this chapter how important the comprehensive assessment is to the processes of goal setting and the selection of intervention tasks.

TASK-CENTERED PRACTICE

The problem-solving model of practice was described in detail in Chapter 2 but is reviewed here because it provides the basis for an intervention strategy known as task-centered practice. The steps in problem solving involve the social worker and client:

- Articulating the problem as specifically as possible, with a present-focus
- Analyzing the problem by breaking it down into its component parts
- Identifying any significant other people who are affected by the problem and who may be included in its resolution
- Brainstorming a range of alternatives with the purpose of generating all possible solutions for a presenting problem
- Discussing each viable alternative as to its advantages and disadvantages
- Selecting and implementing a strategy for problem resolution that appears to maximize benefits over costs for the client
- Evaluating the outcome of the strategy

This final step is particularly important. If the problem is not resolved to the client's satisfaction, the social worker and client return to the sixth step and select another option for implementation.

Task-centered practice (TCP) is a focused, time-limited, systematic approach to intervention that is conducive to a variety of cognitive and behavioral interventions with individual clients (Reid, 2000; Reid & Epstein, 1972; Reid & Fortune, 2002). It represents a process of the social worker and client articulating and recording goals and objectives, and together developing plans for goal attainment through shared tasks. It is recommended for generalist practice because of its *clarity* for the client. It incorporates the use of a form that lays out the intervention process in a step-by-step, session-by-session manner. It also incorporates an assumption consistent with social work values—that clients are respected and empowered when they are actively involved in the change process. With this model the social worker and client share responsibility for the client's goal attainments. Because it is collaborative, it is an empowering activity. Task-centered practice is one of few practice models that was originally developed by social workers, and it has been shown to be effective with a variety of client populations (Reid & Fortune, 2002).

Figure 8.1 is a form that the generalist practitioner can use when working with the task-centered practice model. Remembering that agencies usually adopt their own forms for use by practice staff, the social worker may elect to use this form in addition to other agency materials. While it may seem counterproductive to add paperwork to one's existing job responsibilities, use of this form is intended to be time-efficient.

The process of task-centered practice is outlined in the following steps, followed by an example. Keep in mind that the social worker and client complete the task-centered practice form together. The client should be given a copy of the updated form at the end of every session because he or she will be working with it between meetings.

The social worker *completes an assessment* in accordance with agency protocols and specifies the client's presenting problem as clearly as possible. The client may have more than one problem for work, and if so these others should be listed. It is advisable that the social worker not focus on more than three problems at one time, because doing so creates a potentially overwhelming situation for the client.

The social worker *educates the client* about the nature of the task-centered process and *elicits his or her commitment* to participate in it.

The social worker and client *identify one or two goals* for each problem. Goals represent the client's ultimate desired outcomes.

The social worker and client *set one or more subgoals (objectives) for each goal statement.* Each of these includes a short time frame (for example, within one day or one week). Recall that objectives are behavioral indicators that an ultimate goal is being approached. Usually the time frame for each subgoal is the time between this and the next meeting between the social worker and client. That is, the social worker promotes the accomplishment of subgoals on a session-by-session basis. This helps the client to see and feel progress regularly, and keeps the intervention focused on achievable tasks.

Problem(s)

1._____

2._____

3._____

Goal #1:_____

   Subgoals (including time frame)

     1._____

       Tasks for client:_____

       Tasks for worker:_____

       Anticipated obstacles:_____

     2._____

       Tasks for client:_____

       Tasks for worker:_____

       Anticipated obstacles:_____

Goal #2:_____

   Subgoals (including time frame)

     1._____

       Tasks for client:_____

       Tasks for worker:_____

       Anticipated obstacles:_____

     2._____

       Tasks for client:_____

       Tasks for worker:_____

       Anticipated obstacles:_____

Goal #3:_____

   Subgoals (including time frame)

     1._____

       Tasks for client:_____

       Tasks for worker:_____

       Anticipated obstacles:_____

     2._____

       Tasks for client:_____

       Tasks for worker:_____

       Anticipated obstacles:_____

Issues for relationship development:

_____

_____

_____

_____

F I G U R E 8.1   A Task-Centered Practice Form

The social worker and client *specify and write down the tasks that each of them agrees to undertake between this and the next session so that each subgoal is met.* These are always cognitive or behavioral tasks. Because this is a collaborative process, it is not only the client who assumes responsibility for activity. Examples of social worker tasks might include making a referral, getting resource information, or performing an advocacy task.

The social worker next *reviews and practices with the client those behaviors, skills, or areas of knowledge that are required for task accomplishment.*

A unique and extremely useful aspect of TCP is the social worker and client's *formal identification of obstacles that might get into the way of their abilities to complete agreed-upon tasks.* Experienced social workers know that it is not unusual for clients to agree to certain activities but then fail to follow through because of forgetfulness, conflicting responsibilities, or ambivalence. Looking ahead to possible obstacles paradoxically helps both parties ensure task completion because it (1) makes the planning process more thorough, and (2) provides a "check" on how realistic the tasks are.

Prior to ending the session the *social worker summarizes the plan with the client,* making sure that both parties are clear on what has been accomplished and what is expected for the next session.

The social worker can make notes at the bottom of the form regarding his or her *relationship concerns* with the client. TCP is a collaborative process that requires trust, and it cannot succeed if the worker and client do not trust or are guarded with each other. The social worker can document his or her sense of the quality of the relationship as it unfolds, and again discuss it with the client regularly.

The discussion thus far has focused on the philosophy of task-centered practice and activities during the first session. The process is organized in much the same manner throughout the client's participation. During all follow-up sessions, the social worker attempts to maintain a clear focus on the client's goals, objectives, and tasks, by:

- Beginning each session with a review of the task activities established during the previous meeting

- Comparing the client's perspective on task accomplishment with observations about cognitive or behavioral changes that serve as objective evidence of progress

- Communicating to the client the fact of his or her making gains, even if these are partial

- Encouraging the client to reward himself or herself for gains made

- Analyzing any failures of either person to follow through successfully with a task, not to place blame but to understand obstacles more clearly and work past them

- Discussing, agreeing on, and then recording on a revised form tasks that each party will undertake for the following week

- Discussing how closely the client is coming to achieving his or her stated goals, and in so doing keeping a time frame in mind for the intervention

- Discussing the possibility of adding new goals, or new objectives, to the intervention plan, depending on the client's desires

- Monitoring the quality of the relationship, perhaps with discussion if there are concerns

The intervention ends when the client is satisfied that he or she has achieved his or her goals. When the social worker and client attend to the intervention process in a task-focused manner, they are both likely to be aware when the end is nearing and thus experience a smooth ending process.

Case Illustration: Robert's Vocational Training

Robert was an Italian American high school graduate who had recently become physically disabled in an automobile accident. His cognitive faculties were intact except for short-term memory problems that were anticipated to be permanent. He also needed to use a walker because of nerve damage that affected his lower extremities. Robert was referred to a bureau of vocational counseling (BVR) service as a part of his overall physical and psychological rehabilitation. Margaret, the social worker at that agency, utilized the task-centered practice model with all of her clients. She felt it was important that clients work systematically and concretely toward specific goals related to their employment. In Robert's case, the model would also facilitate the management of his memory problems, as their session topics would be written down each week, with a copy for the client to take home.

Robert was agreeable to participate in this model and he was motivated to get a job. Many of his young-adult friends were also becoming independent of their families. His strengths included a drive to earn a steady income and to live in an apartment. Margaret was also aware that Robert experienced depression as he struggled to make adjustments to his disabilities, and she was concerned that this might present an obstacle to his progress.

Robert's first goal was to select a suitable vocation. He and Margaret specified two subgoals, or objectives, related to this—to complete an interest assessment (and thus achieve a clear picture of his abilities and aptitudes) and to get the support of his parents (both financial and emotional) in pursuing his career interest. The social worker estimated that these objectives would require four to six weeks for completion. As stipulated in the TCP model, both the social worker and client took responsibility for tasks each week. Margaret's activities included referring Robert to an appropriate testing source, sending required information to that agency, gathering information about training organizations and schools in the region, and talking with Robert's parents about the rehabilitation process. These represented the generalist practice roles of direct practice, environmental practice, and service access advocacy. Robert's tasks included reading information on careers provided by the social worker, having weekly conversations with his parents about his vocational preferences and writing down their expectations of each other, and attending all testing appointments on time. One obstacle became Robert's variable enthusiasm about persisting with the steps in this process, related to his moderate depression. Margaret and Robert agreed that she could consult with his psychiatric nurse about the mood disorder at these times with the hope of successfully regulating his mood with medication.

Once this goal was achieved, Robert set another major goal of securing part-time paid employment as a plumber. His subgoals became regular attendance at vocational school for a one-year term and the acquisition of a steady volunteer experience as a plumber's assistant within three months. Regarding the first subgoal, Robert agreed at each session (now held only once per month) to maintain the activities of daily school attendance and prompt completion of all assignments. In her role as advocate Margaret agreed to talk with his instructors prior to the first semester about Robert's status with the BVR and then on an as-requested basis by Robert, the instructors, or his parents about his needs for any accommodations. Regarding the second subgoal, the social worker agreed to provide the client with resources about volunteer opportunities and to provide potential mentors with letters of reference and appropriate case information. Robert agreed to review newspaper and Internet sources on jobs and volunteering, read all materials shared with him by his social worker related to volunteering, and make the inquiries about potential positions on his own. Through all of these structured activities, Robert eventually achieved his goal of working for a plumbing company and moving into a friend's apartment.

Next we consider an intervention that includes both behavioral and cognitive strategies.

SOCIAL SKILLS DEVELOPMENT

Social skills development is a process of helping clients *learn* and *rehearse* new behaviors to replace other behaviors that have caused them problems in interpersonal situations (Chang, D'Zurilla, & Sanna, 2004; Greene & Burleson, 2003). Effective social skills can help clients adjust their behaviors in such areas as work, school, friendships, and other social interactions. These skills include assertiveness and anger management, among others.

This intervention technique can be used with all age groups but is particularly appropriate with children and adolescents (Hennessey, 2007). People in that age range are in the process of developing a variety of basic life skills, and many of the behavioral problems and emotional stresses they demonstrate are related to a lack of adequate social skills to help them negotiate normal life challenges. This absence of social skills is an example of a cognitive *deficit,* or lack of knowledge, as opposed to intentional deviance from social norms. Social skills development can be helpful for children and adolescents who are depressed, anxious, or exhibit conduct problems (Bloomquist, 2006). Their behavior may be characterized by aggression, destruction of property, deceitfulness, defiance, theft, and rule violations (such as skipping school). Conduct problems may appear along with hyperactivity, academic problems, and interpersonal conflicts. The social worker's goal as a direct practitioner is to help the client acquire the skills that will enable him or her to manage these various challenges more successfully.

All children and adolescents experience rapid developmental changes (Allen-Meares, 2003). Biologically, they must adjust to growth spurts and the onset of puberty and sexual maturity. Cognitively they are becoming able to engage in more complex reasoning, separating reality from fantasy, predicting the consequences of their actions, and developing moral principles. Their psychological and social changes include conforming to peer groups in taste and behavior, criticizing their parents, and formulating their own opinions. They seek a sense of identity and self-worth but at the same time are insecure about breaking away from the family unit. Depending on the person's cognitive skill level, interventions may tend to focus on changing thought patterns (through education and discussion) or behaviors (rewarding more positive behaviors).

Regarding the *cognitive* aspects of social skills development, the social worker first assesses the assumptions that seem to lie beneath the client's attitudes about relationships, or how he or she interprets the social world. For example, does the client's perspective incorporate social interactions as presenting opportunities for growth, or do other people represent threats? What thoughts contribute to the client's conclusions about this? The social worker may challenge the client's assumptions as reflecting cognitive distortions or deficits. After this process the social worker educates the client about the following topics, many of which can be approached with videos and written materials (stories, for example).

The nature of relationships. What they are, why they are important, how they develop, and the prevailing social norms that influence them

How to make decisions in social situations. Different strategies for deciding when and how to approach other people, depending on the purpose of the contact

How to assess social situations. How to evaluate possible explanations for the behavior of others in social situations when those behaviors are unclear; in other words, becoming more sensitive to the thoughts and motivations of other people

Regarding *behavioral* interventions in social skills training, the social worker helps the client to rehearse and refine skills in the areas of:

Self-presentation, to enhance the likelihood of positive responses from other people

Social initiatives, or how to start conversations

Conversational skills, including talking, listening, and taking turns

Maintaining relationships over time, including keeping in touch with other people, understanding boundaries and how they may change over time, and understanding cues related to becoming closer or more distant

Conflict resolution, including managing disagreements and disappointments

These skills are taught and rehearsed through a systematic training process that includes the following steps (Bloomquist, 2006). Notice that these are similar to the steps involved in problem solving:

- Through assessment, determine what skill the client wants or needs.

- Discuss the rationale for learning the skill with the client.

- Describe the skill.

- Outline *all* of the "steps" involved in using the skill. Generally, all social skills, even those that seem basic to people who possess them, include many steps. The social worker must list out each of these steps with the client.

- Model the skill in its entirety for the client through role-play, the use of videotapes, or other media resources.

- Role-play each step in the skill (as written down) with the client. This involves the social worker demonstrating and then role-playing each of these with the client.

- Evaluate the role-plays, repeating them until the client demonstrates competence with them.

- Combine the steps of the role-plays into a full rehearsal of the social skill.

- Ask the client to apply the skill in one or more specific real-life formats.

- Evaluate and refine the skill by discussing the client's efforts to practice it in subsequent meetings. Refine the skills until the client achieves mastery of it.

Case Illustration: The Angry Adolescent

Jake was a 13-year-old Hispanic middle school student who was frequently in trouble for fighting with classmates and arguing with his teachers. These were serious behavioral problems because Jake was spending much time in detention, was failing several courses, and had alienated many of his peers and teachers. The school social worker became aware that there were several reasons for Jake's long-standing problems, many of them involving an unstable home life. One source of his difficulties, however, involved cognitive deficits. Jake had never learned how to manage disagreements or conflicts with other people in nonaggressive ways. Nate, the social worker, decided to include conflict resolution skills training in Jake's intervention plan. Jake did not enjoy interacting with the social worker, but he was agreeable to do so because he was tired of being in trouble and was bothered that his peers were avoiding him. He wanted to have friends.

Nate explained to Jake that conflict resolution skills would help him to avoid trouble, get along with his teachers, and keep friends. The social worker described that the following steps were involved in the skill:

- Recognizing the physical signs that accompany negative feelings (which for Jake included butterflies in the stomach, dry mouth, and tense facial muscles).

- Putting labels on feelings experienced at these times (anger, frustration, shame). This step includes Jake's learning about differences between feelings.

- Calming himself with breathing exercises (described in more detail later in this chapter).

- Making a decision not to fight physically (and in the process demonstrate personal power and self-control).

- Waiting 10 minutes before acting on thoughts and feelings. During this time period, composing a clear statement of what he wants to communicate to the other person.

- Considering the circumstance of the other person prior to approaching him or her. For example, does the teacher have time now to discuss the conflict? Is the other student also angry and likely to respond physically? Select a time for conflict resolution when the other person will most likely be calm.

- Approaching the other person and communicate the statements composed earlier. Begin by saying, "I want to clear something up here but not have an argument." Use no profanity and maintain a calm voice tone. Come no closer than three feet to the other person.

- Allowing the other person to speak after expressing each idea. Listen to what the other person is saying.

From this point in the process, Jake's responses would depend on what was transpiring between the two parties. The social worker taught and rehearsed each of these steps with Jake. They eventually improvised responses as part of the role-plays that were likely to emerge. The total skills training process took four weeks to complete.

Learning and practicing new skills is usually challenging for a client and creates stress, at least in the short-term. What follows is a discussion of several interventions that specifically target clients' stress experiences.

STRESS MANAGEMENT

For all people, whether or not their problems bring them to the attention of a social worker, life is full of stress. Some of it is minor and some is considerable. Sources of stress can range from being late to school or not finding a parking spot near the classroom building to needing to consider dropping out of school because of financial pressures. All people can manage their lives better if they have good stress management skills. These include their learned strategies for reducing levels of biological, psychological, and social stress (as described in Chapter 2).

For some clients, a major aspect of their presenting problem includes difficulties with managing the stresses they experience (Davis, Eshelman, & McKay, 2000). This is not to suggest that all of their problems can be resolved with stress management skills, but many problems related to fear, anxiety, and depression can be ameliorated with stress management practices. Even for more serious situations, problem solving can be more focused if the client can reduce his or her level of subjective stress. For these reasons the social worker's ability to teach present stress management skills is important. These practices can work well for clients of all ages. The interventions can be categorized into the two general types of relaxation skills—training and stress prevention training (Davis, Eshelman, & McKay, 2000).

Relaxation Skills Development

For any client who might benefit from controlling his or her subjective level of stress, the process of stress management includes the following steps.

Explain the rationale for the skill. The social worker and client must first agree that the client's current methods of coping with stress are not sufficient, and that additional skills may help the client function better. The social worker helps the client to understand the benefits of stress management practice, both generally and with respect to the presenting issue.

Identify and articulate as clearly as possible those situations in which the client needs to better manage stress. Some clients benefit from an outsider's (social worker's) perspective in narrowing down their awareness of what causes stress in their lives. It may be a specific situation at work or school, a particular type of conversation, a social situation, an expectation, and so on.

Select a relaxation technique and describe its components. In this step the client and social worker should be creative. First, the social worker should take a strengths perspective and explore with the client his or her current relaxation practices that are helpful at times. This may include listening to music, reading, exercising, and other behaviors. All people are different in how they relax themselves. The present author, for example, uses deep breathing techniques to relax, but becomes agitated when attempting to use progressive muscle relaxation activities. The social worker should not assume that any one or several strategies can work for every client. If the client already has a suitable method of relaxing, the social worker should build on it, helping the client to adapt it to the problem situation.

Instruct the client in the relaxation technique. As in social skills training, the social worker breaks down the practice into discreet steps and reviews them with the client. Even if the client already relaxes in a certain way, he or she can benefit from understanding the steps more clearly, as this may help the client generalize the practice. In deep breathing, for example, there are eight steps: (1) lying down or finding a comfortable position in a chair, (2) scanning the body for tension, (3) placing one hand on the abdomen and another on the chest, (4) inhaling slowly through the nose, (5) holding the breath for five seconds when the intake is complete, (6) slowly exhaling through the mouth, focusing on the sound of the breathing, (7) continued breathing in this manner for five minutes, and then (8) scanning the body again for tension.

Assign the client to practice the technique(s) on his or her own. The client should practice the relaxation strategy in a variety of situations, including those related to the presenting problem. The client is reminded that all skills take time to learn well, and that he or she should not be discouraged if the new technique does not work at first. The social worker should add that the technique they have chosen may not turn out to be effective for the client, and that they may need to consider other techniques.

Teach and practice abbreviated techniques. All skills become easier and can be used more efficiently when practiced. Clients can use a relaxation technique in more situations to greater effect once they can implement them efficiently. The social worker should thus promote the client working toward this level of mastery. Again using deep breathing as an example, the client can be asked to practice the technique each day for a specified amount of time (10 to 20 minutes) in "natural" positions (not necessarily lying down or sitting in a comfortable chair). The client can practice shortening the time of each breath, so that others will not notice the technique in "real" situations.

Other formal relaxation strategies include progressive muscle relaxation, meditation, visualization, thought stopping, and biofeedback (Davis, Eshelman, & McKay, 2000).

Case Illustration: The Niece and the Nursing Home. Mabel had been the primary caregiver for her aunt, Jesse, before the older woman needed to move into a nursing home because of declining health. It was soon discovered that Jesse, who had a strong German heritage characterized by a stoic dealing with physical threats, had a terminal illness and would die within three to six months. The social worker at the nursing home became aware that Mabel was terrified of facing her dying aunt to whom she was so devoted. Mabel had no experience with this type of loss. Among the social worker's interventions was teaching Mabel relaxation techniques so that she could manage the stress when visiting her aunt. Following an assessment of Mabel's usual relaxation habits, the social worker recommended that Mabel take brisk walks in her neighborhood just before coming to visit her aunt, and that she listen to a compact disc of soothing music on her way to the facility in the car. She and Mabel worked out a specific routine, and Mabel practiced it for several days to test its suitability. Mabel was able to use the relaxation techniques with some success, and maintained her regular visitation with a positive mood. Mabel was also pleased that the walks were beneficial to her overall physical health.

Now we can consider interventions that are concerned with preventing stress from becoming a problem issue.

Stress Prevention Skills Development

This intervention strategy is related to that described previously, but includes a cognitive component of proactive planning for problem resolution (Saunders, Driskell, Hall, & Salas, 1996). Many clients have developed habits related to their ability to manage stress that are no longer functional, and with more positive or constructive planning they can learn to more effectively anticipate and perhaps avoid certain stressful situations. For example, if a client has difficulty managing job stress, he or she may benefit from this intervention strategy. Perhaps the job is such, or the client's physical or emotional characteristics are such, that some level of ongoing job stress is to be expected. This client cannot eliminate the stressful situation, but may be able to manage it more effectively with relaxation skills coupled with a different perspective about his or her job situation.

The first step in this process is to educate the client about the nature of core beliefs, automatic thoughts, and cognitive restructuring as described in Chapter 2. The social worker then explores the client's thoughts relative to the problem situation with such questions as:

- How stressful is the situation? (It may be useful for the client to rank the perceived level of stress on a scale of 1 to 10 to provide a baseline for later evaluating progress.)

- Why is the situation stressful?

- What does it mean to the client to be in the situation, regarding his or her immediate and long-range goals?

- What aspects of the presenting situation are the most threatening? Why?

- What strengths does the client possess that could be mobilized to eliminate or reduce the significance of the stressful situation?

- What other resources (including other people) can the client mobilize to confront the stressful situation?

- Is the client inclined to ask for appropriate help with the situation? Why or why not?

- What personal vulnerabilities is the client concerned about?

- What is the source of the client's self-assessment of these vulnerabilities?

- What is the nature of the evidence that the client may not be able to manage a stressor?

Once the client is able to consider the stressful situation as rationally as possible, the social worker can help the client develop plans for minimizing the stress and developing new relaxation strategies. These strategies can be quite varied and may begin with techniques the client already uses to manage stresses in other areas of his or her life.

As with all cognitive–behavioral interventions, the social worker asks the client to rehearse relaxation skills and problem-solving skills in two stages. First, the social worker and client role-play situations in the office, giving the client the opportunity to implement new behaviors and cognitions in hypothetical situations and thus refine his or her understanding of them. Next, the social worker and client plan together for the application of the skills in "real" social situations, including those involving the target problem. The worker and client review the client's functioning during subsequent meetings until the client is able to develop a sense of mastery. The social worker reminds the client that these new strategies are not meant to represent perfect solutions.

Case Illustration: Every Day Was Overwhelming.   Bethany was a 16-year-old African American woman living in an adolescent residential treatment center. Her mother had enrolled her in the program because of chronic unruly behavior.

Bethany had received inconsistent parenting, and her impoverished family had dealt with frequent crises involving jobs, money, and housing. Bethany lived in a "reactive" manner. She had never learned to plan ahead, and her coping style was characterized by ineffective distancing and escape strategies. Neither did she have good organizational skills. As a result of her background, Bethany was easily overwhelmed when expected to assume responsibility in her residential program for household upkeep, school attendance, and school assignments. When overwhelmed she broke down into tears, became angry, and ran off to her room.

Her social worker, Cynthia, included stress prevention content in Bethany's intervention plan. She wanted to teach Bethany that planning ahead for daily task completion could prevent stress and advance her personal development. The issue was addressed primarily through Cynthia's teaching of time management skills. Bethany learned to (1) make a list every night of what she was expected to accomplish the next day, (2) keep an ongoing log of how long it took to complete her activities of daily living, including her school schedule and assignments, cleaning her room, and preparing meals (when it was Bethany's turn to do this), and (3) fill out a daily appointment book with her required activities and the times of day during which they would be addressed.

Through this process Bethany also came to learn that she could preserve several hours each day for leisure activities. The social worker also explored her client's recreational interests and encouraged Bethany to plan these into her day. Finally, Cynthia taught Bethany the differences between proactive and escape coping strategies (see Chapter 2). The social worker helped Bethany practice several problem-solving rather than escape and avoidance strategies. These included attention to Bethany's social skills, and the client was helped to develop a greater range of conversational skills. Bethany learned that negotiation rather than angry outbursts could resolve problems at times. As a result of these interventions, Bethany's behavior improved and her general level of subjective distress declined.

Our final intervention strategy in this chapter for individual clients is crisis intervention, which involves the social worker's quick and active strategies for assisting clients who are experiencing overwhelming stressors.

CRISIS INTERVENTION

A *crisis* is a major upset in one's biological, psychological, social, or spiritual equilibrium due to some hazardous event that is experienced as a threat, challenge, or loss, and with which the person cannot cope (James & Gilliland, 2001). The crisis poses an obstacle that is important to a personal goal, but it cannot be overcome through usual methods of coping. The person temporarily lacks either the necessary knowledge for coping with the situation or the ability to focus on the problem because of feeling overwhelmed. A crisis episode often develops when the person faces a serious stressor with which he or she has no prior experience.

It may be environmental (including natural disasters such as floods and fires) or interpersonal (the sudden loss of a loved one).

Crises include three stages, as follows (Caplan, 1990):

The client experiences a sharp and sudden increase in tension, including shock, denial, and a failure of coping. The client enters a vulnerable state.

The failure of usual coping efforts increases the client's tension further, and produces additional reactions of confusion, depression, anger, hopelessness, and the sense of being overwhelmed. In this stage the client is receptive to receiving help.

The crisis episode ends with the implementation of solutions that are either maladaptive (physical or emotional breakdown) or adaptive. With a positive resolution, the client will be better prepared to manage future stresses.

The three stages of a crisis necessarily occur in six weeks or less. Crises are time-limited because one's body simply cannot maintain a state of alarm any longer. From a physiological perspective the crisis *must* be resolved, either in an adaptive or maladaptive way. One person's means of resolving a crisis might include increased drinking or drug use, while another person might instead acquire assertiveness skills. Timely, focused intervention is critical so that the client may resolve the issue in a health-promoting manner.

The process of crisis intervention is characterized by four principles, including time limits, a here-and-now orientation to the problem situation, a high level of practitioner activity (perhaps exceeding what is typical of the worker in other contexts), and the use of tasks as primary tactics of change. The goals of crisis intervention are to alleviate the client's distress and either return the client to the previous state of equilibrium or enhance the client's functioning.

The social worker's assessment and intervention activities in crisis intervention can be guided by the following questions (Myer, 2001):

- What crisis stage is the client experiencing?
- What is the meaning of the hazardous event to the client?
- What is the impact, both positive and negative, of cultural factors on the client's perception of the crisis?
- What is the full range of precipitating factors for the crisis?
- How vulnerable does the client appear to be to negative effects of the situation?
- What are the client's potential and actual support systems?

Assessing Suicidal Ideation

People in crisis are often at risk for suicide attempts. Assessment questions for use with clients who may be suicidal include (Hawton, 1989; Macgowan, 2004):

Why is suicide being considered? Areas to investigate include the nature of relationships with significant others, employment or school concerns, finances, housing, legal issues, social isolation, use of substances, physical health, social adjustment, loss, and bereavement.

Does the client have access to the means for a suicide attempt? Determine whether the client has guns, knives, other weapons, or drugs that could be lethal if improperly used.

What are the person's support resources? The numbers and types of people in the support network may be assessed as adequate or inadequate to provide the client with a safe environment.

Crisis Intervention Strategies

The social worker's level of task activity with a client in crisis is high, particularly in stages one and two of the crisis episode (Roberts, 2000). The social worker pursues more reflective activities with the client during the third and final stage, to promote learning and planning for the future. But in general, in the roles of direct practitioner, service accessibility advocate, and environmental practitioner, the social worker's interventions at all three stages should be characterized by:

- Availability
- Communicating caring, confidence, and competence to the client
- Offering a plan for help and social support that includes choices for the client
- Obtaining a commitment to the plan, perhaps including an anti-suicide agreement
- Following up with the client and any referral sources

More specifically, in stages one and two, the social worker should:

- Provide reassurance about the availability of help and encourage the client to persist through the crisis.
- Make social support arrangements by mobilizing supportive people in the natural environment.
- Engage in environmental work to secure necessary material supports for the client (such as income, food, housing, health care).
- Engage in advocacy activities with other systems (because the client will be at least temporarily unable to self-advocate).

In stage three, the social worker should:

- Help the client to understand the nature of the precipitating events, so that he or she can plan ahead to control or avoid them.
- Help the client connect the experience of current stress with patterns of past functioning, so that he or she can initiate new behavioral patterns.

- Initiate improved modes of coping through problem solving, stress management training, social skills training, or other interventions (described in this and in subsequent chapters).

- Near the end of intervention, review with the client what he or she has learned about coping skills and social supports (this is sometimes called "anticipatory guidance").

What follows is an example of crisis intervention. We emphasize that there are many directions that the intervention may take, depending on the client's particular circumstances.

Case Illustration: A Mid-Life Crisis.   Justin was a 44-year-old Caucasian man who had experienced several losses in the past few years. First, his wife of 20 years divorced him. Next, the printing company where he worked announced that it would soon go out of business. Seeking a new career, Justin came to the community services agency for vocational counseling. Frank, his social worker, noticed that Justin seemed uninterested in the options presented to him. Justin displayed a negative attitude and little motivation to find an alternative career. Frank concluded that Justin was a sad, lonely man. One day, Frank learned that Justin had been admitted to a psychiatric hospital after a suicide attempt (an aspirin overdose). The moving away from home of Justin's only child, an adult son, precipitated the nonlethal attempt. His son's move devastated Justin, even though it was not unexpected. Justin had been in the first stage of crisis when he came to the community agency, and now was in the second stage.

Frank visited Justin at the hospital. Justin was touched by Frank's gesture and, in his desperation, appeared more open and more motivated to make changes. He admitted that it was difficult to admit his loneliness, but that he might die if he did not take more social and vocational initiatives. Frank took advantage of Justin's new motivation and, once Justin came home from the hospital, embarked with him on an intensive vocational intervention plan. Justin also had a psychiatrist and psychologist working with him on other issues related to his depression.

Frank was very supportive of Justin's desires to find suitable work, and he gave Justin many tasks related to exploring job opportunities. Frank kept in close touch with the other service providers, and advocated with his supervisor for a two-week extension of the agency's standard time limits for intervention. He helped John look to others for emotional support at the church where he was a member. Frank became a primary confidante as Justin risked more honest participation in those relationships and activities. Frank's acknowledgement of the inevitable anxiety associated with taking risks helped Justin to feel better about himself. Justin had always assumed that emotional struggles were evidence of maladjustment.

In the third stage of Justin's crisis, Frank helped him understand the meaning of his son's moving away, and why it was so devastating. Almost anyone would become depressed by the kinds of losses Justin experienced, but given Justin's background, their impact was more profound. Growing up in the shadow of a "perfect" older brother favored by his parents, Justin had become an angry, inse-cure youngster. He had always put himself into no-win situations wanting rela-tionships of mutual caring while basing most of his major life decisions (about jobs, where to live, and whom to spend time with) on a desire to avoid close contact with others. As a result Justin did not manage *any* relationships well, al-though he managed formal relationships best and was most comfortable at work.

It was predictable that Justin's ending with Frank and the agency would be difficult for him, even though he had found a new job. Frank pointed out that with his increased insight and confidence Justin was likely to maintain an improved level of functioning. Because Justin felt sad, he was not able to fully appreciate this affirmation, but he might do so in the future if he experienced vocational successes.

Before closing this chapter we will consider one example of an ethical di-lemma that may arise in working with individual clients.

AN ETHICAL DILEMMA: THE SOCIAL
WORKER–CLIENT RELATIONSHIP

Gordon was a single, 27-year-old social worker who provided counseling ser-vices to community college students. He was one member of a four-person team in the human services department at the college. The purpose of the counseling services was to help students resolve interpersonal conflicts and their adjustments to college. Clients were rarely seen more than five times. If the so-cial workers, along with their supervisor, determined that a student needed in-tensive counseling, the student would be referred to an outside mental health agency.

Gordon was assigned to work with Ellen, a 22-year-old Lebanese student who was floundering in school because, as she said, her parents were having a hard time letting her go. She was an only child living away from home for the first time, and her parents were demanding that she maintain daily contact with them by phone or e-mail, and visit them every weekend. Ellen wanted to be-come more independent of her parents but struggled to manage her guilt about leaving home. She had no one else to talk with about her concerns and wanted the social worker to listen to her problems and give her "an outsider's perspective."

Gordon was a seasoned professional, well respected as a person of talent and integrity by his peers, but in this instance he felt himself becoming sexually at-tracted to his client. Gordon was aware of these feelings, but his ethical dilemma was his reluctance to process his feelings with the supervisor, because of his em-barrassment, and his assumption he could work out the issue on his own. Still, Gordon scheduled a higher than average number of meetings (10) with Ellen. For her part, Ellen was attracted to Gordon as well. She was lonely and desiring of companionship. Interestingly, the social worker and client never spoke of their feelings openly. The "affair," such as it was, played itself out beneath the surface of their work on Ellen's concerns. During their 10 meetings, however, Gordon allowed himself to disclose more personal information than was typical, letting Ellen get to know him better than most of his other clients knew him. On several occasions when Ellen cried about her family conflicts, Gordon hugged her, justifying to himself that these were therapeutic interventions for a young woman who needed personal affirmation. Their relationship finally concluded at the end of the semester. Ellen decided that during the break she would apply what they had discussed and try to set clear limits with her parents regarding their expectations of her.

Throughout the intervention Gordon had in fact been struggling with an ethical dilemma regarding sexual relationships with clients. The first standard of the NASW Code of Ethics (1999) prohibits sexual relationships and inappropriate physical contact between social workers and their clients. What is interesting about Gordon's situation is that he did not actually have sexual relations with his client, and he would have argued that their few instances of physical contact was within the bounds of appropriate professional behavior. After the relationship ended, however, Gordon came to realize with perspective that he had behaved inappropriately.

There is nothing wrong with feeling sexual attraction to a client, but Gordon should have informed his supervisor of the feelings. He would have been helped to manage the feelings better or perhaps been asked to refer the client to another practitioner. But as a result of his feelings Gordon exercised poor professional judgment. It is possible that Ellen was harmed in some ways by his failure to deal openly with his feelings. For example, Ellen may have been uncomfortable with the situation and developed a distrust of helping professionals. Gordon's actual interventions may have been less effective than they might have been because of his preoccupation. His client did seem to make progress, however, as Ellen continued in school and set clearer limits with her parents. Gordon learned from this experience that the sexual aspect of relationships with clients is not confined to actual physical contact, and that he needed to trust his supervisor to share some of these very human feelings when they arise.

SUMMARY

There are a variety of intervention strategies and techniques for use with individual clients that are consistent with the perspective of generalist practice. All of those described here derive from the cognitive–behavioral theory of practice. In this chapter the models of task-centered practice and crisis intervention have been described. Within these models, students were introduced to the techniques of social skills training, stress management, and stress prevention. These techniques are additive to those that were introduced in Chapters 5 and 6. The techniques described in Chapter 10 for group intervention may also be used with individual clients. Next we will consider a variety of family intervention techniques that are also consistent with our theoretical perspective.

TOPICS FOR DISCUSSION

1. From a holistic perspective, does task-centered practice overlook any important aspects of client functioning?

2. Discuss some common obstacles toward goal attainment presented by clients with different types of presenting problems, different personalities, or different lifestyles might face. Which of these are predictable, and which are not?

3. What range of client challenges or problems may be due in full or in part to social skills deficits? How do these deficits contribute to the presenting issue?

4. Consider the various ways that you and other students try to manage and prevent stress. What does this suggest about how clients' natural relaxation and stress management tendencies can be assessed and utilized?

5. What range of crises have your clients faced in their lives? How did they manage them? Which appear to be positive or negative coping strategies?

ASSIGNMENT IDEAS

1. Utilize the task-centered practice format provided in this chapter to construct an intervention plan with a real or hypothetical client. You must first provide relevant assessment information about the client.

2. Select a particular social skill that is often appropriate to teach and rehearse with certain types of clients. Develop a four-session skills training protocol for that client group that attends equally to the cognitive and behavioral elements of the particular social skill.

3. Interview a human services or medical professional who (at least occasionally) provides crisis intervention services to clients. Write up a description of the professional's practices and compare them to the assessment and intervention procedures outlined in this chapter. Conclude the assignment by noting whether there is anything relevant to crisis intervention (a) that the professional could add to his or her practices, or (b) that should be included in this book chapter.

4. Interview a social work practitioner about any ethical dilemmas he or she has experienced in the context of worker–client relationships. Ask the social worker about any common ethical dilemmas for professionals in his or her position, and how these can be successfully resolved.

Chapter 9

Practice with Families

Generalist practitioners frequently work with families, or parts of families, even at times when an individual is identified as the primary client. The range of interventions that social workers may provide for families includes case management, collateral family contact, family therapy, advocacy, family group work, and family education and support. In this chapter we will review concepts from *structural* family theory, a useful perspective for working with families, especially those who are experiencing multiple challenges (Minuchin & Fishman, 1981). Structural family theory includes many practical strategies for family intervention, and it is consistent with our cognitive–behavioral framework for small systems.

Defining "family" has become more difficult in the past 25 years or so, as the nature of family life in this country has changed so much. Perhaps a broad definition is best, with families understood as two or more people who are drawn together by bonds of sharing and intimacy (Hepworth, Rooney, Rooney, Strom-Gottfried, & Larsen, 2006). Families may be classified as nuclear, single head of household, extended, multigenerational, blended, adoptive, foster, and step. There are many types of couples as well, including unmarried partners living together, couples who do not live together, and gay and lesbian couples. A former student of mine argued that his primary family consisted of his fraternity brothers, because he felt closer to them than to any other people in his life. His was a surrogate family—a "psychological kinship" (Ahern & Bailey, 1996). Many people experience these kinds of attachments.

SELF-AWARENESS IN FAMILY WORK

Working with families can generate strong emotional reactions in the social worker (Goldberg, 2001). We tend to evaluate family structures and processes from the perspective of our own backgrounds. What we see in clients may remind us of issues with our own families, and this can make us sensitive to client family processes in positive or negative ways. Our natural tendency may be to either re-create a family system we are familiar or comfortable with, or that is consistent with our ideal. To prepare for family work it is useful for the social worker to reflect on the following questions:

> What was (or is) my family like? What values and behaviors are (were) emphasized? What positive and negative feelings do I have about the members of my family?
>
> How does my idea of an ideal family compare to this family?
>
> What are the values of the family I am working with? How comfortable am I with these?
>
> What does this family want for itself? Can I support their goals?

Ongoing self-awareness, facilitated by peer and supervisory consultation, will help the social worker to maintain appropriate emotional boundaries with the members of a client family.

STRUCTURAL FAMILY THEORY

Structural family theory has been an influential, widely utilized, and effective theory of family assessment and intervention since the 1970s (Walsh, 2006; Aponte & DiCesare, 2000). Case studies in the literature indicate that it has been useful with Hispanic, Chinese, Vietnamese, Jewish, West African, Native American, Mexican American, and Italian American families. Its proponents focus on the external "architecture" of the family and assert that when a family establishes appropriate authority, rules, and boundaries, the emotional lives of its members will be satisfactory. Structural family theory was developed by Salvador Minuchin and has continued to evolve through his ongoing work and that of others (Minuchin, 1974; Minuchin & Fishman, 1981; Minuchin, Lee, & Simon, 1996). It is consistent with the cognitive and behavioral interventions described earlier.

The focus of this theory is family *structure,* a concept that refers to the invisible and often unspoken rules that organize how members of a family interact. The theory developed in response to a perceived need for intervention methods that could be used with families having multiple problems, including nontraditional inner-city families dealing with poverty (Wetchler, 2003). Structural family theory is particularly useful when working with families experiencing crisis and disorganization (Sori, 2006). Its interventions are suited to families plagued by illness, acting-out members, and problems such as drug addiction, crime, single-parenthood, and violence. The theory can, however, be used with any type of family.

Major Concepts

The family structure concept was described earlier. The other major concepts, all of which make up that structure, are described next, and are drawn from Wetchler (2003) and Minuchin and Fishman (1981).

Executive authority. Effective family structure requires that some person or people assume a position of primary decision-making power. This executive authority characterizes the people in that role. Structural theory asserts that in every family consisting of more than one generation, adult members should exercise primary authority. Other family members may share authority in some circumstances, such as in deciding how to spend a weekend or what kind of restaurant to visit. During assessment the social worker should determine who has power, whether power shifts depending on circumstances, and how decisions are made. Regarding decision making, the social worker should assess the extent to which the opinions and needs of all members are taken into account, the ability of the family to problem solve as a unit, and the family's flexibility in adjusting decisions when appropriate.

Subsystems. In any family that is comprised of more than two people, some members develop patterns of interaction in certain contexts that exclude other members. Examples of these subsystems include parents, adult members, nuclear versus extended family members, siblings, older and younger siblings, and some adult–child alliances. Subsystems are normal and usually functional. For example, adult members need to act as a subsystem in establishing behavioral standards for children, and siblings learn social skills and ways of negotiating conflict through their interactions. Subsystems may be problematic, however, when serious conflicts develop between them (parents versus children, for example), or if they inappropriately exclude certain other members. A problematic parent–child subsystem may develop as a strategy by one parent to avoid interacting with, or dilute the influence of, the other parent.

Alliances are conditions in which two family members or subsystems interact cooperatively. These are positive when they contribute to the overall well-being of the people involved, and to the family unit. In families that include two spouses, their alliance around child-rearing practices are positive if those practices contribute to the health of the children. Alliances are negative when they are rigid, exclusionary, or otherwise contribute to family problems. Two siblings can form an alliance against a third sibling, or against a parent, with the purpose of enhancing their power and the result being cruel or unfair treatment of the third person. Two terms that reflect family problems in this regard are *enmeshment* (two or more members behaving in collusion with one another to the extent that they cannot function with autonomy) and *disengagement* (two members being isolated from one another).

Boundaries. Families are systems, but they must preserve some physical and emotional separateness for each member in order to insure their effective functioning. These boundaries are both internal and external. *Internal* boundaries are the barriers that regulate the amount of contact members or subsystems are expected to have with each other. In some families, for example, each member is entitled to the privacy of his or her own room, while in others it is desired that the members share rooms. Likewise, some families engage in many social activities together, while in others the members interact infrequently. Boundaries may be rigid (members being physically or emotionally isolated) or fluid (members being too close to each other, and therefore denied privacy or separateness). *External* boundaries refer to the separation of the family unit from outside systems such as community groups. Most families believe that much of their internal business (finances, conflicts, illnesses, religious practices, child-rearing practices) should be kept private from people (and agencies) outside the family.

Rules are the behaviors and responsibilities to which each family member is expected to adhere. They are different for each member depending on life stage and family position (parent, child, extended family member, and so on) and are usually established with reference to age-appropriate social norms. The executive authority has primary responsibility for rule development but all members may participate in the process. A parent may decide rules about driving practices among adolescent members, but the adolescent may be permitted to set rules about his or her study and work routines. Rules may pertain to such issues as curfew, household upkeep, academic standards, who is expected to work, how money will be spent, and with what other people family members may interact. Some rules are openly articulated while others may be acquired through habit. For effective family functioning, rules should be clearly understood by all members.

Roles. A family member's roles refer to his or her functions within the system. Each family member must manage several roles. These may be *assigned* by the executive or some external source (usually reflecting social norms) or be *assumed* by members because of particular family circumstances. Examples of typical roles include the breadwinner, money manager, caregiver, housekeeper, and social director. Other roles may include the family hero (who presents a positive image of the family to the outside world) or scapegoat (the source of all family problems). Roles change over time and in different contexts. The social worker needs to assess how a family's roles are defined, whether they seem appropriate, how satisfied members are with their roles, and whether any member experiences stress due to role overload, or being responsible for a number of possibly conflicting roles.

Triangles represent a type of alliance in which two family members turn their attention to a third member for relief or support when in conflict with each other. As examples, two adults in conflict may choose to blame a child member for creating their problem (that is, scapegoating) or an adult and child member may join forces to block the power of another adult member. Negative triangles often develop outside of the parties' awareness. Triangles are often a natural process of seeking relief from tension, but they may cause structural problems if they become disruptive to other members in a family system.

Flexibility. For effective functioning, all families frequently need to adjust their structures to accommodate the predictable and unpredictable changes in the lives of their members and in the environment. Predictable changes may include the movement of members into new life stages (childhood to adolescence, adulthood to older adulthood) and the addition and loss of members through birth, death, coming home, and moving away. Unpredictable changes may include a member's abrupt job loss, physical injury, illness, incarceration, pregnancy, and changed relationship with significant others in the external environment. Flexibility refers to the ability of the family system to make adjustments that preserve its positive functions. This idea is not in opposition to that of structure. The opposite of structure is chaos, which represents a family's structural breakdown in the face of system challenges.

Communication. The ability of people in relationships to engage in clear and direct communication, those practices for conveying messages, is important in every practice theory. It receives extensive attention in structural family theory, however, because the practitioner is interested in the *structure* of communication. Functional family communications are characterized by verbal and nonverbal congruence and consistently observed rules. The structural practitioner will assess and may help the family to become aware of its rules (for example, *who* is permitted to talk to *whom* about *what issues* at *what times* and in *what tones of voice*). Many family problems are caused or sustained by unclear or unbalanced communication, or by its absence. If communication skills are enhanced, other restructuring activities are facilitated.

Other Concepts

Other factors not specific to structural theory must also be taken into account during family assessment. These are described next.

Cultural considerations. Diverse family cultures may feature differences in structure regarding communication style, family hierarchy and power structure, how much authority the family wishes to grant the practitioner, member preferences for formal versus informal interaction (with each other and the practitioner), and the issue of dual identity (the family's relationship to the dominant external culture) (Fong & Furuto, 2001). Social work practitioners need to be aware of cultural norms when a family's background is different than their own so that the assessment will not be biased.

Family goals. Families do not always openly articulate a set of goals, but members nevertheless tend to develop a sense of purpose regarding their place in the family and how they can be mutually supportive of those goals (Pimentel, 1996). Family goals may include raising responsible children, developing loving bonds, developing a shared sense of spirituality, or amassing material resources. The social worker should assess the family's awareness of and level of consensus about goals and their functionality.

Family life cycle stage. The nature and quality of a family's functioning is variable depending in part on whether it is comprised of unattached adults, new partners, or is a family with young children, adolescents, adult children, and people in later life (McGoldrick, Heiman, & Carter, 1993). It would be expected, for example, that a family with adolescents features more ongoing tension than one comprised only of new partners.

Family myths. This refers to shared family beliefs that evolve in a family's effort to define itself, set boundaries with the outside community, and perhaps protect members from both internal and external conflict (Coleman, 1992). They are called myths because they are not "true" in an objective sense, but reflect traditions and possibly cultural factors. Example of family myths are that "outsiders are not to be trusted," "people should always stay close to home," "children should take care of their parents," "Dad's violent behaviors are not to be questioned," and "Mom doesn't really abuse drugs." Myths tend to be problematic for outsiders (including social workers) when they serve a defensive function.

External systems influences. It has been noted that the family is a primary social institution, but there are others with which families routinely interact, including religious, educational, economic, and political institutions (F. Walsh, 2006). Further, families exist in the midst of other identifiable systems such as the neighborhood and larger community. All of these entities contribute to conditions that influence a family's structure and the quality of life of its members. Structural family theory developed in a context of serving the needs of families that were socially disadvantaged by external systems. The social worker must always assess the effects of a family's interactions with these other systems and possibly direct some of his or her interventions to create a more mutually facilitative environment. The social worker's extra-family activities may include linkage, referral, mediation, and advocacy activities.

The Nature of Problems and Change

These concepts direct the manner in which structural practitioners define the problems experienced by their clients (Nichols & Schwartz, 2007). Many problem situations lie on a continuum of functionality. It is not easy to conclude without a careful assessment whether, for example, a boundary is rigid or fluid.

Power imbalances describe situations in which the "wrong" (less mature or responsible) members have the most power in a family system. Perhaps young members of the family can get adult members to acquiesce by throwing temper tantrums or making threats. Young members may also assume power when the adult members choose not to exercise it. Further, adult members in a family may be inconsistent in their expectations of members or disagree about major decisions and behavior limits. When the "wrong" family members have the most power, the system often moves toward chaos (a lack of structure) because it lacks an executive authority with reasonably mature judgment about family functioning.

Subsystem boundaries that are too rigid or too diffuse produce situations in which some members are either emotionally or physically isolated from each other or too involved in each other's lives. Examples of problems related to diffuse boundaries include the sexual abuse of a child by an adult and parental overinvolvement that prevents child and adolescent members from developing age-appropriate independent living skills. Adult and child subsystems may intrude into each other's personal affairs to the extent that none are assured of privacy, and as a result they act out their frustrations with negative behaviors. Problems related to rigid boundaries include a lack of availability of adult members to their children and a lack of communication and interaction among members of subsystems (adults, children, extended family, and so on). When boundaries are rigid members may experience high levels of tension due to an inability to find support to manage their everyday challenges at school, with peers, or at work. Members of subsystems also fail to benefit from the learning that might otherwise come from their interaction.

The following two sources of family problems are related to the boundary issues just described but refer to the behaviors of individuals rather than subsystems. *Disengaged (isolated) members* do not interact with other members or with the family system in general. When one spouse is disengaged from the other each person may feel lonely or depressed. Another example is commonly seen in an adolescent member "shutting out" the rest of the family and organizing her life around peer activities. This diminishing of the family's influence prevents it from providing appropriate guidance and limits to the disengaged member. Of course, the person may feel angry with or pushed away by the family. On the other hand, *enmeshed members* rely too much on one another for support and assistance rather than developing their own life skills. They may be at risk for failure to develop through expected stages of social development and become unable to assume socially appropriate roles.

When members of a family lack good communication skills, they may develop a family atmosphere of *pervasive conflict or tension* related to the *avoidance* of processing conflict. It was noted earlier that good communication practices are an essential component of successful family systems. It is the "currency" of family interaction. Because conflict is also a natural part of interpersonal life, an inability to process it sustains even small problems. For example, if a parent cannot resolve anger with a child related to poor grades in school, the resulting tension may persist and spiral into resentments that blow up at times into harsh physical punishments.

Family problems may derive from a *failure of the system to realign* (or resume productive and cooperative individual and family roles) after a stressful event such as the birth, death, injury, illness, or separation of a member. While making adjustments to change can be challenging for any family, rigid families have particular trouble, essentially holding onto roles and rules that are no longer functional. With the death of one parent, for example, the father may be unable to make changes in his roles and routines to devote more time to nurturing the children. The children may not be inclined to increase their support of the remaining parent by taking over some household responsibilities. This failure to adjust may result in a variety of presenting problems such as increased tension, other emotional distress among members, substance abuse as a coping strategy, and behavioral acting out.

Member resistance to normal family change processes is related to this issue but indicates a lack of flexibility in the family system to accommodate *any* changes.

This issue—being able to recognize when one member is moving into appropriate new roles and a changed relationship with the family, and making adjustments in the rest of the family to accommodate that change—presents a challenge for many families. Parents typically struggle with these change issues when considering when to allow younger members to work, drive, stay out later, and spend more time away from the home. Siblings struggle with adjusting to one member's moving away, and to the changing expectations for those remaining in the household.

The goals of intervention in structural family theory are to change the existing family structure so that it becomes more functional. Change may also involve increasing the available supports for members outside the family system. A basic principle of structural family intervention is that *action precedes understanding* (Nichols & Fellenberg, 2000). One or more family members must take action, with the guidance of the social worker, to change the nature of family interactions, rather than simply *talk* about taking action. Through restructuring processes that include practicing new ways of interacting and communicating, family members may experience permanent relief from the presenting problem. Insight about the problem situation may occur after the fact, but this is not considered to be a necessary aspect of change. Again, this perspective is consistent (but not identical) with those of the cognitive and behavior theories.

Assessment and Intervention

Beginning Procedures.   Before considering specific family structural intervention techniques, we will first consider beginning procedures that are common to all types of family intervention (Janzen & Harris, 1997). These are based on the principle that the social worker is becoming involved with a system of which he or she is not a member, and thus has outsider status in the eyes of the other participants.

   Plan for a high level of activity. Take charge. The social worker must become recognized as the leader in the process.

   Relieve the normal anxiety of all family members who are present. Ask each person to share his or her reactions to the meeting being scheduled, and empathize with all responses.

   Anticipate reactance from at least some family members, and accept their negative comments without defensiveness.

   If appropriate, *use exercises to promote family participation*. These may include icebreakers that are commonly used by your professors on the first day of a new course.

   Clarify member expectations and choices about intervention. Ask what they expect will happen during the intervention, what they would like to see happen, and how they would organize the intervention. The social worker is not obligated to adopt the family members' ideas, but he or she may decide to incorporate some of them into the process.

Relate to individual members and to the group. Identify the needs and wants of all members. This "balancing" of individual and system perspectives will be an ongoing challenge.

Focus on interactions. Encourage members to talk to each other, rather than directing their contributions to the social worker (which typically happens in first meetings).

Work toward problem consensus. Elicit problem definitions from all members and validate their perspectives (they are, after all, the experts about their own processes). Try to articulate what their different perspectives have in common.

Discourage the blaming of any individual members. Promote the problem issue as a family issue without stigmatizing any member.

Highlight member and family strengths, and communicate hope.

Promote positive communication. Help members relate to each other in positive ways.

Specify which family members should be included in the ongoing intervention. It is often difficult to secure the participation of all members because of differential availability or, more problematically, an unwillingness to participate. As a general rule, all members of a household except for infants are asked to participate, and members from outside the household (including extended family members) may be requested to come if they play a significant role in the system.

At the end of the session, *negotiate an agreement for additional meetings with the family.*

If the social worker is able to successfully apply these principles, he or she will be in a good position to facilitate family change. Now we will turn to a description of specific intervention strategies that can help to promote that change effort.

An Assessment Outline for Families.   Prior to problem exploration, it is often useful for the social worker to conduct a structured warm-up exercise to promote the family's comfort. These may include traditional icebreakers such as having members introduce each other, talk about their favorite hobbies, describe the figures from popular culture they most admire, and so on (see Barlow, Blythe, & Edmonds, 1999).

Structural family theory does not rely on a lengthy process of formal information gathering in the form of specific questions. The social worker asks all members of the family to describe the issue that brought them all to the agency, and some details about its background, but always in a conversational tone. The social worker then attempts to get information about the following issues, not by asking them specifically, but by observation and nonthreatening interchanges.

I have developed the assessment areas in the following paragraphs.

Referral statement. This will be the same as in the individual assessment outline.

Identifying information. List all nuclear and any relevant extended family members, their cities of residence, and ages; which members are living in the home; and the family type (nuclear, blended, single parent, extended, and so on), living arrangements, and type of residence (house, apartment, shelter, and so on).

Problem identification and definition. List the problem issue(s) as perceived by individual family members, the social worker, and the referral source. Survey all participating family members to identify what factors precipitated the issue. Determine whether the issue reflects ongoing system characteristics or is rooted in recent circumstances; whether the family is in crisis; what the family has already tried in order to resolve the issue (such as involvement with other helpers outside the family, internal problem-solving strategies, or support networks); the family's view of appropriate issue resolution, or what they think should happen; which (if not all) of the family members are willing to participate in the intervention; and whether the family demonstrates confidence in its capacity to resolve the issue.

A *visual portrayal of the family system.* A major tool in assessment is the *genogram* (see Figure 9.1, later in the chapter, for an example). This is a visual representation on one sheet of paper of a family's composition, structure, and relationships (McGoldrick, Gerson, & Shellenberger, 1999). It typically covers two or three generations. Information that may be provided on a genogram includes basic facts about family members (dates of birth and death, marriages, and illnesses), the primary characteristics and levels of functioning of each member (age, gender, education, and occupation), and relationship patterns among members (closeness, conflicts, and cutoffs). Family characteristics that may be assessed include structure (roles, rules, and boundaries) and relationship patterns across generations. The advantage of the genogram as an assessment tool is its presentation of complex family data on one page.

In addition to helping the social worker develop an understanding of family structure, the genogram may help family members gain insight into their interactions. They may learn about interpersonal patterns and how triangles operate within the family. Family members learn to appreciate that their behavior is related to larger system processes, and the ways in which those processes support or inhibit member functioning. With the information provided, family members may be able to offer their own ideas for enhancing family functioning. Another way in which the genogram serves as an effective early intervention is that, during its construction, each member is physically observing a diagram rather than each other. This brings a shared focus to the discussion and may displace any negative feelings onto an object rather than another person.

Cultural factors and transitions. This will be the same as in the individual assessment guide.

Significant events in the family's life cycle. List the family life cycle stage (adults with young children, adults with adolescents, an adult family, children with aging parents); significant events in the family's history (deaths, divorces, separations, adoptions, medical illnesses, and handicaps) and how these events have affected family functioning; survival factors in the family's life (employment, finances, outside relationships, community participation, and other resources); factors that enhance or inhibit the family's functioning; and the family's everyday interactions with its environment (agencies, schools, churches, employers, leisure activities, and so on).

Dynamics of family relationships. Because this category is highly specific to structural family intervention, we provide a detailed listing of issues for the social worker to explore:

What are this family's patterns of interacting? Who spends time with whom, what do they do together, and what do they talk about?

How does the family present itself structurally? What roles do the members seem to occupy? How do these roles play out in the session?

Where does power lie in this family? Who makes decisions and who enforces them? Is authority or decision making shared in any ways?

What subsystems appear to be prominent? What members appear to be bonded, and for what reasons? Are alliances rigid or fluid?

Does the presenting problem appear to serve a function for the family? Does one (or several) members' behaviors absorb the family's attention?

What are this family's typical patterns of managing stress? How do they respond as a unit to everyday stress as well as crises and members' normal life transitions?

How sensitive are family members to each other's feelings and needs? Do they listen to each other and take each other seriously? Are certain members ignored?

What do members seem to expect from each other? What is their sense of shared responsibility for family functions?

Do members accommodate each other's needs? Are they capable of flexibility in their responses to each other?

Is the family involved with external systems? What formal and informal institutions do they interact with, like churches, civic associations, recreational centers, or perhaps legal and welfare agencies? Are they welcoming or suspicious of outsiders?

It should be evident that there is a great deal of information to be gathered in this portion of the assessment. Because it involves the social worker's judgment as much as factual information it can rarely be gathered in one visit. As the social worker gets to know the family over time, he or she can gradually come to some valid conclusions about these issues.

Evaluation of resources for problem solving, the *diagnostic statement, goals,* and *plans* are addressed in the same way as in the individual assessment guide.

The social worker begins rather quickly to assess the family structure and presenting issue by encouraging members to *enact* rather than merely *describe* their significant interactions. This is facilitated through role-plays. During these enactments the social worker focuses on the nature of member interactions with respect to the questions previously listed.

During enactments the social worker begins to identify both positive and negative patterns of interaction within the family. The practitioner alerts family members to any observed problematic communication patterns and asks if they wish to change them. The practitioner also identifies and articulates any structural characteristics of concern such as weak bonds between spouses or others, conflicts between subsystems, alienation or enmeshments of any members, and alliances outside the family that contribute to internal problems.

Assessing Involuntary Families.　In previous chapters we have outlined some complications of working with involuntary or reluctant client systems. These issues may be more common when working with families, because there are likely to be some (or many) family members who do not identify themselves with the problem issue, even when one is acknowledged (Rooney, 1992). This will be evident in the examples included later in this chapter. Many families do not think in terms of systems interactions, and tend to single out one or several individuals as "identified clients" rather than share responsibility for a problem situation. In response to this possibility, the social worker should openly elicit each family member's level of motivation to participate in the intervention. The social worker can then educate the family about the effects of family systems on the functioning of each member, highlighting the potential of each member to constructively move the family forward. The social worker must be careful to do this in a manner that does not label any member as pathological, and accentuates each member's strengths. Still, it may not be possible to engage every member of a family in the intervention process.

Intervention.　It must be emphasized here that, when implementing all of the interventions described next (adapted from Nichols & Schwartz, 2007; and Kilpatrick & Holland, 2006), *repetition* is often necessary for structural changes to become internalized into a family system.

Supporting system strengths refers to the social worker's providing compliments about aspects of family functioning that are going well. This includes affirming the dignity of the family with empathetic responses and nonjudgmental comments about its behaviors.

Relabeling, or normalizing, a problem helps family members to develop a new perspective about themselves that is more constructive. For example, behaviors that are now seen as problematic may have initially represented members' caring for each other. A parent's harsh treatment of a child may now be a problem, but it also indicates that the parent cares about the child. When relabeling, the social worker does not excuse behavior but places it into a context that reduces defensiveness and the stigmatization of any member as "the problem."

Problem tracking encourages the family to track its target behaviors between sessions so that members can more clearly identify their structural patterns and get accustomed to working actively on problem resolution. A part of each family meeting will include a review of these observations as well as reports of new activities undertaken between sessions. At the same time members are asked to give up their exclusive focus on past events that have been problematic and look ahead toward the future of family life.

Manipulating space, or assigning family members to stand or sit in certain configurations, can highlight important structural characteristics. For example, adults who lack power in setting limits on child behavior may be asked to sit closely together so that they can provide support to each other. Likewise, two estranged siblings might be instructed to sit next to and even face each other, as a means of encouraging their interaction. Space manipulation, also known as *sculpting,* can also be used to visually highlight family structural characteristics. The plight of a child who feels ignored by his parents, for example, can be illustrated by the social worker's turning the child's chair around while his parents talk between themselves about the child. The goal of these activities is always to promote the development of more functional structural arrangements.

Teaching stress management skills can enhance the self-control of members prior to initiating any anxiety-provoking interactions. This was described in the last chapter. Practices such as deep breathing and progressive relaxation can help members manage any tensions that emerge during family intervention.

Helping the family to modify its rules is achieved through *discussion and mutual decision making.* The potential for a family to resolve its presenting problems is usually high, particularly in the relatively formal environment of the social worker's office where interactions may be less emotionally charged. As a part of this process, the social worker should help to correct any cognitive distortions or myths regarding what family life should or should not provide for the members.

In *communication skills training* the social worker instructs families in methods of clear speaking and listening to communicate their needs, ideas, and feelings. It was stated earlier that the quality of communication is a primary determinant of family functioning. Functional families are characterized by a shared understanding of messages between senders and receivers and rules about communication that are consistently observed (the range of topics that are appropriate to discuss, when they can be discussed, and who can participate). Communications intervention includes the following activities:

- Pointing out confusing messages ("I don't understand something. You tell your son that he should spend time with his friends, but then you won't let him go out on weekends.")

- Teaching members to make clear requests of one another

- Teaching members how nonverbal behaviors (expressions, tone of voice, physical distance) may enhance or disrupt communication

- Disallowing interruptions, so that all members have the opportunity to be heard

- Helping clients learn to disengage from unproductive conflict (to stop its escalation before reaching the point of negativity)

Directing *role-plays,* simulations of actual or possible family situations, is a means of adjusting family interactions. During role-plays the social worker asks the entire family, or certain members, to act out a specific episode that has relevance to the participants. For example, if a parent has difficulty setting limits with an adolescent child, the social worker may ask the two members to role-play a conversation in which the parent tries to establish a curfew agreement. Afterward the social worker and family members evaluate the exchange and make suggestions about how the members might behave differently to be more consistent with the family's goals. Role-plays may be brief (less than a minute) or more lengthy (10 to 15 minutes). In *role reversals* members are asked to play the roles of other people in the family to sensitize them to the feelings of others with whom they may be in conflict.

A major practice strategy from this theory is to *assign tasks* for members to complete between sessions. These tasks are always intended to strengthen or loosen alliances and subsystems in accordance with the family's goals. The practice insures that the family works actively toward its goals in the natural environment. As examples, two spouses who have become disengaged may be asked to spend one evening together each week without other family members. A sibling who is enmeshed with an adult may be asked to undertake a household maintenance task with another sibling or adult. There is much room for the social worker and family's creativity in devising any tasks. The social worker should leave it to the family members to decide on the specific elements of tasks so that they will be suitable to the people involved. At some point during the follow-up meeting the social worker should review whether the tasks have been completed, whether they were helpful, and what other tasks might be useful.

Ending Structural Family Interventions

Structural interventions focus on behavioral change, and thus indicators that the process should end can be ascertained through family member behaviors in sessions and family self-reports of activities between sessions (Walsh & Harrigan, 2003).

The social worker can use time measures to see how alliances change among family members. For example, toward the goal of developing rules for appropriate boundaries, a child may be asked to monitor how much time she is permitted to spend alone in her room or out of the house with friends without parental interruption. The issue of permanence of change can be addressed by evaluating the consistency of these measures over some specified length of time. At the end of the intervention the practitioner can summarize in concrete terms (time, frequency, and content) the manner in which various subsystems have changed.

As a family's functioning improves, the social worker can utilize role-plays more flexibly to help members anticipate possible future challenges. He or she can ask family members to respond to difficult situations they have not yet faced. Their ability to do so flexibly indicates that the family has acquired the ability to respond to new challenges.

Throughout the intervention the social worker and family will be sharing impressions of how well they are managing their target behaviors related to task activities in the natural environment. When there is consensus among all or most participants that they have mastered these behaviors, the intervention can end unless the family sets additional goals.

We will now look at several case illustrations to see how these intervention strategies can be applied.

CASE ILLUSTRATIONS

The Dalton Family

Nita Dalton was a 41-year-old Caucasian married mother of three children living in the rural outskirts of a large city. A case manager at the county human services department who had been managing her requests for financial assistance referred her to the family agency. The referring worker was concerned about Nita's reports of family conflict that included emotional detachment from her husband and acting-out behaviors from her two sons. The social worker met with Nita once and decided that the client's concerns could be best addressed if the entire family came for a second appointment. All of the household members agreed to do so except for Nita's husband, who remained uninvolved throughout the five-session intervention. The members who did participate included Nita, her two sons (ages 22 and 20), their new wives (ages 20 and 18, respectively), and her 8-year-old daughter (see Figure 9.1). The genogram in Figure 9.1 is simplified to only provide information about family composition, alliances, and conflicts.

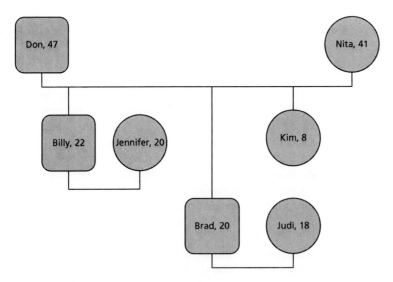

F I G U R E 9.1 The Duelin' Daltons

The social worker observed that the family was highly conflicted. Nita's husband was employed part-time as an auto mechanic but was estranged from the others, living several miles from the house and maintaining minimal contact with them. He was also said to have a drinking problem. Nita was over-functioning as the de facto head of the household, trying to manage it on the limited income her husband provided. As a result she was continuously stressed, anxious, and depressed. She complained that her two sons were irresponsible, working sporadically and always trying to borrow money from her. It was hard for Nita to set limits with them—they were able to wear her down with persistent cajoling. The social worker noticed that the older children were cheerful in the session, seeming to feel entitled to the family resources and having little sensitivity to their mother's distress. Nita felt close to her young daughter and spent most of her free time with her. She wanted to work outside the home (and had done so in the past) but felt that she had no time. She said that if her sons would leave home and take care of themselves she could get a job.

Nita and her family came from an Appalachian cultural background. In that culture, women were expected to assume the role of household manager and survive with little material support, all for the good of the family. Men maintained primary power but were less involved in day-to-day family interactions. Marital infidelity was not uncommon among members of their community. In fact, women often came to view themselves as martyrs (as Nita did), accepting that it was their fate to suffer for the sake of the family.

The sons, feeling a need to defend themselves against their mother's criticisms, agreed to several sessions of family counseling. The social worker decided that the Daltons were suitable for structural family intervention, and assessed them as follows.

Locus of power. Dad maintained absent, passive control over the family. He maintained the authority to do what he wanted, which was usually to stay away. He took the money he wanted out of his paycheck and gave the rest to his wife. Nita could not predict how much of his pay would come into the household each week, but maintained it was too little. She was ambivalent about whether she wanted the marriage to continue (they had been separated several times in the past), and felt it was up to him. In Dad's absence the boys were able to team up to exert power over Mom.

Problematic boundaries. Nita and her husband were disengaged. Nita and her sons were enmeshed; that is, despite their conflicts they seemed to need each other. Nita's relationship with her daughter was positive, but there was a potential for enmeshment because of Nita's reliance on her for emotional support. Living in a semi-rural area the family was moderately isolated from its external environment. This was typical of families in the region with Appalachian roots. The children all had friends, but Nita was only close to a sister who lived nearby.

Relevant subsystems. There was an absence of an adult couple system and a related lack of partnership regarding parental authority. The brother subsystem was strong, and the mother–daughter subsystem was also strong. Only the last of these seemed to be functional with regard to family structure. There did not seem to be a daughter-in-law subsystem—these young women appeared to share a congenial but not close relationship. Nita's own daughter seemed to be an out-sider sibling because of her age, although she enjoyed the others. The social worker felt that Nita needed support from another adult (her husband, a close friend, or other extended family member) to strengthen the adult subsystem.

Relevant triangles. Three problematic triangles within the family included: (1) Mom–Dad–daughter (Nita relied on her daughter to meet her needs for companionship that she did not get from her husband); (2) Mom–Dad–oldest son (Nita tried to rely on this son for assistance with family management, al-though this was frustrating for her); and (3) new spouse–son–Mom (the older son's spouse encouraged her husband to make demands of Nita for money and other material resources).

Context. This was an Appalachian family in which women were expected to fill certain traditional roles. Nita accepted her caregiver role and despite her stress level got attention from her sons with the current arrangement. Additionally, Dad was attempting to recover from alcoholism, which may have accounted for his desire to avoid internal family stresses. Another important issue was the family's poverty. Even if Dad invested his entire paycheck into the family, it would have been difficult to cover the basic financial needs.

Family stage. As young adults, the sons should have been working and leav-ing home, particularly to support their new wives. Nita and her husband wished to begin relinquishing their day-to-day parenting roles so that they could attend to some of their own interests.

Function of Nita's symptoms. In her current role, in which the others blamed her for being the unstable member, Nita served to absorb the family's chaos. She served a function for her husband as well by keeping the rest of the family's focus away from him.

Overall nature of the family structure. The social worker concluded that the Dalton family had become *chaotic,* characterized by an absence of appropriate ex-ecutive authority, subsystem functions, and boundaries.

The social worker had moderate success with helping the Dalton family re-structure itself into a more functional unit. While Dad's refusal to participate was an initial concern, the social worker was encouraged by the motivation of the other members. Several of them were angry with each other, but they shared an interest in resolving their conflicts, if only for selfish reasons. Nita was in con-flict with everyone but her daughter, the sons and older wife were in conflict with Nita, and the daughter was angry at her brothers (for monopolizing their mom's attention) and her sisters-in-law (for not spending enough time with her). With this assessment the social worker provided the following interventions.

Reframing. The social worker summarized Nita's symptoms of anxiety and depression, and her feelings of anger, as evidence that she was working too hard to be a good parent, and perhaps caring too much about her adult children. Nita accepted the reframe, which helped her feel affirmed and also suggested to the others that their mother was interested in their well-being. None of the chil-dren challenged this perspective.

Developing a shared definition of "family challenges." After hearing each mem-ber's point of view about the family situation, the social worker summarized the problem as a lack of sufficient *emotional* and *material* resources to go around the family. He shared his belief that the family members had the capacity to work toward expanding those resources. Those members who had few material resources might make up for this with task contributions to the family unit. This problem definition was relatively nonthreatening to the children, so they agreed with it.

Practicing clear communication skills with all family members. The Daltons (except for Nita) shared a habit of arguing with and interrupting each other. Even the social worker had trouble containing their interruptions, so he formalized their interactions during the first two visits. He called on members to speak in turn, silenced any interruptions that occurred, and assured everyone that he or she would have the opportunity to respond to others' comments. The social worker was authoritative but not abrupt in this task, and he was careful to repeatedly explain his rationale for this controlling behavior. After awhile the Dalton children's interactions became more peaceful.

Positioning family members to highlight appropriate alliances. As examples, the sons were separated from their wives at times (to break up a problematic alliance or triangle), and the daughter (who idolized her sisters-in-law) was seated next to them, to encourage their relationship development. Nita was seated next to various of her sons and daughters-in-law at times when the social worker wanted them to carry on conversations to establish new household rules about money and personal responsibilities. The social worker supported the parental subsystem by sitting next to Nita at times and taking her side (joining) in conversations about family authority, roles, and rules. This was important because Nita was the only adult member without an ally in the household. At these times the social worker shared his concern that Nita was still on her own at home. Nita had mentioned that her sister and two other friends always tried to be helpful to her. The social worker encouraged her to collaborate with any of them when making household decisions.

Role-playing to practice new styles of family interaction. For example, Nita role-played a hypothetical situation with her son (in which he was requesting money she could not afford to give) so that the social worker could assess their behavior and help them to improve their abilities to control anger and bring discussions to constructive closure. During all role-plays, the social worker assigned the uninvolved members to pay attention and comment on the participants' behaviors. This tactic brought all members into the process of problem solving and promoted their sense of mutual participation in family activities. In *role reversals* certain members were instructed to take the role of another family member in discussions of specific problem situations so that they could perceive their own behavior more clearly and better understand the point of view of the other person. As one example, Nita was asked to portray her son and ask him (playing the role of Mom) for money. Her son (as Nita) was assigned to reject her request and articulate the reasons why she should not get any more of the family's limited funds.

Task assignments between family meetings. These were intended to support the development of appropriate alliances and clarify boundaries between family members and subsystems. The social worker assigned Nita (with her approval) to spend two hours away from the family, two times during the coming week, doing whatever she wanted. He assigned her this same task each week, because it proved difficult for her to disengage from the household. The sons were asked to spend a certain amount of time alone with their spouses each week talking about future plans. The social worker hoped that this activity would help the young couples to realize that they might benefit from greater self-reliance. The daughters-in-law were asked to include the daughter in one social activity each week, to strengthen that bond and to reduce the potential enmeshment of Nita and her daughter.

The family made significant gains. Their communications became less conflicted, some new household rules were developed, and the roles of the children expanded. Nita spent more time with her friends, the sons were looking for work more regularly, and the daughters-in-law assumed some responsibility for taking care of the daughter. The level of tension was lower in the social worker's office and in the Dalton home. The social worker would like to have seen the family for several more sessions, but the family (primarily the sons) wanted to terminate because, in the social worker's view, their motivation and interest had waned. He was disappointed but felt good that they had made some progress.

We continue with two additional, briefer descriptions of family interventions.

The Family Drawings

Cynthia's agency provided in-home intervention services to families identified "at risk" for child emotional and behavioral problems. These were generally single parent families living in poverty. The families tended to feature a lack of strong authority and consistency in the behavior of parent figures, and poor limit-setting on the behavior of the children. Cynthia worked with the Paulson family for six months. The family included Kendra, a 20-year-old single African American, and her three sons—a 7-year-old, a 5-year-old, and a newborn. Her mother had moved in with Kendra when the new baby was born, and the two adults often argued. Grandmother tried to take on the traditional parent role because Kendra was away working, sometimes at odd hours. Kendra was a strict parent when she was home, but Grandmother was permissive and set few limits with the kids. The two women could not agree on how to manage the kids. Damon, the 5-year-old, began to develop behavior problems of aggression in the home, neighborhood, and school.

After the assessment Cynthia decided to work with Kendra and her mother on improving their relationship. She infrequently included the two older children in the process. She felt that if the adults could get along better and agree on appropriate parenting strategies, the children would respond with improved behavior. Cynthia met with Kendra and her mother weekly for three months and then twice monthly when the situation began to improve. Her goal was system restructuring as evidenced by both adults assuming appropriate roles of authority in the family. She taught them how to communicate clearly, directly, and frequently with each other. Cynthia also helped Kendra resolve the lingering anger she felt toward her mother. Kendra was bitter about the lack of supportive parenting she received as a child. The pair was able to learn and practice a process for resolving their differences and agreeing on household and child-rearing rules. Cynthia developed role-plays based on possible conflict situations that the adults practiced during her visits. Occasionally the social worker brought in the older boys to talk about what they were doing and to let the adults practice what they had learned with them.

One day when Cynthia was visiting the children were behaving rambunctiously. To calm them down she suggested that the older boys draw a picture of the family. To Cynthia's surprise, the pictures portrayed the family's problems. They indicated where each child saw himself in relation to the others in the size of the figures, their expressions, and their positions. Because the boys seemed to enjoy drawing, it occurred to Cynthia that this might be a good way to monitor the family's changes over time. Every month or so she asked the boys to draw family pictures, and then discussed with them and the adults what the drawings showed. As the weeks went by the pictures demonstrated that the family system was stabilizing. The figures of the family members, including the baby, became more equal in size and closer to each other.

When Kendra and her mother became able to consistently problem solve without the social worker's assistance, and Damon's behavior improved as well, it was time to end the intervention. As a closing activity, Cynthia asked the four family members (excluding the infant) to each draw a picture of what they wanted their family to be like. Afterward she used the pictures to review the work they had done together during the previous six months. All of them had made changes that the social worker felt were likely to persist. Cynthia took the pictures and had them mounted together on a mat board. The family members all agreed that the board should hang on the wall of their home.

A Mobile Home near the Woods

Andy's agency, Family Preservation Services, provided in-home counseling and case management services that were time-intensive and financially expensive. A regional Family Assessment and Prevention Team (FAPT), made up of public agency representatives, made referrals to the agency for families that exhibited severe behavioral problems. Social workers went to the clients' homes three or four times per week, spending a great deal of time with all family members to help them resolve their problems. An average visit was two or three hours, and the full intervention process might take six months or more.

Andy worked with the Davidson family for a full year. The mother, her live-in boyfriend, two adolescent sons, and adolescent daughter came to the attention of several legal and human service agencies because of their physical violence with one another. The mother had filed assault charges against each of her sons, but she also initiated fights with them and with her daughter. The Caucasian family had recently relocated to their current home, a two-bedroom trailer in an isolated rural area, from another state in the rural South. The family members were estranged from each other and disconnected from the nearby community. The FAPT team hoped that it could teach them alternative ways to work out conflicts.

Andy was in the Davidson home frequently. The entire family was ambivalent about his visits. Sometimes they were happy to see him, and other times he seemed to annoy them. The in-home services were highly invasive. Still, the family made good progress. Through the social worker's teaching, conflict mediation, role-playing, and modeling, they reduced their use of violence and increased their sense of contentment with each other. They became able to step back and think about their behaviors more clearly and control their impulses. After six months Andy initiated a step-down process, in which he gradually reduced his amount of contact with the family. Agency professionals routinely moved into step-down stages to find out if the positive changes they had seen would be lasting. Andy's contacts generally moved from 10, to 6, and then to 3 hours per week. Andy made fewer visits, until ending with a family completely. The process typically took two months.

Unfortunately, the Davidsons' violent behaviors began to escalate as Andy's time with them decreased. He resumed seeing them for an additional month at nearly his previous level of intensity. Their behaviors improved as Andy put more of his focus on strengthening the family's connections to outside support resources, primarily with the school and church. He realized that their inability to maintain change was related to a lack of support outside their family to provide outlets for stress. Andy moved into another abbreviated step-down procedure, and the family's gains persisted.

We now turn to the issue of ethical dilemmas. Family systems present many situations where the social worker might be uncertain about how to proceed ethically, partly because there are more people involved whose interests and goals may differ and even be in conflict.

ETHICAL DILEMMAS IN FAMILY WORK

There are several common ethical dilemmas that arise when working with families (Dolgoff, Loewenberg, & Harrington, 2005). One pertains to the challenge of managing confidentiality among members, particularly when some are participating with the social worker and others are not. Social workers also face dilemmas at times when making decisions about how to intervene when the behavior of one or more family members is significantly disruptive to the intervention process. Several illustrations are included here.

Consuela, a 15-year-old high school student, was referred to the school social worker by her mother, who was concerned about the child's withdrawn behavior. The young social worker had difficulty helping Consuela feel comfortable enough to talk but felt that the student was hiding a major problem. After several meetings the social worker promised Consuela that whatever she wanted to share would be kept confidential. While well meaning, this was a promise that the social worker should have known she might not be able to keep. Consuela reported that her father was sexually abusing her. The social worker was shocked at this revelation and knew immediately that she needed to report the allegation. Still, because of her promise to the client the social worker struggled for one week about what she should do. She finally told her supervisor about the situation and of course had no choice but to file a formal report. The situation turned out to be more traumatic for the child than it needed to be, for although it was important that the abuse be dealt with, the child learned that she could not trust helping professionals.

There are laws mandating that suspected child abuse be reported, but there are no such formal stipulations regarding the abuse of adults. John was a social worker who was helping a couple named Brad and Jan to register for medical benefits. He became aware during this intervention that Brad was physically abusing Jan, and that this was emotionally devastating to her. Still, Jan did not want to leave Brad or report the abuse. John became very angry. He confronted Brad, who minimized the seriousness of the situation. John then refused to work with the couple on the grounds that he would not be an enabler of abuse. His supervisor told John that he could not deny the services being requested on the basis of the domestic behavior if the wife did not want to file charges. Still, John refused, and the couple was referred to another social worker at the agency. The second worker was not pleased about his assignment, but finished the task after being reminded that the couple's rights to self-determination needed to be respected.

Mary Beth provided in-home counseling to a family of four that had been identified as at-risk for serious behavioral problems. She interacted primarily with Latoya, a 28-year-old newly married biracial mother of two children (a 7-year-old girl and a 1-year-old boy). Latoya was rigid, controlling, impulsive, and easily angered. She had a history of lethality, including a felony conviction, and this fact became central to the social worker's ethical dilemma. Latoya's new husband, the father of the younger child, lived in the home but did not initially participate in the counseling. He worked two jobs, partly to escape the highly charged home situation. The couple argued often and almost violently. The 7-year-old appeared to be aligned with Latoya against her stepfather.

The intervention went well at first. Mary Beth initiated a structural family intervention. Latoya's husband soon joined them for counseling and the social worker helped the three older members assume more appropriate roles in the family system. She also supported the development of a positive parental alliance. The family began to get along better and the husband began to stay home more often. But then, after five weeks of progress, Latoya's husband informed his wife that he was having an affair. She became angry and threatened him with physical harm. He moved out of the house and Latoya's behavior became erratic. She was obsessed with punishing him for the affair. Latoya informed the social worker during one of her visits that she planned to kill him, and she shared with Mary Beth her plan for doing so. This was a woman with a prior conviction for assault. She had never tried to kill anyone, but the situation was explosive, and the social worker felt that she might follow through. Mary Beth struggled with the issue of whether to warn the husband because of her confidentiality agreement with Latoya. After two days, however, she decided that her duty to warn took priority over the value of confidentiality.

Mary Beth informed Latoya that there were limits to their confidentiality and that she needed to inform her husband that his life was in danger. The social worker explained her reasons as thoroughly as she could. Latoya became furious, and demanded that Mary Beth leave the house immediately and never contact her again. The social worker felt terrible but left and attended to her duty to warn. She spoke to the husband and then called the local community mental health agency to request an evaluation of Latoya for possible hospitalization. Despite her efforts, the agency chose not to investigate. Fortunately Latoya did not act on her impulses, but her husband did stay away.

Mary Beth tried to make contact with Latoya numerous times during the next few weeks, but the client did not respond. Mary Beth sent Latoya a letter to again explain her actions and to request additional contact, again in vain. This was one of the most troubling outcomes Mary Beth had ever encountered, as Latoya had been progressing so well. The social worker felt that she had done the right thing, but with so many mixed feelings, she felt uneasy. Months after the event Mary Beth felt comfortable about her choice, and in fact wondered if Latoya had meant for her to warn the husband as an indirect way of controlling herself.

SUMMARY

Structural family theory provides a useful perspective for clinical social work practice with diverse family forms. It is focused on the external "architecture" of families, including their rules, boundaries and subsystems rather than the inner psychology of members and their interactions. A functional family structure will result in a system in which members will get their basic material and emotional needs successfully met. Structural family interventions were specifically developed to help the kinds of families encountered by social work practitioners—those experiencing multiple problems such as poverty, illness, unemployment, physical abuse, substance abuse, absent members, and acting out. With this theoretical approach social workers can also continue to provide the environmental interventions (through case management) that make the profession so distinctive. In fact, the theory is outstanding in its promotion of social justice activities.

TOPICS FOR DISCUSSION

1. Discuss examples (both functional and nonfunctional) of the eight major concepts of structural family theory that students have observed in their professional and personal lives.

2. With family structures taking on such diverse forms, how can a social worker discern whether an observed "executive authority" in a family is appropriate or not?

3. It is understandable that a social worker might be inclined to take sides with a family member or subsystem when members are in conflict. How can the social worker minimize this possibility?

4. Discuss applications of the various intervention strategies from family systems theory using real or hypothetical examples.

5. It is argued in this chapter that structural family theory can facilitate the social worker's social justice activities. Do you agree? If so, share some examples of how this could be done.

ASSIGNMENT IDEAS

1. Prepare a detailed assessment of a family, using all of the major concepts of structural theory. Indicate in a concluding statement whether these concepts seem adequate for understanding the "fundamental nature" of the family.

2. Interview a social work practitioner about how he or she ideally likes to end family interventions. What challenges does he or she tend to experience in trying to facilitate an appropriate ending?

3. Structural family interventions include supporting system strengths, relabeling, problem tracking, manipulating space, teaching stress management skills, discussion and mutual decision making, communication skills, directing role-plays, and assigning tasks. In a short paper explore in detail the uses of one of these with a real or hypothetical family. This assignment can also be done in role-play format.

Chapter 10

Group Interventions

G roup interventions represent an appropriate and effective means of service
delivery in many agency settings. They may be conducted for convenience
(to accommodate large caseloads, for example) or as the intervention of choice
for people with certain needs who might benefit from an interpersonal process
(see Figures 10.1 and 10.2). The general purposes of treatment groups are to
meet the social, emotional, or educational needs of participating members
(Corey & Corey, 2006). All types of groups can be provided in formats that are
consistent with our cognitive and behavioral theoretical principles. Effective
group leadership always requires that the practitioner have an understanding of
systems, however, because member interactions are often the most significant aspect of their utility. Groups are fundamentally different from individual and family interventions in other ways as well. One of their important characteristics is
that, when effective, they represent a small but positive sense of *community* for
the members. Even if temporary, this community may be more supportive
than other natural groups with which the members are involved. In this chapter
we will consider principles of group organization, leadership, intervention, and
monitoring for generalist practitioners.

TYPES OF TREATMENT GROUPS

Listed next are five types of treatment groups (Toseland & Rivas, 2005), although there is often overlap in the goals they promote. We emphasize that all
of these can be developed as self-help groups, without the participation of a human services professional.

> *Support groups* promote mutual aid, help members cope with stressful life
> events, and enhance the general coping skills of members. Examples

Peer pressure—The presence of many "like-minded" others with change expectations can help a member feel open to change.

More support—A greater range of empathic responses is likely, and each member may be helped to appreciate his or her strengths.

Broader feedback—A range of alternative perspectives can be offered in response to a member's problem situation.

Greater influence—An increased likelihood that each member will develop attachments to one or more others.

Sense of belonging—Each member may feel less alone or isolated with his or her problem issue.

Mutual aid—A greater range of possibilities for problem resolution can be shared.

F I G U R E   10.1   Advantages of Group vs. Individual Intervention

Instillation of hope from other members
Greater self-understanding
Positive role modeling (imitation)
Learning from interactions (verbal and nonverbal feedback)
Universalizing of one's experience ("You are not alone.")
Group as a reflection of society (reality testing)
Acceptance by others
Support for "healthy" self-disclosure
Opportunities to help others (altruism)
Sharing useful information with others

F I G U R E   10.2   Helpful Factors for Clients in Groups

include single parents sharing the challenges of raising children and children meeting after school to discuss the effects of divorce on their lives.

Educational groups help members to acquire new information and learn the skills to use it. Examples include an adolescent sexuality group sponsored by a family planning agency and a prospective foster parents group sponsored by a child welfare agency.

Growth groups provide opportunities for members to become aware of or change their thoughts, feelings, or behaviors regarding themselves and others. Examples include an adult psychotherapy group focused on general relationship issues and a values clarification group for adolescents.

Therapy groups help participants make positive adjustments or rehabilitate after experiencing a social or health trauma. Examples include Alcoholics Anonymous and a first-offenders group in a juvenile diversion program.

Socialization groups help member develop social skills and new behavior patterns. Examples include a Catholic youth organization activity group and a social club for people with serious mental illnesses.

FORMING INTERVENTION GROUPS

Regardless of their level of formality, intervention groups need to be carefully planned, with clear purposes and procedures. What follows are the steps involved in forming treatment groups (Zastrow, 2006).

Articulate the purpose of the group. This requires a concise statement that clarifies for staff, administration, and clients what the group will attempt to accomplish. As one example, my Family Education and Support Group was developed with the purposes of helping families to:

- Become educated about current theories of the mental disorders that affect their relatives, including causes, course, degree of impairment, interventions, and prognosis

- Become educated about the purposes and actions of the medications used to treat their relatives

- Act as an ongoing mutual support system in day-to-day interactions with relatives, with an emphasis on reducing and controlling behaviors disruptive to the family

- Become informed about all local agencies that provide relevant services to clients and families

- Become well educated enough about the mental health service system that they can advocate for quality services on behalf of their relatives

- Reduce their feelings of guilt and social isolation

- Become able to pursue activities that do not center on the client member

Keep in mind that the sponsoring agency may have additional goals for the group. My agency director saw these as a means of better integrating our agency with the network of other agencies in the city by offering a unique program.

Identify a guiding theoretical framework. This refers to the general approach (such as cognitive or behavioral) that the leaders will take in delivering the service to group members. The importance of selecting a theoretical approach is to bring consistency to group activities. Cognitive theory, with its emphasis on learning, is pertinent to educational groups, and behavior theory is relevant to groups that are intent on changing member behaviors, such as skill-building groups. The Family Education and Support Group utilized both perspectives—the second one to help the members reinforce their impaired relatives' behaviors differently. Groups may be based on other theories not highlighted in this book, of course, such as ego psychology and solution-focused therapy.

Articulate the roles of the leaders. Leaders should decide what roles they antici-pate playing during the meetings. These will depend on the purposes and mem-bership of the group. It is possible that group leaders will be highly directive and active, more facilitative, or perhaps more focused on monitoring the activities of the members. Certainly the leader roles may change over time depending on the group membership, and through trial and error about finding out what works best. Leaders should always be flexible in how they approach their roles.

Select techniques and activities for the group. This is related to the theoretical framework, but refers more concretely to how the leader will use time in the group. That is, what will the leader and members do? In the Family Education and Support Group, the coleaders divided up each 90-minute session into pro-viding lecture material, discussion handouts, and the informal discussion of mem-ber concerns. By the time recruitment begins, leaders should have most of these materials selected, even though they may make changes as the group unfolds.

Locate space for the group. Space is often at a premium in agencies, so the social worker should not forget to take the step of reserving adequate space for the group. I once had a nightmarish experience with this issue, as I mistakenly as-sumed that a certain room on a certain evening would be available for my group. I was forced to make some last-minute inquiries and ended up conducting the group in the meeting room of a nearby church.

Consider the financial aspects of conducting the group. What will be the costs to the agency of adding the group to its range of services, in terms of staff time and supplies? Along the same lines, what will be the financial benefits to the agency? My director was willing to take a financial loss on a new group (not charging clients any money) because he saw a long-term financial benefit in terms of pos-itive agency exposure. This, however, is not always possible, so the leader needs to consult with administration about funding or any charges to members.

Composition of the group. Some groups will be homogeneous, meaning that members will be much alike in their presenting challenges and perhaps demo-graphic characteristics, while other groups will be heterogeneous, with wide var-iability in member characteristics. Heterogeneous groups are challenging in that the members have less in common and therefore do not connect as easily. In the Family Education and Support Group, membership was primarily homogeneous, including middle-aged parents with children who had mental illnesses. This pre-sented problems at times for younger parents or siblings who wanted to join the group because they tended to feel out of place in the general context.

Open versus closed status. Open groups are willing to accept new members after they have begun. These groups incorporate the benefits of accommodating more participants, providing immediate support to members, putting less pressure on members for personal disclosure, and tolerating a changing membership. On the negative side open groups are less stable and members are slower to trust each other. Closed groups accept no new members after beginning. They tend to encourage more intensive interactions, are more stable and cohesive over time, and ensure greater predictability of member behavior. On the negative side they require long-range commitments from members and are more ad-versely affected by member dropouts. The Family Education and Support

Group was closed, as it took members several weeks to feel safe enough to talk about their personal issues.

Group size. Some groups are as small as four or five members, while other intervention groups can be quite large, with 25 to 30 members or more. The leader will often have an ideal group size in mind, but this may need to be compromised depending on the success of recruitment and other unpredictable factors. Clearly, how the group operates will depend very much on its size. With more members, the interventions tend to be less personal. Group leaders need to be aware that the group size should not be such that its purposes are defeated, or that the leaders cannot present group material effectively in ways that they desire. The Family Education and Support Group appeared to function best with 10 to 16 members, which encouraged participation but also helped members feel that they would never be "put on the spot" about sharing.

Frequency and duration of meetings. Most groups function with a regular schedule, although some are time-limited and others may be open-ended. As a general rule, no session should last for more than 90 minutes, as members will begin to tire and their attention spans will wane. For young clients, who are physically restless, sessions of 30 to 45 minutes may be sufficient. The Family Education and Support Group featured nine weekly meetings of 90 minutes each.

Recruiting strategies. This refers to methods that will be used to advertise the group, how extensive they will be, who will be involved, and whether a budget is required for this service. The Family Education and Support Group's developer, an agency social worker, assumed sole responsibility for recruiting. He wrote and distributed flyers to all of the mental health agencies in his metropolitan area, gave presentations to staff at those agencies about the program, and called all prospective members to discuss the group after they were referred. He devoted two months to these activities before starting his first group. Additional groups did not take so long, as a referral network fell into place.

Screen candidates in advance. This allows the group leaders to provide all interested candidates with an orientation, in person but perhaps by phone, about the group. They can learn about the program, get to know the leader, and ask and answer questions related to their suitability for such a group program. They may describe their previous group experiences, their presenting concerns, their specific goals, relevant background information relative to group content, and any potential obstacles to their participation in the group. In the Family Education and Support Group, candidates were screened during a phone call from the leader that followed their referral.

Set rules. These are sometimes set in advance by the leaders, and can be communicated as part of the screening process. It is also considered advantageous to group process to help members take responsibility for the group, if some rules are set with the members' participation. Rules generally include such issues as attendance expectations, behavioral guidelines, policies about visitors and new members, policies about individual member contact with the social worker between meetings, and details such as eating, use of language, and cleaning up.

Many intervention groups are formal and structured, and include sequences of topics and activities that are neatly paced from beginning to end. Other groups are established with only general topics and goals. Their leaders may intend for discussion themes to emerge from the membership. In every type of group, however, it is useful for leaders to think of the intervention as including a number of stages. With an awareness of these predictable stages the leader can better monitor how well the members are progressing toward their goals. It must be emphasized, however, that not all groups do, or even have the potential, to progress through all stages. But some leader activities are particular to each stage, so this awareness is important.

GROUP STAGES

While there is no single standard outline of group stages, the four-stage model presented here is useful to consider (adapted from Anderson, 1997).

The *pre-affiliation* stage is characterized by a mixture of approach and avoidance behavior among the members. They do not know each other well, and may not know the leader, so they will likely feel normal anxiety and ambivalence about participating in the new group.

In the *power and control* stage members work out issues of status and role with the leader and each other. Put another way, they integrate their personalities into the group system. Those people who are relatively dominant will tend to present as such, and those people who are more passive will fall into those roles. Some members may test their influence with other members and the leader, and test the leader's limits with regard to rules and discussion topics. The social worker must tolerate any such challenges, as this is a normal process that can have a constructive outcome in how patterns of interaction evolve.

The *shared working* stage is characterized by the members working together constructively on the group's purposes. After they have been together for awhile they may fall into a predictable, relatively comfortable pattern of interaction. It is possible that the leader is not quite as active in this stage, at least with regard to managing group process. The members achieve a sense of group identity.

The *separation* stage is characterized by member awareness of the upcoming end of the group, or perhaps their own ending with the group. Members begin to break away physically or emotionally in ways that may be quite distinct from each other. The leader becomes more active in order to insure that all essential group material is covered and the members have time to reflect on their experiences with the group.

Each of these four group stages tends to be characterized by a different set of processes, or patterns of interactions among members. The social worker is generally quite active in the beginning two stages, before a comfortable process of member interaction develops. The leader needs to orient members to the group's format and mediate the predictably awkward interchanges that characterize the early meetings. The leader may also need to enforce group rules and retain primary control of the meeting agenda. The leader may become less active, or less dominant, during the shared working stage if members assume more responsibility for group functioning. The leader becomes more active again during the separation stage, as noted earlier, to lead members toward appropriate closure.

Again, it is important to emphasize that not all groups progress through the stages just described. They, in fact, represent an ideal type. In some educational groups, for example, such as an adolescent conflict resolution group, the social worker may be highly active for the duration. Further, some client populations may not be expected to move fully into the working stage. Children with behavioral problems, people with mental retardation, and people with serious mental illnesses may have limited interpersonal skills or cognitive ability that inhibits their moving much beyond the second stage. In every group the leader should consider the goals, timeline, and characteristics of its members, and with this information think ahead to the type of group process that will be most desirable.

GROUP LEADERSHIP SKILLS

The specific leadership skills and intervention strategies required of the generalist social worker will vary, depending on the type of group. We will specify these later in the context of our six examples. Still, there are some leadership tasks that tend to be common across the stages, as follows (Hepworth, Rooney, Rooney, Strom-Gottfried, & Larsen, 2006):

Pre-affiliation stage. The leader presents the group goals and general structure to the members, clarifies expectations for member interaction, assures all members of their opportunities for participation, encourages members to discuss any anxieties or ambivalence they feel about the group, encourages the development of trust, and models desired member behavior.

Power and control stage. The leader encourages regular attendance and membership stability (unless it is an open-ended group), encourages balanced member participation, draws out less involved members, provides feedback about the quality of member communication, encourages member-to-member rather than member-to-leader exchanges, creates and models norms for group behavior, promotes decision making by consensus, and discourages the formation of subgroups (which tend to marginalize some members and detract from the "whole group" process).

Shared working stage. The leader becomes less verbally active (as members take more responsibility for the agenda), supports the development of positive internal leadership, highlights common group themes, balances time allotments among members, keeps members focused on goals and tasks, and makes statements to help members appreciate both their individuality and their value to the group.

Separation stage. The leader becomes more directive in bringing the group to a constructive conclusion, encourages members to look toward the

Guide Interactions	Link common elements in communication; accentuate similarities
	Block undesired behaviors
	Set limits (define boundaries; provide structure)
Consolidate	Synthesize group themes
	Summarize core points (usually at end)
	Partiailze (for focus and manageability)
	Reframe comments (to promote less rigid, more creative thinking)
Support	But do not "rescue" too quickly
Confront	Raise discrepancies in members' actions, thoughts, and values (may involve the group or individual members)
Process	Raise underlying themes and issues for discussion
	Stay with the "here and now"

F I G U R E 10.3 Group Leader Interventions

future, helps members review their learning or rehearse new skills, identifies areas for each member's continued work, shares his or her re-actions to the group's ending, and asks members to evaluate the group.

See Figure 10.3 for a summary of group leader interventions.

MONITORING GROUP PROCESS

Ongoing group assessment includes the leader's observations about the function-ing of the group over time. It includes elements of *content* and *process*. Content refers to the verbal statements of participants, and process refers less concretely to the ways members interact with each other (Reid, 1997). Further, member roles in a group, while varied, may be classified as task-focused (keeping the group moving toward its explicit goals) or process-maintenance (being more concerned with how members are interacting and getting along). Monitoring may be done formally or informally, perhaps with a coleader or supervisor, through file chart-ing, summary notes made after the group, or occasional meetings between the leaders. The following topics are relevant to group monitoring:

Presentations of the group members. This includes notes about each member with regard to his or her attitudes about the group, and strengths and limitations as they pertain to the group's functioning.

Group structure. Does the group work together as a unit? Are there subgroups of members who tend to talk with each other and exclude the rest? Is this acceptable? How active must the leader be in helping the group function as a unit rather than a collection of disconnected individuals?

Communication and group interaction. This includes the exchange of verbal and nonverbal messages, the extent to which members seem to like or dislike each other, the relative attention or inattention of members to each other, the assertiveness vs. passivity of members, and the intensity or lethargy of their interactions. These characteristics are determined by group size (some people may become lost in a large group), the power and status relationships among members, their emotional bonding, any subgroups that may develop, and the expectations and reinforcements that members receive from the group experience.

Decision making. To what extent do group members share responsibility for decision making as relevant issues come up? What are the group norms for making decisions? Is it primarily the leader's role? Do a few people tend to monopolize the process?

Group cohesion. This is the relative sense of unity among the members. It is determined by their needs for affiliation, their perceived incentives to coalesce, and their expectations about the consequences of the group. In other words, what's in it for them?

Group norms. These are the standards of acceptable and unacceptable behavior, both formal and informal, that preserve order. These result from, and also reflect, member attitudes toward task orientation, the shared sense of responsibility for goal attainment, their attitudes toward the leader(s), attitudes about receiving feedback, the subject matter of the group, accepted ranges of emotional expression, and members' personal characteristics (their values, beliefs, and traditions).

Leadership style of the social workers. This refers to how active the leaders are (of course there may be only one), the topics about which they tend to be more or less focused, their sensitivity to each member, how they differentially interact with each member, and how they divide up roles and tasks.

Summary. Based on these considerations, the leader can write a concluding statement about how well the group is moving toward goal achievement. This should include impressions of its overall strengths, weaknesses, and ongoing potential. Following this process the leader will be better prepared to make any leadership or strategic adjustment for upcoming sessions.

A WORD ABOUT INVOLUNTARY GROUPS

Involuntary groups are those in which the members participate because of some legal mandate or the encouragement of another person. Working with involuntary clients in groups is much like working with them individually, although there are some advantages for groups with this population (Rooney, 1992). That is:

- The group may provide a rare source of support for members.

- Members may learn to be helpers, which can be a new positive experience for them.

- Members may experience positive role models, in the leader and in each other.

- With empathic confrontation members may learn new, more constructive ways to interact with others.

There are also disadvantages to involuntary groups. Members may react negatively to an imposed agenda. There may also be negative peer modeling and a potential for disruptive behavior by some members. To maximize the positive potential of involuntary groups, social workers need to plan a group with clear structure, expectations, mandates, and choices for the members. Social workers must identify and focus on member motivations and strengths, which are almost always present.

COGNITIVE–BEHAVIORAL INTERVENTION IN GROUPS

While group interventions may feature a variety of guiding theoretical perspectives, almost all groups can be provided in formats based on cognitive and behavioral theory. This is because many groups conducted by generalist practitioners are developed to provide members with education, new skills, new behaviors, and new ways of understanding themselves and their surroundings. All groups by nature may also attend to the interpersonal needs of members through mutual support and perhaps social learning, in which members imitate the positive behaviors of their peers. Role-playing, which has already been described in this book as a featured cognitive–behavioral technique for mastering new behaviors, is well suited to the group format.

EXAMPLES OF INTERVENTION GROUPS

What follows are examples of five very different types of social work groups, chosen to emphasize the different formats and purposes of this intervention modality. The first example is the most detailed, while the others (several of which were conducted by social work students in their field placements) provide a more general overview of their subjects. A summary of leader tasks during the first and final sessions of most group types precedes these examples (see Figures 10.4 and 10.5).

Give a brief opening statement
Clarify the social worker's role (compassionate distance)
Encourage comments, questions, feedback; accentuate member similarities
Clarify client roles (perhaps later in session)
Help members develop an agenda and goals (explicit, realistic, measurable)
Clarify mutual expectations (confidentiality) and norms (by word and example)

FIGURE 10.4 Leader Activities During the First Session

"Label" the onset of the ending stage
Become more active and directive
Encourage a future orientation in conversations
Consider the group less as a unit, more as individuals with distinct agendas
Address separation issues if appropriate
Process any member's (or leader's) departure
Resolve unfinished business prior to the final session
Structure the final session (possibly including member reflection activities)
Celebrate the group's significance

FIGURE 10.5 Endings in Group Intervention: Leader Tasks

The Family Education and Support Group

The Family Education and Support Group is a nine-session, nine-week program for adult family members of people with serious mental illnesses like schizophrenia. The purposes of the group are to provide families with education about their ill relative's disorder and to provide a setting in which they can support and problem solve with each other. The group format features a mixture of formal presentations and informal discussions among group members regarding their day-to-day challenges in living with an impaired relative. It can be classified, perhaps obviously, as both an education and a support group.

The single group leader contacts each referred family prior to its acceptance into the group (see Appendix A). He first sends each family a short letter describing the course, and follows up one week later with a phone call. During the conversation, the leader answers questions the family member has about the program and, if the person decided to join, he conducts a brief survey to solicit input into the group's content. This information helps the leader to plan sessions in accordance with member needs. Families who join the group are asked to make a commitment to attend at least three sessions.

Members generally move through all four stages of the group process described earlier. The leader must be well educated and experienced in the area of mental illness and family intervention. He must also be willing to receive much of the members' frustrations about their family stresses, especially in the early weeks, without becoming defensive. The nine sessions are structured as follows:

Week #1:   Orientation and introductions

Week #2:   Group discussion on the range of services available in the county for people with mental illnesses, and the feelings of family members about the quality of the service agencies they have dealt with

Week #3:   Formal presentation about the current theories about the causes, course, and treatment of the severe mental illnesses

Week #4:   Follow-up group discussion on last week's presentation, including applications to one's own family

Week #5:   Formal presentation on the uses and limitations of medications in the treatment of mental illness

Week #6:   Follow-up group discussion on last week's presentation, including applications to one's own family

Week #7:   Group discussion about the various intervention modalities commonly used in mental health agencies, and how families can best involve themselves in that process

Week #8:   Formal presentation on the family advocacy opportunities for quality services from mental health professionals on behalf of client relatives

Week #9:   Wrap-up discussion on any matters of interest to family members. Evaluation forms will be distributed for completion and then discussed

The leader provides a high level of structure for the first two sessions but tries to become less directive and more facilitative as the weeks pass. At the first meeting he introduces himself, reviews the goals of the group, and summarizes the input given by members during the phone survey. He then asks the members to introduce themselves. Many participants are reluctant to say much about their struggles, being unaccustomed to doing so and feeling anxious in the new setting. Near the end of the first meeting, the leader asks members to complete the pretest of an evaluation form (see Appendix B). He will compare these responses to responses collected at the group's final meeting to determine what effect the group has had on (a) the functioning status of the impaired family member, and (b) the types of support developed by the group members.

Group topics are sequenced in an effort to gradually build member cohesion. At the second session the topic of community resources is covered. This topic is not so sensitive that it intimidates member participation, so it usually stimulates much sharing. The group process is significantly enhanced during this session. The emerging group norm of interaction usually continues through the coming weeks. The third meeting consists of the leader presenting information on the topic of psychiatric diagnosis. The following week's meeting, however, features an open-ended discussion of issues related to having a family member with a mental illness. It is the first session devoted to mutual support rather than education. It establishes a pattern of meetings being alternately devoted to formal presentations and informal discussions. The leader encourages the family members to rely less on him and to focus more on sharing their knowledge and experiences with each other. During the fifth session the leader makes a formal presentation on psychotropic medications, and this is followed one week later by another open-ended discussion. The seventh meeting includes another presentation, this time about the nature of roles provided by various professions in the health care system.

The group members usually move from a position of ambivalence and anxiety about the group to feeling comfortable with each other's shared experiences, with which they can all tend to relate. There is often much expression of anger that occurs early, as members are encouraged to vent their frustrations about service providers who they feel have not been helpful, or who have not been empathetic to their challenges. The group leader may be the target of this venting, but he best serves the group by letting the process unfold, because it soon passes. There is often a positive bonding around shared experience that develops by the later stages of the group, and this includes the leader.

During the eighth (second-to-last) meeting, the leader begins attending to the ending process. Group members are self-directed by this time, and the leader offers two options for the evening's agenda. He can help the group organize a discussion about a new topic in which they had expressed interest, or they can devote the meeting to additional sharing and open discussion. He keeps in mind that there is only one session remaining and tries to bring recurrent group themes to closure. In preparing for this meeting he reviews the group's evolution and identifies topics about which there have been particular interest and might require additional attention. The leader also becomes more directive this week than he has been for a while.

The final meeting does not include a great deal of formal content. Leader responsibilities included introducing a speaker from a local family organization, directing an ending discussion, and collecting evaluation forms. There is a 30-minute presentation by a representative from a consumer group such as the Mental Health Association or Alliance for the Mentally Ill so that members have a direct link to another family organization in case they would like to join. In the second half of the meeting the leader asks members to share their impressions of the group experience. He reviews the nine-week course, including its goals, what emerged as significant themes, what information was presented, and what members had shared with each other. He then asks members to respond to the following questions as a means of formal evaluation:

- What did they learn that was important to them?
- How comfortable did they feel about sharing personal concerns with the group?
- How can they apply their learning to situations outside the group?
- How can they generate support systems for themselves outside the group?
- How do they feel about termination?

Finally, members are asked to complete and return the evaluation forms (see Appendix B). Thirty minutes of social time is reserved at the end of the meeting, including light refreshments, so members can chat informally and say good-bye to each other.

The Art Therapy Group

The Art Therapy group is provided at a short-term, inpatient substance abuse treatment facility, and is led by one social worker. It is an open-ended therapy group for five to eight members that is one part of the facility's intervention milieu. The average stay in the setting is only seven days, just enough time for clients to become medically stabilized. The Art Therapy groups focus on the three goals of promoting clients' emotional expression, interpersonal connections (client to client, client to staff, and client to outside resources), and behavior change. These changes often include new coping responses to environmental cues related to drinking and relapse prevention. The leader tries to generate several sources of therapeutic support for clients, and she focuses on their learning to utilize new community supports to broaden their repertoire of helping relationships. Toward this end, the power of the group can be significant. Art experiences can provide a wonderful forum for identifying and developing supportive relationships.

An example of a directed arts activity that helps clients identify needed changes and promotes supportive social networking is the recovery-related gift exchange. Clients are paired and asked to create a recovery-related gift for the partner, based on what they think the partner needs. Clients are directed to remain present-focused. Examples of drawn gifts include candles that represent spirituality and wisdom, groups of family and friends that represent needed support structures and community connection, toolboxes that represent learned coping strategies, and clocks that represent an increased mindfulness of purposeful daily activity. One client created a three-dimensional oyster with a "pearl of wisdom" inside, sharing with his partner his need to look inside for the power and strength to guide his recovery. Clients often find humor and comfort in such interpersonal exchanges, benefiting from both the giving of oneself and the ability to accept the gifts of others.

Because the Art Therapy group is short-term and open-ended, it does not neatly pass through the four stages of group process. The leader must possess art skills but also have the abilities to maintain a high level of activity and direction, as the group is rarely stable and members look for support from outside themselves. Each new member's entry promotes a brief "power and control" phase, as new members always disrupt the cohesion of a group, and their personalities need to be integrated. Members move quickly, though, into a working phase, which for most of them represents comfort but not necessarily a sense of intimacy. This is facilitated by the group's project-focus. Members do not always have to talk or even attend to each other until they feel comfortable doing so. Yet they all work on projects that enhance their emotional expression. The separation stage, which arrives quickly for each member, is important because the leader wants the member to preserve his or her gains. In fact, there is always a focus on termination as each session is usually the last for one or two members.

A challenge in the short-term setting is managing a client's profound sense of loss that comes with becoming intimate, even in a short amount of time with the group, and then leaving, often abruptly (discharge may be sudden). One ending ritual that supports the client's appreciation of the power of community involvement is a good-bye ceremony. The client who is leaving sits in the middle of the group and each member reflects on his or her relationship with the client. Afterwards the client communicates his or her feelings back to the group. This is a constructive process as members always emphasize strengths and remind the departing client of challenges that he or she will face as a recovering substance abuser. This activity is affirming for the departing client but also for those who remain, as they witness over and over again the significance of the community.

Another favorite activity that activates clients' emotions related to transition involves their artistic illustration of what they need to leave at the treatment facility and what they need to take with them. Examples of things to be left behind include panic, isolation, chaos, anger, fear, clinging to pain, depression, sadness, emptiness, negativity, betrayal, and resentments. Things to be cultivated from treatment often include serenity, peace, happiness, appreciation, gratitude, hope, a positive attitude, support, willingness, and courage.

One young male client, when asked to complete this activity, chose themes of "chaos" and "serenity." He used a blue marker in his picture to symbolize both of these concepts, with a similar line quality to represent the seemingly disparate feeling states. Serenity was illustrated as a smooth, clear line, untangled from the web of chaos drawn on the paper's opposite side. The group discussion about his products focused on the parallels that exist between the two ideas, proposing that serenity can, in fact, be found in and arise out of chaos. The group engaged in a dialogue about the line organization within the picture. It suggested the client's awareness of his own responsibility for emotional transformation and the existence of hope in the midst of addiction chaos. The group decided that active, personal responsibility coupled with a developing sense of faith in the recovery process would contribute to the chaos–serenity transformation that was visually represented in the client's artwork.

An Anger Control Group: The Franklin Court Conflict Resolution Group

Franklin Court Elementary School was located in a large public housing development in an urban city. The school consisted of 400 students between the ages of 4 and 12 years old. Two student social workers there developed the Conflict Resolution Group in response to faculty concerns about frequent fights that broke out in the halls. The social workers became aware that 20 students had been referred to the office or suspended from school for fighting during the first semester of that school year. They decided to develop their group as a pilot program for some of those 20 students. They chose social learning theory, which is related to cognitive–behavioral theory, as a perspective for understanding students' problem behaviors and devising group intervention projects. This theory proposes that learning takes place through a person's tendency to observe and imitate the behaviors of others. The social workers postulated that the students' fighting behaviors represented their modeled methods of coping with violence in their communities. The goal of the group was that participating students in the Conflict Resolution Group would have fewer future referrals for disciplinary problems. The social workers hoped that they could teach alternative behaviors and coping mechanisms that might be attractive to these students so that their chances for school success would be enhanced. The social workers assumed the role of teachers in the group, and used material on anger management from a handbook from the local school system for their teaching material.

The Conflict Resolution Group met for one hour weekly for six weeks. Six students were chosen for referral for the initial group by school administration on the basis of their apparent motivation to change their behaviors. Each of these students was given a 15-item pre-group questionnaire designed by the students in which they provided information about why they fight, what they think about fighting, what makes them angry, and what they do that makes other people angry. The social work students relied exclusively on the group members' questionnaire responses to select topics for group discussion.

This was a closed, time-limited, highly structured group. Each week, the leaders oriented the six students to the plan for that day's session. The social workers began each meeting with instructional material about conflict resolution. This was followed by role-play or discussion activities, whereby the students could discuss and rehearse a variety of ways to resolve conflict that did not include physical fighting. One activity required the members to watch a favorite TV show at home and write down how some episode of conflict was presented and addressed. Another activity was an exercise in which the participants were asked to focus on their feelings in a variety of conflicted situations, and how they responded to the different feelings they experienced.

Regarding group process, the members never really got past the power and control phase, which was not unexpected given their developmental level and the nature of the presenting problems. Still, the social workers were pleased at the level of participation by the group members, who did consider and experiment with new behaviors. The students agreed that it was important to have coleadership, as the members became easily distracted from the topics at hand. The social workers concluded that the group was successful because all six participants experienced a reduction or elimination of disciplinary referrals for the rest of that school year.

An Education Group: The Living Skills Group

Four social work students who shared a field placement at a county mental retardation services agency observed that the agency might benefit from a program that taught parenting and living skills to clients who had children. Given the average caseload size of 60 clients per case manager, it did not seem feasible for the full-time case managers to individually spend adequate time with their clients for these types of specific skill-building activities. The students researched the topic and found empirical evidence that mothers with mental retardation are indeed capable of acquiring most of the parenting skills required to provide a safe environment for a child. The students, with the approval of their field supervisor, decided to develop and colead the Parenting Skills Group.

The social work students met with the case managers to find out what kinds of skills would be most important for the mothers to acquire. The identified target areas turned out to be quite practical: proper use of a baby car seat, child safety techniques, basic child discipline techniques, and ways to help children develop socially. The students decided on a four-week group for reasons of feasibility, so that they could devote one complete session to each of the four topic areas. The students prepared a pre-test for group participants, with the assistance of their field instructor, to see how the clients rated themselves in these areas. The recruitment process involved asking the agency case managers to recommend clients for the group from their caseloads. The students were hoping to recruit four to eight mothers, thinking that this would be a manageable size for a new group, and they ended up with six participants. Through telephone interviews with the participants, a suitable meeting time and day was determined. To insure the participation and regular attendance of each mother a second group was formed for childcare purposes (which included eight children). The students received permission from agency administration to transport the mothers and their children to and from the groups.

Because of their numbers, the social work students were able to rotate group leadership responsibilities. Each week a different student facilitated the group and a second social worker assisted. The structure of each meeting involved the presentation of information, a few handouts, a discussion of related concerns in the participants' own families, and role-play rehearsals of new parent–child behaviors. The two other students led the children's group, engaging with the kids in play.

The four group sessions ran smoothly. Following the introductions on the first day there was very little "power and control" activity. The mothers were all motivated and cooperative, and responded well to the high level of group structure. They wanted to listen more so than talk, although this changed as the weeks went on. The mothers discussed with each other their limitations and frustrations with parenting and their desires to be more effective parents. The "working" phase of the group unfolded nicely, although there was relatively little in the way of sustained member interaction. The mothers participated more like classroom students. The ending stage was uncomplicated as well. It seems that the mothers shared a natural bond in that they participated in similar agency programs but they seemed to move into and out of the group experience without much intensity. This group program appeared to be successful in educating the mothers about all the targeted parenting skills, as evidenced by the posttests in which the mothers showed greater comfort in all four target areas.

Education, Growth, and Socialization: The Multiple-Family Weekend Retreat

The Weekend Family Retreat is a program for homeless families with children. These families are in the process of moving into permanent housing and are referred to the program by the housing agencies with which they are involved. The goal of the group intervention is to strengthen families by providing training in communication, stress management, and decision-making practices. These are all cognitive–behavioral activities. Having parents and their children meet together to address common concerns is seen as an effective means of providing family mental health services. A major assumption of the modality is that family growth is promoted more fully when peers are included in the intervention. The group leaders believe that the Weekend Retreat format is preferable to traditional agency-based weekly groups because they are more intensive and, as such, promote greater cohesion. Regular attendance at weekly groups is often problematic for families as well. The family retreats include about 10 families with their young children, usually 30 to 40 people in all. The two coleaders of the program, who are also its administrators, recruit approximately 10 social work students to help implement the specific retreat interventions.

The Weekend Family Retreats are held at a park from late Friday evening through late Saturday afternoon. The program, and the specific small groups, focus on two themes, "strengthening families" and "families have fun together." There are four formal group sessions held with different configurations of family members on the topics of building trust, effective communication, managing stress, and decision-making practices. During the instructional portion of each session parents are presented with information to help enhance their parenting skills, followed by a discussion of how this information might be pertinent to each family's unique situation. Some groups are held specifically for the children. Between the four formal sessions various activities are held with the purpose of having fun and adding practical meaning to the session content.

Of all the groups described in this chapter, the Weekend Family Retreat demands the most flexibility of its leaders. It is unpredictable how the families will behave in the setting. Their progression through the four group stages is also unpredictable. Family members are oriented to the program in a large group when they first arrive at the retreat and have dinner. During the actual group sessions they usually move through stage two (power and control) and into stage three (intimacy), although the stage two issues may persist. It is probably best to consider the weekend retreat to be one group that involves all of the families and leaders, while the small groups are subgroup activities. It is during the many large-group social and discussion activities that intimacy is best developed.

The issue of leader flexibility cannot be overemphasized. For example, it is rare that all of the families who have signed up for the experience show up for the bus. Thus, the composition of the intervention groups must be adjusted just before they begin. Secondly, family members may not show up on time, or at all, for their groups, or they may not remain for the entire 90 minutes. When children are misbehaving in one group, a family member may need to leave another group to help take care of the situation. Thus, while the specific groups are structured, the leaders expect to diverge from that structure in order to accommodate the needs of the members.

The Weekend Family Retreat is intense; the leaders pay careful attention to the closing ceremonies so that families can feel energized and affirmed as they go back to their normal lives. The ceremonies are also intended to encourage the families to continue the work they have begun at the retreat. There is a closing ceremony at the end of each day. On Friday evening, after the families have been together for only a few hours and participated in one of the four scheduled groups, there is a "positive statements" activity. Each family is asked to sit in front of the other families. One member is given a candle, and holds it while he or she makes a positive comment about each other family member. When that person is finished, the candle is passed to another member who does the same thing. Once the entire family finishes, the candle is passed to the next family who continues the same process. If any member cannot think of a positive comment (this is not unusual with young children) the other participants are invited to offer suggestions. The passing of the candle symbolizes the connections of the families with each other.

The final two hours of the second day are focused on the ending of the retreat. Each family works together to create a banner, a collage created from linen sheets with drawings and magazine pictures, on which they depict their family strengths. An alternative activity is the creation of scrapbooks about the weekend in which families can include photographs of themselves at the retreat. After a short period of completing the formal evaluations, the families take turns sharing their banners with the rest of the participants. Other people can comment about the family's strengths. They keep their banners, and it is hoped that they will display these in their homes.

All Five Types of Groups: The Wilderness Group

The Wilderness Conquest program is a 42-day group experience conducted in the canyon lands of Utah. The clients are boys and girls between 14 and 21 years of age. These adolescents and young adults have serious problems with such issues as substance abuse, truancy, violence, and other acting-out behaviors. Outings typically consist of five adolescents, both male and female, and two staff, also male and female. Other support staff participate at times (for example, to make food and supply drops). Wilderness Conquest is an intensive program of hiking, camping, and primitive living for young people who might never have experienced anything of the kind before. They learn to make fires, shelters, animal traps, and maps. It is above all a therapy program. The setting and activities are means to help the participants improve their practical and social skills, gain confidence, learn to be responsible, learn how to address their problems in constructive ways, and set healthier goals. One of the striking features of the program is that participants are abruptly thrown together into this strange, shared experience, and when it is over they are abruptly returned to their previous environments.

The program leaders must be experienced campers who have also received training in this kind of leadership. They function as models, teachers, mediators, facilitators, and enforcers of discipline. The group experience consists of a highly structured set of adventure activities in which the participants are forced to rely on each other, and to contribute their special skills to the group process. This group program is unique in that the process is related to survival. There are almost no life and death risks to this program, of course, with the structured supports being in place, but there is a practical reality that the group can only function well with everyone's contribution.

The leaders engage in skill building and educational activities. They are active with the group throughout the experience because their expertise is so critical to the learning of the participants. The group truly does pass through all five group stages described earlier. At the outset the members tend to be quiet and anxious about the daunting task ahead of them. They must be given a set of rules in order to insure everyone's safety and well-being. Once the hike gets underway, there is a lot of jockeying for position, power, and the leaders' favor. Finally, once members are into the pattern of hiking and learning some new skills, they become closer with each other. There is finally an extended ending process in recognition of the fact that this was such a unique experience, and they will need to readjust to their normal lives.

During the fifth week in the desert, each participant must set up his or her own campsite. The purpose of this activity is to help each person use what he or she has learned in the program and show himself or herself that he or she is competent to survive alone. This begins with a five-mile hike alone at night with a fluorescent tube. The participant marks a trail along the way from the base camp and then sets up the campsite. The adolescents return to base camp that evening, but the next morning all of them return to their own campsites with some supplies and spend three days alone. They set up mailboxes amidst piles of rocks at the edge of their camps so that staff can check in with them daily without interrupting their solitude. After the third day the participants return to base camp in silence. That evening they all sit around a fire and, finally breaking the silence, share their experiences.

Next a series of rituals based on Native American traditions are implemented involving the entire group. During a fire ceremony, each person writes down a negative life pattern that he or she wants to leave behind in the desert. These are thrown into the fire and burned. The next day the group builds a sweat lodge of hot rocks placed in a hole surrounded by a shelter, like a sauna. Before entering the sauna each person lights bands of sagebrush, and the smoke is intended to release the person's negative energy before he or she enters the lodge. This experience symbolizes a cleansing of the old self and the rebirth of a new self. The rituals are all part of a summing up of what each adolescent has accomplished in the desert, and to prepare each person to carry positive aspects of the experience into his or her normal life. Each person is reminded of his or her debts to the other members of the group, as he or she clearly has relied on others' support to succeed in the demanding program. On the last day, support staff bring a feast to the campsite in the desert and they all celebrate the end of the six-week journey with a sumptuous meal.

The desert adventure is not the entirety of the adolescent's therapeutic group experience. The group goes directly from the desert to a small-town inn, where they are met by the adolescents' families, and initiate a three-day workshop. During the three days the kids and their families set goals, make amends, own up to their previous negative behaviors, get all of their secrets out, and arrange linkages with follow-up agencies in their home areas. The final program activity is a graduation ceremony, much like a high school commencement. From there, the families scatter to all areas of the country.

ETHICAL DILEMMAS IN GROUP WORK

Working with clients in groups can create ethical dilemmas for social workers due to the need to balance the interests of individual members with those of the entire group. Some member behaviors need to be limited (this is normal during the "power and control" stage) and sometimes limits can become so firm that a member must be released from the group.

Tina was a social work student who was conducting a "values clarification" group for older adults at a local community center. This was a closed, eight-session, weekly group experience for high school boys and girls who were in the process of developing life values around such topics as relationships with peers, relationships with family members, and attitudes toward substance use, sex, and careers. Discussion topics that emerged from within the group were almost always relevant to the members' life situations, and Tina, in her facilitator role, was pleased with the group's development.

By the fourth session, however, one member named Susan was creating serious problems for the group. She was the most verbal member and not only tried to initiate the major topic for discussion each week, but she also tended to respond to any other comments made by other members. Tina could see that the other members resented the amount of time Susan took within the meetings. They began ostracizing her by not delivering any comments to Susan and trying to ignore her when she spoke.

Tina first intervened by asking Susan to allow other members the opportunity to talk, and asking other members to comment on Susan's behaviors. The other group members openly confronted Susan about her monopolization of their time, but when it appeared that Susan was not going to adjust her behavior, they seemed to give up. Tina noticed that group absences were becoming more common, and she suspected this was due to member frustration with Susan.

Next, Tina met with Susan outside the group to discuss the problem and ask her to become less verbal. Tina did not like talking to Susan outside the group, because she always wanted to deal with group issues with all the members present. While Susan listened respectfully to Tina, she did not seem to get the message. Susan was not an insightful person and was not aware of the effects of her behavior on others. While a group is often a good place for a person to learn this kind of information, Tina was concerned that Susan's dominant behavior was endangering the future of the time-limited group.

After one more unproductive group meeting, in which three of the eight members did not attend, Tina met with Susan again and asked her to drop out of the group. She referred Susan to an individual counselor for additional services, but reluctantly had decided that the life of the group needed to take precedence over Susan's personal situation. Tina wondered if a more skilled group leader might have been able to moderate Susan's behavior, and she wondered if her growing negative feelings about Susan had been a major factor in her decision. Not all clients are suitable for certain kinds of group interventions, but it is not always easy to come to that conclusion with confidence.

SUMMARY

Generalist practitioners can effectively deliver educational, supportive, therapeutic, growth, and socialization services to small groups of clients. All groups can be provided through a cognitive–behavioral theoretical base. The specific skills required of group leaders are different depending on the group's focus, but there are some common leadership skills that are applicable to all types of groups. There are also stages through which groups tend to pass from beginning to end, although again how and whether these unfold will depend on the type of group. Knowledge of these group processes can help the generalist practitioner to plan a group and evaluate its process over time. This chapter has included examples of six groups that may serve to capture the broad range of formats that small groups can assume in human service agencies.

TOPICS FOR DISCUSSION

1. Present and discuss other examples of the five types of treatment groups. Be alert to the many types of groups that seem to combine several of the five types.

2. Describe and discuss examples of groups that do not pass through the four stages presented in this chapter. How important is it for some groups to work though all five stages?

3. Based on your experiences, what are the pros and cons of having a coleader in a group? Would it be more important depending on the "stage" of the group?

4. From a hat, draw typical group member roles (over-sharer, blamer, withdrawn one, intellectualizer, and so on) to comprise some type of intervention group. Rotate out of the leader/coleader chairs, utilizing the leader

interventions summarized in Figure 10.3, to role-play parts of the group process.

5. In small groups, select one of the five types of intervention groups described in this chapter. Select (from one of your field placements) and discuss an example of that type of treatment group. Focus on the following questions as a means of clarifying the group characteristics. At the end of the discussion period, discuss as a class whether the different types of groups tend to have distinct norms.

- What are the expectations of members about the outcomes of the group?
- What range of topics is relevant for inclusion in the group?
- What range of emotional expression is anticipated in the group?
- What member patterns for working on problems and staying on task are considered functional?
- To what extent do members consider it their responsibility to make the group experience successful?
- What are the members' attitudes toward the leader(s)?
- What leader interventions are utilized in the group?

ASSIGNMENT IDEAS

1. Develop a proposal for a new treatment group, using the outline provided in this chapter. While it should not be an expectation that you will actually implement the group, select a type of group that would be relevant to a field placement agency.

2. If you are, or have, participated in an intervention group, write an assessment of the status of that group using the group monitoring guide included in this chapter.

3. Develop a group intervention program.

Scenario: The social services department in which you are employed at the medical hospital has identified a need for a new group in the community. The number of AIDS patients at the hospital has been increasing markedly in the past three years, and the social workers are being called upon to provide more support services to the families and friends of those patients. Of particular concern is that no special services exist for the adolescent relatives and friends of the hospital's AIDS patients. Many teachers in the community have reported that these adolescents feel ostracized by their peers, confused about the implications of the disease for their own lives, and anxious about the unpredictable course of the condition in the lives of their parents, aunts, uncles, cousins, or friends.

Due to this perceived need, you have been asked to develop a time-limited (5- to 10-week) information and support group for adolescent family members or peers of people being treated for AIDS-related illnesses. The hospital wants to provide this service for free, but understands that some outside funding will eventually be necessary to continue the group if it proves to be successful. The challenge to your team of social workers is to design a group of this type. Your supervisors hope that the program will lend itself to evaluation. If it is shown to be effective for the adolescent participants, arguments for new funding can be presented to the United Way and other charitable organizations.

While you may know little about AIDS issues, or have limited group experience at this point, please speculate about the goals, leadership skills and strategies, topics, group tasks, and possible evaluation strategies that could be relevant to a group of this type. Assume that there is a list of 10 adolescents ready to be referred to the group once it is developed. Finally, one of your tasks is to recommend meeting space for the group outside the hospital.

Appendix A

Sample Phone Survey for Prospective Group Members

<u>Opening Remarks</u>: In order to be most helpful to you, I am interested in learning how much you understand about your family member's mental disorder, and what kinds of help you are seeking. I would appreciate your taking a few minutes to answer some questions. All of your responses will be confidential. The answers that you and other new group members provide will enable me to prepare subject matter most relevant to your needs.

Name: _____ Relationship to Client: _____

1. How long has your family member been in treatment at this and other mental health agencies?

    _____ years   _____ months

2. How long has your family member been living with or close by you?

    _____ years   _____ months

3. Clients of mental health agencies are given a diagnosis, which is a professional term used to describe their problem. Are you aware of the diagnosis that your family member has been given?

    _____ yes   _____ no

    If so, what is it? _____

4. Have you ever been invited by your family member's case manager, physician, or other providers to participate in joint meetings?

    _____ yes   _____ no

    If so, please explain the nature of your participation. _____

    _____

5. Is your family member taking any medications as part of the treatment program?

    _____ yes   _____ no

    If so, what kind? _____

    Can you describe what the medication is supposed to do? _____

    _____

6.   Is your family member involved with any other social service agencies to get help
     with his or her problems?

     _____ yes   _____ no

     If so, which ones? _____

     _____

7.   Have you heard of any other social service agencies that you would like to learn
     more about?

     _____ yes   _____ no

     If so, which ones? _____

     _____

8.   What are some of the main challenges you experience in living with or near your
     family member?

     a. _____

     b. _____

     c. _____

     d. _____

     e. _____

9.   In what ways do you hope that the Family Education and Support Group can be of
     help to you?

     a. _____

     b. _____

     c. _____

     d. _____

     e. _____

10. Do you have any other questions or comments about the group, the agency, or me?

_____

_____

_____

Appendix B

Sample Evaluation Form

THE FAMILY EDUCATION AND SUPPORT GROUP MEMBER ASSESSMENT

Name: _____   Date: _____

In this first series of statements, please assess the independent living skills of your family member with mental illness. Please remember that these can be possessed in degrees and do not necessarily indicate that your family member is living on his or her own at the present time. As you consider each item, use the past month as a time frame in deciding on your response. Circle the response that most closely matches your assessment of each statement as demonstrated by the example.

Example: My family member is a   Very   Rarely   (Occasionally)   Frequently
           friendly person.   Rarely

This respondent feels that the family member is sometimes friendly, but not as friendly as he or she might be. Now, please proceed to complete the scale below, and elaborate on each of your responses in the space beneath each item.

My family member with mental illness:

1. Uses money to pay his/her personal   Very   Rarely   Occasionally   Frequently
   expenses in a reasonable way.   Rarely

Explain: _____
_____
_____

2. Takes care of housekeeping tasks   Very   Rarely   Occasionally   Frequently
   without being reminded.   Rarely

Explain: _____
_____
_____

3. Maintains an adequately balanced   Very   Rarely   Occasionally   Frequently
   diet.   Rarely

Explain: _____
_____
_____

4. Arranges for transportation promptly   Very   Rarely   Occasionally   Frequently
   when needed.   Rarely

Explain: _____
_____
_____

5. Spends time with friends outside   Very   Rarely   Occasionally   Frequently
   the home.   Rarely

Explain: _____

_____

_____

6. Engages in recreational activity   Very   Rarely   Occasionally   Frequently
   outside the home.   Rarely

Explain: _____

_____

_____

7. Makes an effort to secure income   Very   Rarely   Occasionally   Frequently
   from a source outside the family.   Rarely

Explain: _____

_____

_____

8. Keeps his/her clothing clean.   Very   Rarely   Occasionally   Frequently
                                           Rarely

Explain: _____

_____

_____

9. Maintains reasonable expectations   Very   Rarely   Occasionally   Frequently
   of the family for companionship.   Rarely

Explain: _____

_____

_____

10. Takes the initiative to achieve   Very   Rarely   Occasionally   Frequently
    or maintain a job.   Rarely

Explain: _____

_____

_____

11. Takes medication as prescribed.   Very   Rarely   Occasionally   Frequently
                                              Rarely

Explain: _____

_____

12. Has a physician whom he/she   Very   Rarely   Occasionally   Frequently
    visits when physically ill.   Rarely

Explain: _____

_____

13. Purchases his/her own clothing   Very   Rarely   Occasionally   Frequently
    and household supplies.   Rarely

Explain: _____

_____

14. Meets at least monthly with a   Very   Rarely   Occasionally   Frequently
    mental health counselor or case   Rarely
    manager.

Explain: _____

_____

Next, rather than thinking about your family member, please consider your own situation. Listed below is a series of statements reflecting various types of personal relationships and activities. These refer to different ways in which people may cope with the stresses associated with mental illness in the family. There are no right or wrong answers to these items, since all people cope with stress differently. Next to the statements below, please circle the response which best describes your level of participation. Again, you may elaborate on your responses in the space below each item.

Example: I exercise to work off   Very   (Rarely)   Occasionally   Frequently
            tension.   Rarely

This respondent hardly ever gets exercise, if at all. Please go on now to complete the scale items below.

1. I engage in personal hobbies outside the home.

Very Rarely · Rarely · Occasionally · Frequently

Explain: _____
_____
_____

2. I participate in at least one community social group.

Very Rarely · Rarely · Occasionally · Frequently

Explain: _____
_____
_____

3. I have contact with my family member's mental health service provider.

Very Rarely · Rarely · Occasionally · Frequently

Explain: _____
_____
_____

4. I spend time with my friends for purposes unrelated to my family problems.

Very Rarely · Rarely · Occasionally · Frequently

Explain: _____
_____
_____

5. I can devote uninterrupted time to my job or my own routine daily activities (if unemployed outside the home).

Very Rarely · Rarely · Occasionally · Frequently

Explain: _____
_____
_____

6. I visit a mental health professional for help with my own problems.

Very Rarely · Rarely · Occasionally · Frequently

Explain: _____
_____
_____

I confide in the following people about my family problems:

7. Neighbors   Very Rarely   Rarely   Occasionally   Frequently

Explain: _____

_____

_____

8. Extended family members (aunts, cousins, grandparents, etc.)   Very Rarely   Rarely   Occasionally   Frequently

Explain: _____

_____

_____

9. My physician   Very Rarely   Rarely   Occasionally   Frequently

Explain: _____

_____

_____

10. My pastor   Very Rarely   Rarely   Occasionally   Frequently

Explain: _____

_____

_____

My family member with a mental illness is my:

_____ SON   _____ BROTHER

_____ DAUGHTER   _____ SISTER

_____ MOTHER   _____ SPOUSE

_____ FATHER   _____ OTHER (please specify:_____)

He/she lives in:

_____ MY HOUSE OR APARTMENT

_____ A GROUP HOME FOR PEOPLE WITH MENTAL ILLNESSES

_____ AN AGENCY-MANAGED OR SUPERVISED APARTMENT

_____ HIS/HER OWN HOUSE OR APARTMENT

_____ OTHER (please specify: _____)

He/she is now _____ years old and has received services at this and other mental health agencies or psychiatric hospitals for approximately _____ years.

Other comments?_____
_____
_____
_____

THANK YOU VERY MUCH FOR YOUR COOPERATION.

Chapter 11

Organizational Practice

*S*cenario #1: "I love my job at the community center. There are lots of social workers and other professionals working there, and everything feels like a team effort. I work with older adult clients but there is variety in my job. My supervisor encourages me to come up with new ideas for our programs. We have a lot of contact with the neighborhood residents and some of them make good suggestions about improving our services."

Scenario #2: "My job at the county children's services agency is exactly what I wanted after getting my BSW degree because I wanted to help kids who were abused and neglected. But after three years I'm wearing out. It's important work, and I love the kids, but the hours, the large caseload, and the endless paperwork frustrate me. I feel like I spend half my time filling out forms. All my supervisors seem to care about is whether I get my required number of client contact hours each month."

Scenario #3: "As a case manager for clients with mental illnesses, I get frustrated when other agencies in my community are slow to help my clients. For example, we have a center for vocational rehabilitation that many of my clients rely on for job training. But the waiting list is so long! My clients and their families complain when it takes three months or more to get a vocational assessment done. I try to move things along by complaining to the agency director, but I don't seem to make a difference."

The scenarios described illustrate some positive and negative aspects of human service organizations. An *organization* can be defined as a group of people gathered together as a unit to serve a purpose (Netting, Kettner, & McMurtry, 2004). Based on the assumption that people working together can achieve more than people working independently, it is no surprise that organizations are *everywhere* in society!

They range in complexity from the federal government (which includes a number of subagencies, to put it mildly), to schools of social work, to your local chapter of the Justin Timberlake fan club. In all organizations policies and procedures must be established to coordinate the activities of participants, and also to institute rewards and sanctions for member performance that promote its ongoing effectiveness. Social workers almost *always* provide their services within the context of employing organizations. Generalist practitioners, because they often serve clients with multiple problems, further operate in the context of *networks* of organizations. They refer clients to, and receive referrals from, other agencies for some services, and then they must coordinate those interagency efforts. Social workers may understandably feel overwhelmed by the numbers of organizations with which they interact.

In this chapter we will present strategies for agency-level assessment and intervention by social workers, but first we will consider the nature of organizations. The purpose of social work is to facilitate matches between clients and their environments (Segal, Gerdes, & Steiner, 2007), and this requires that social workers have the ability to connect client systems with supportive agencies. Further, the NASW Code of Ethics states that the social worker "should work to improve the employing agency's policies and procedures, and the efficiency and effectiveness of its services" (1999, p. x). It is thus important that social workers understand how agencies *do* and *should* work. Effective generalist practice requires that social workers have the ability to interact with people from other agencies and have good working relationships within their own employing agencies, so that they can carry out the mission of the profession. Direct service social workers should never underestimate the importance of their "front line" perspective as a source of essential knowledge about service delivery improvement.

THE NATURE OF HUMAN SERVICE ORGANIZATIONS

Human service agencies may be *public, private,* or a combination of the two (Netting, Kettner, & McMurtry, 2004). Public agencies, which are established by government bodies with public money, are generally more dependent on outside organizations (rather than paying clients or donors) for monetary and other supports. These outside organization include city, state, or federal government sources. The public schools and city departments of social services are examples of public agencies that employ social workers. They are subject to many outside regulations and as a result often have less independent discretion to decide how their services can be provided. Private agencies are established with private money from contributors, often by church organizations. My first place of employment as a social worker was a private facility operated by the Seventh

Day Adventist Church. These organizations originate with and are operated through private donations, although they may receive public money for some services. They are sometimes expensive for clients to use. These agencies often include a staff position with the sole function of raising money for ongoing agency operation and development.

Agencies in which social workers are employed can also be categorized with regard to how they work with clients (Bruggemann, 2002). *People-changing* agencies, such as mental health centers, provide clients with knowledge and coping skills so they can conduct their lives in new, more effective ways. *People-sustaining* agencies help clients optimize a certain quality of life after the onset of a threatening problem. Examples include rehabilitation centers, medical centers, and foster care agencies. *People-processing* agencies are focused on providing clients with material benefits. Welfare and housing departments are examples of these. All of these agencies are appropriate for social work service delivery. Depending on a social worker's professional goals, one type of agency may be more attractive than the others.

Agencies may further be differentiated as *primary* or *host* settings for social workers (Meenaghan, Gibbons, & McNutt, 2005). In the first type of agency social workers comprise a majority or near majority of the total professional staff. A child and family guidance center, due to the nature of its work, may be staffed predominantly with social workers. In host settings social workers are in a clear professional minority. The public school system, mentioned earlier, qualifies as a host agency because the teaching profession is far more widely represented than social work. A school may employ only one social worker, or one social worker may serve several schools. Social workers in host agencies tend, because of their numbers, to have less influence with regard to agency operations. They may experience more ethical conflicts (due to their unique value perspective) and status conflicts with members of other professions.

Practicing social workers (and members of other service professions) often have uneasy relationships with their employing agencies because of their uniquely client-centered perspective on its mission. Social workers may in fact see their employing agencies at times as both a *resource* and an *obstacle* to service delivery (Dolgoff, Loewenberg, & Harrington, 2005). This is not to say that administrators are not client-centered, but their different responsibilities can pull them in different directions at times. For example, practitioners want to *maximize* resources for their clients, but administrators must necessarily *limit* the scope of services to some degree, to preserve typically scarce resources. Also, criteria for worker and program evaluation often tend to reflect *administrative* concerns (outputs, costs, caseload sizes, units of service, fee collection, and so on) rather than *professional* concerns (client goal achievement, the amount of time that can be spent with clients, support for advocacy activities, and so on). Further, because of the limited budgets of human service agencies, practitioners are often required from year to year to do more with less, which may be necessary but is also frustrating.

To summarize, there seem to be some inherent conflicts between the roles of *professionals* of all types and *bureaucrats* in many organizations. These conflicts may include:

- Conflicting loyalties to the profession and its values versus loyalty to the organization and its survival needs

- A client-centered orientation versus adherence to rules that at times appear to be agency-centered

- The desire to have discretion in decision making versus recognizing the authority of agency administration

- A focus on service *effectiveness* versus service *efficiency*

It is certainly possible for social workers to be employed in agencies where the goals of professionals and administrators are largely consistent. When conflicts exist, however, the range of social worker reactions may include a first loyalty to the profession or dual loyalties to the agency and profession. The social worker's pursuit of administrative power and personal security at the agency may be problematic if this reflects a loss of professional purpose. For example, a social work practitioner who wishes to earn an administrative promotion may focus his efforts more on adhering to instrumental agency policies (getting reports completed, collecting fees, opening the required number of cases, terminating with clients who do not pay fees or keep appointments) rather than the quality of client service delivery. While agency policies are important, this social worker may become quick to terminate with clients who sometimes do not appear for scheduled appointments rather than explore the reasons for their non–adherence. Ideally a social worker must learn to balance his or her loyalties by helping the agency meet the needs of clients and appreciating the importance of discretion and diplomacy when working for change within the agency.

All agencies, public and private, operate within larger social service and community systems. They are never autonomous and must be responsive to the expectations of many relevant outside organizations for their survival. These outside influences, known as agency *sanctions,* include people and organizations that support and legitimize the existence of the agency, and to whom the agency must be accountable in some ways. Some sanctioning bodies are highly influential (such as a primary funding source like the United Way) while others are less so (the school of social work that only places a few students in an agency). All of them are important, however, and social workers should be aware of them in order to fully comprehend the functions of the agency. Sources of agency sanctions may include (Long, Tice, & Morrison, 2006):

- Clients (actual and potential)

- Community agencies that make referrals, receive referrals, and participate in the coordination of services for clients

- National credentialing organizations (for example, the National Council of Community Mental Health Centers)

- Professional organizations (such as NASW and practitioner licensure boards)

- Key community supporters (government, business, and community leaders who serve as board members or support the agency with financial and political support)
- Foundations and other funding sources (such as the United Way)
- Government bodies (that set policies and possibly provide funding for agency functioning)

Organizations are intended to be effective and efficient means for the participants to achieve common goals. This is, however, an ideal principle. Not all members of an organization share the same goals, and even when they do so they may disagree on the means to achieve them. Larger organizations tend to have more complex hierarchies and more impersonal roles. A larger proportion of members may be at odds with its operations, if only because with more people, more types of activities, different levels of power, and different rewards, the possibility of different opinions increases. As an example, social workers most often participate in host organizations such as public schools. They may hold to different priorities than teachers and administrators with regard to the attention given to special needs students. They may wish to advocate for more individual time with students and more formal programs that include parents. When managed well, such different perspectives on service delivery may contribute to creativity in work with clients, but they may also give rise to conflict related to the mission of the organization.

Characteristics of Formal Organizations

The following paragraphs describe general characteristics of *all* formal organizations (Bransford & Bakken, 2001).

Structure incorporates sets of policies and procedures that organize how members of the agency should interact. Social workers and all other agency employees are assigned specific *roles* or job tasks that are usually articulated in their position descriptions. Interactions among members that relate to the organizational mission are intended to be largely formal.

Hierarchy is the formally established levels of authority in an organization. Social workers may occupy positions in an agency that are largely autonomous or require them to be accountable to another employee with regard to job performance (possibly another social worker, but just as likely a member of another discipline or even a nonprofessional staff member). People in higher positions tend to have greater responsibility for decision making about policies and procedures, and broader levels of authority.

Power is the ability to influence the actions of others in an organization. *Formal* power is articulated in a job description or organizational chart. A social worker may be given considerable or little power in an organization with regard to, for example, making decisions about service provision. *Informal* power, which represents real but unofficial influence in an organization, is not formally scribed, and may result from agency traditions as well as a person's charisma or ability to intimidate. It is often said, only half-jokingly, that the secretaries are the most powerful members of some organizations because of their access to information.

Specialization is the principle by which staff from each department are expected to have unique knowledge and skills that make them capable of completing their job requirements effectively. The generalist practitioner, for example, may be considered to have special expertise in client assessment or community linkage activities in an agency. The sum of all specialized roles insures the agency's capacity to fulfill its mission. Members of one specialization, such as social workers, are not expected to intrude on others' levels of expertise (such as the nurses or vocational counselors), and vice versa.

Qualifications are staff credentials related to knowledge, training, and experience to merit their appointment to job positions. Job assignments are not supposed to be based on personal considerations. Social workers should be hired and promoted based on their demonstrated competence and overall contribution to agency function. An agency that hires generalist social workers should require that the applicant has earned a college degree in social work, although there may be other qualifications as well.

Detachment refers to functional impersonality in staff interactions. This is considered to be desirable as it separates professional relationships, intended to focus only on organizational issues, from personal relationships, which are much broader in scope. People can be more productive in an organization if they only interact around their formal roles. This is a challenge, however, for workers in many organizations, and perhaps even more so for social workers, who place such a high value on human relationships. Most administrators understand that employees are usually happier with their jobs when they can enjoy the company of their coworkers, but they will discourage excessive social interactions on the clock. Many organizations have formal policies prohibiting staff from dating or being in a partner relationship. This is a difficult issue to balance, because clearly a personalizing of job relationships can give rise to the inequitable use of informal power, differential attention to agency rules, the inefficient use of time (when staff engage in excessive socializing), and differential treatment of employees.

Rules are formal procedures that are outlined for the coordination of activities, and to which all staff are expected to comply. Rules are intended to be unbiased, functional, and for the protection of clients and staff, but there may be situations where staff view a rule as constraining. Social workers may learn that going outside the rules sometimes facilitates service delivery for their clients (for example, a male social worker making home visits by himself when policies require that a female staff member also be present), although this practice may be the source of many ethical dilemmas.

Productivity is a measure of the performance standards that all staff are expected to maintain in order to adequately contribute to the agency mission. Meeting or exceeding these standards results in positive evaluations, rewards, and ongoing employment. For social workers, productivity is often set in terms of number of clients seen, number of hours of client service provided, number of new cases open, number of cases closed, and so on. Social workers often experience conflict when pro-

ductivity related to quantity (also known as *outputs*) is given priority over productivity related to quality (client *outcomes*).

Documentation is an essential organizational activity, as it satisfies the requirements of sanctioning bodies and facilitates interprofessional communication about
client issues and other procedures. On the negative side, social workers sometimes
perceive that record-keeping demands become so time consuming that actual
service quality for clients is compromised.

Agency planning and goal setting is an essential activity for the agency's adapt-
ability and survival. Some staff are charged with the responsibility of monitoring
the agency's functioning and its interactions with the environment and planning
for the short- and long-term future. This sometimes involves adjusting the mission of the agency and its programs in response to environmental conditions.
Social workers may perceive that an organization, in an effort to survive, is moving closer toward, or further away from, the interests of the clients it was originally intended to serve.

Culture refers to the unique and perhaps idiosyncratic patterns of behavior
within an agency that evolve over time. These patterns are considered valid
and are modeled as correct ways for employees to think and behave. They
tend to reflect the personal qualities of powerful members of the agency who
have come and gone. They are also the values and norms that guide agency behavior. For example, a spirit of collaboration or a spirit of authoritarianism can
characterize an agency's culture. An agency's culture may or may not be consistent with the social worker's value base. Still, every employee has influence on
the culture by introducing new ways of behaving.

Task Groups in Agencies

All agencies incorporate the regular use of task groups, whose purposes are to
accomplish a specific task or carry out an agency mandate (Toseland & Rivas,
2005). These groups, like almost everything else in the organization, are characterized by formal procedures related to the scope of communication, prescribed
roles, and levels of participant self-disclosure. Their composition is ideally based
on talent and expertise, and there is often a division of labor within them. As
members of agencies, social workers may participate in any of the following
types of task groups:

> *Committees* come together by appointment or election to accomplish a task.
> They are often short-term in duration. (Example: Social workers who
> meet to consider ways to improve service delivery to pregnant
> teenagers.)
>
> *Administrative* groups tend to be ongoing and help agency staff and programs
> to carry out their goals. They typically have authority to make decisions
> and act on them. (Example: A weekly meeting of social work staff and
> the social services director at a municipal hospital.)
>
> *Delegate councils* are comprised of appointed or elected members who repre-
> sent the interest of their agencies at interagency meetings. (Example:

Mental health agency representatives who meet regularly to improve interagency linkage communications.)

Agency teams are comprised of individual staff members with particular knowledge and skills who come together to share expertise for a particular purpose. These also tend to be ongoing. (Example: Interdisciplinary treatment teams.)

Social action groups engage in planned change efforts to alter some aspect of the social or physical environment. (Example: Social workers lobbying for increased funding for social services.)

Some professionals enjoy task groups, seeing them as an opportunity to constructively participate in the organization's activities. Other staff dread them as cumbersome and ineffective. For example, I always enjoyed the weekly case conference at one agency where I worked, which featured a free and comfortable exchange of ideas about providing direct services to challenging clients. On the other hand, I dreaded a social work departmental meeting, where the leader was (in my opinion) ill prepared (with no written agenda) and tended to delegate tasks to the rest of us without much discussion. A social worker's motivation to participate actively in task groups depends on several factors, including his or her feeling valuable to the project, feeling secure with the other members, and perceiving that there is an opportunity to grow professionally from the experience.

Common Administrative Challenges in Human Service Agencies

Organizations can work quite effectively toward achievement of their goals, often providing creative solutions to social problems. Two examples include those school systems that have developed the capacity to effectively educate children from disadvantaged backgrounds and the mental health systems that first designed community-based case management services for people with mental illnesses. Social workers share the responsibility of improving the quality of the agencies with which they and their client systems interact. Listed here are common challenges experienced in human service agencies that may lead to significant client care problems (Hepworth, Rooney, Rooney, Strom-Gottfried, & Larsen, 2006):

A lack of clarity that develops over time about the agency's mission or program purposes. External pressures, changes in the environment, changes in clients, and organizational rigidity can sometimes result in the agency's losing focus on the clients it was intended to serve. Strategic planning can help to prevent this problem.

Variable program quality within the agency due to such factors as differential resource investment, staffing patterns, workload, standards for staff competence, and the relative emphasis on efficiency versus effectiveness.

Difficulties insuring that all clients whom the agency is intended to serve have access to those services. Members of the target population should have awareness of the agency and its services, be able to make convenient contact with the agency, have access to competent staff, and not be denied services due to racial, cultural, and language differences.

Upholding client dignity with regard to eligibility requirements, admission protocols, confidentiality practices, and staff attitudes.

Recruitment and hiring practices that foster staff demographic resemblance to the client populations they serve.

Efficiency of resource use (such as time and money) so that all members of the target population can be served. Some agencies, for example, promote short-term interventions to insure that all clients in high-demand programs can be served.

The quality of interprofessional relationships. Specialization and hierarchy can lead to members of different departments not working together cooperatively. Differences in status among the professions (social workers vs. nurses or doctors, for example) may impede the potential for collaborative work.

The quality and range of interagency relationships. Staff need to maintain constructive linkages with other agencies for referral purposes.

The challenge to agency managers of regularly accessing information and feedback from all relevant stakeholders (people with a vested interest in the agency), both inside and outside the organization, when making decisions about policies and procedures. Sometimes information is *not* pursued because, unfortunately, people in power may not wish to entertain perspectives that might differ significantly from their own.

The use of evaluations of staff performance, program quality, and agency functioning. Evaluation processes do not always receive substantial attention because resources tend to be invested into service provision. When they are done, evaluations may be based on criteria that social workers perceive to be relatively insignificant (numbers of clients served vs. clients' quality of life).

Staff alienation and burnout (emotional and physical exhaustion) may be brought on by adverse work conditions. Staff may lose their enthusiasm for their jobs (and clients) because of perceived oppressive agency policies including paperwork, high caseloads, lack of rewards, and a lack of opportunity for career development.

With this overview of characteristics that are common to all organizations, we now consider several theories of how organizations are, or should be, structured. The type of organization in which a social worker is located, and the other agencies with which he or she interacts, have implications for how change activities can be pursued. The reader is encouraged to decide which type of organization described here most closely resembles his or her own.

ORGANIZATIONAL THEORIES

Four specific organizational theories are described next. They are not exhaustive of the literature in this field but are intended to provide a range of perspectives. The theories are described in chronological order of their development.

Scientific Management

This theory was developed during the early years of the 20th century. As implied by its name, it is a highly rational theory of organization, operating with the assumption that there is "one best way" for an organization to achieve its goals (Waring, 1991). Agencies that are organized in this manner are rigidly structured with clear hierarchies, decision-making processes, and levels of power. All employees are considered to be cogs in the machine, and relatively few of them participate in policy making or problem-solving activities. Inherent in this theory is a one-dimensional view of people as technology. It is assumed that employee productivity and loyalty results only from monetary incentives. Good work is rewarded, and agency loyalty is enhanced, with the carrot of more money.

This theory fits well in the context of its era, emerging during the early years of mass production in the United States. Efficiently maintaining such delicate operations as assembly lines for the production of material goods required well-coordinated systems of task-focused human input. The theory of scientific management is considered to be out of date now, particularly in human service agencies that are not in the business of producing material outputs. Its elements, nevertheless, continue to exist in many agencies. Some social workers in highly bureaucratic social services programs may feel, for example, that their primary value to the agency is in the production of service hours that enable the agency to draw money from funding sources. Social workers in these agencies may complain that they have little potential impact on the lives of their clients, working as people processors, only seeing them once or several times to complete paperwork in an impersonal manner. When social workers complain of burnout, their feelings may be rooted in the agency's drift toward this type of management.

Human Relations

The human relations approach to organizational management developed in the 1920s. Despite its name it is not radically different from the school of scientific management but it incorporates broader assumptions about employees and their work-related needs. Agency managers acknowledge the importance of social factors and other nonmonetary incentives in the lives of employees (Porter & Bigley, 1995). The agency attempts to secure employee productivity and loyalty by supporting their informal social interactions during the workday—so long as productivity standards are met!

From this perspective social workers and other agency staff should have the opportunity to enjoy the company of their work peers and perhaps organize their workday with some individual discretion. Social workers might be encouraged to participate in supervision groups and other types of staff development activities to maintain their motivation and professional enthusiasm. Administrators might also encourage staff to enjoy social time during lunch or at breaks, or to visit in each other's offices—again, so long as productivity requirements are met!

The human relations management style is criticized because it is still rather rigid and not empowering of employees. Managers are not interested in employee participation in major decision-making activities for the organization, and they are still paternalistic in their expectations of submission to policies and procedures. Social workers and other professional staff in these systems may feel that their roles are circumscribed and too strictly limited, which conflicts with norms of professional autonomy. This approach maintains the negative assumptions about people as employees that were described earlier.

Diversity.   At this point in our discussion it is important to recognize that the diversification of the workforce with regard to gender, race, ethnicity, disability, culture, and socioeconomic status has great implications for how human service organizations are managed. While it was probably never true that all people have similar needs and motivations regarding their work, it is even less true now. The important questions regarding why people work, what they want from their jobs, how they develop organizational loyalty, how their enthusiasm can be maintained, and how they might contribute to the development of the organization are more difficult to answer than ever. Successful organizational management today requires the ability of administrators to nurture a diverse workforce, and it appears that rigid policies and procedures as described in the previous two theories are not effective toward that end.

Contingency Theory

This is an open systems approach to organizations that emerged during the 1960s. Contingency theory assumes that there is no single best way to manage an agency in a given situation. An agency should have built-in flexibility that enables it to respond quickly to changing environmental circumstances (Donaldson, 2001). Variables from both inside the agency and its external environment have continuous impact on organizational practices—perhaps even its primary mission. These variables include the size of the organization; its political and funding environment; the community culture; its resources; managerial assumptions about employees; and existing strategies for service provision. Administrative tasks include analyzing the agency in its total context, taking advantage of opportunities, and minimizing constraints. These agencies are less structured, and more fluid, in an effort to be adaptable to turbulent environments. They are hierarchical but with fewer levels than the other agency types, and their job descriptions allow for some employee discretion in attending to tasks. From this perspective successful organizations must be able to adjust their structures in response to environmental change.

According to contingency theory there are three types of employees in an agency. The *technical* employees carry out the agency's mission and day-to-day activities. Social workers in direct practice positions would likely be a part of this system as they go about the business of working with clients. The *managerial* staff are the people located within the agency who monitor and direct the agency's activities. These include supervisors and program directors. The *institutional* personnel, including such people as the executive director and the board of directors, primarily deal with interactions between the agency and the environment. Social workers are sometimes surprised to find that their executive directors spend little time in the agency, or with "line" staff, but this may be appropriate. Members of the institutional system attempt to influence the environment and prepare responses to events that might affect agency operations. The director who identifies a need for a neighborhood-based intervention for shoplifters, or who secures new funding for helping refugee families, may be working effectively from this perspective. A contingency approach sees the successful leader as one who is keenly aware of the forces most relevant to his or her behavior at any given time, and who is able to behave appropriately in the light of these circumstances.

Contingency theory adds an emphasis on the agency environment that is critical for human service agencies. It recognizes that multiple organizational forms and management styles should be the norm. One of its limitations, however, is its assumption that managers will react rationally in response to organizational threats or changes. It ignores the fact that managers may act politically or pursue agendas that circumvent rational responses to the agency environment. Further, it has little to recommend about activities within agencies. That is, service providers inside the building should be managed in a way that encourages their creativity and builds on their particular strengths, but the theory does not focus on these internal systems. Still, contingency theory is a more empowering theory than the first two, as it promotes the idea of employee flexibility.

Theory Z and Total Quality Management

These two management theories, developed since the 1980s, are similar in that they both emphasize organizational *process* rather than outcomes, and actively encourage the management participation of all employees (Rampersad, 2001; Ouchi, 1981). Theory Z represents an attempt to incorporate organizational practices from productive Japanese companies into the United States. Its basic principle is that *all* staff, not just professional administrators, should contribute to *all* decision-making processes in the agency. The organization builds in regular opportunities for staff to make recommendations about practice, program, and policy issues, and insures that managers will consider them. One feature of this approach is the *quality circle,* where employees set aside time to brainstorm (note this reference to the problem-solving step described in Chapter 3) about ways to improve agency practices. Managers also attempt to establish and model a norm of cooperation among departments and staff levels. In its pure form, this theory includes few formal leaders and a flatter, more fluid organizational chart.

Total quality management (TQM) is similar to Theory Z but has more of a focus on agency outputs rather than internal processes, whether these are goods or services, and gives managers the responsibility to create procedures that will reinforce the agency's primary goals. Still, it values staff discretion in how jobs are carried out and supports the use of quality circles and other team-building approaches. The TQM approach rejects rigidity in the form of rules and efforts to achieve stability, which is considered to be an elusive (and stagnating) state of affairs. One of its attractions to social workers, and their dedication to client empowerment, is that TQM is especially sensitive to consumer input and formal evaluation practices to determine if consumer needs are being met.

Both of these theories hold much appeal for social workers (and other employees) who as professionals feel that they have earned the right to seek opportunities to provide input into program development and management and have discretion in how they intervene with clients. One problem with the approach, however, is that in order to work effectively it must be implemented for all staff within an agency. While no director is likely to object to the idea of staff and consumer input into agency operations, in fact many of them are reluctant to give up the power that comes with their positions. Further, shared decision making takes time, and directors often believe that quick action is required to insure agency survival.

In summary, American organizational traditions are such that managers are not always comfortable giving real power to agency staff and clients. Staff can become resentful if this approach is espoused in principle but not in practice, or if it is open to only a subset of agency employees.

AGENCY POWER AND POLITICS

All of the organizational theories described so far in this chapter assume that agency functioning is or should be based on rational systems of rules and roles. Some theorists believe alternatively that *informal* power and politics should be a greater focus of agency analysis (Ehin, 2004). The example at the end of the last section shows how agency factions (or subsystems) have some unique interests and can become mobilized to action in ways that seem unrelated to agency purpose. Both of these concepts in large part fall outside formal organizational charts. That is, power is the ability to influence the actions of others even when this influence is not formally incorporated into a position description, and politics is the process whereby this influence is used. These two concepts recognize that agency employees may hold diverse goals and interests rather than agree on a single unifying mission. Any action performed in an agency includes two purposes—to further the organization's goals *and* to further the individual's self-interest.

Power often derives from an individual's location in the agency's hierarchy, but it can also derive from other means. Think about a time in the past when another professional influenced your behavior because he or she was persuasive, had charisma, was intimidating, was your friend, or you were accustomed to doing each other favors. These other people may have more influence on a social worker's behavior than a supervisor may. For example, you may notice (as I have) that your clients are languishing on a nearby housing agency's waiting list while a colleague, who is the friend of a program director there, always receives quick placements for her clients. Learning how power is acquired and used in an agency can be the key to understanding how it operates. It is rare that the exercise of agency power and politics can ignore formal agency procedures, but it can work around them in various ways.

A Note on Interprofessional Relationships

The importance of efficient and productive staff relationships is acknowledged in every theory of organizations. Promoting positive relationships among professional staff, which have implications for the well-being of agency clients, is a particularly complex challenge in "host" human service organizations. Professional staff there usually maintain certain boundaries between themselves and members of other professions. These boundaries represent demarcations of areas of expertise between groups and are based on bodies of knowledge, language, values, histories, and intervention preferences (Teram, 1999). Professionals tend to assert that the problems relating to their specialty should be kept within their domain. Further, members of different professions often occupy different positions and levels of power in the organizational hierarchy. Still, separation from other staff may also result in a sense of exclusivity that inhibits the sharing of information, or any real sense of partnership, about clients (Petronio, Ellemers, Giles, & Gallois, 1998).

The social worker's ability to successfully coordinate interventions for clients requires an ability to manage these boundaries—to work with members of other professions in a way that respects areas of expertise but also facilitates cooperation. This is not at all an easy task and requires special tact and social skills. This theme will recur as we continue to describe intervention techniques and case applications.

AN AGENCY ASSESSMENT OUTLINE

Organizations rarely reflect the ideal types listed. With their unique histories, purposes, personnel, and environments they may contain elements of all four types. Using Figure 11.1, a social worker may determine, for example, that his agency is characterized by a relatively small size and flat hierarchy, but at the same time has power concentrated in the hands of a few managers and little emphasis on staff processes for decision making. Another agency may have a steep hierarchy but also many social incentives for workers and a strong focus on consumer interests. While this is a subjective exercise, estimating how features of one's agency would be placed on the grid can help the social worker understand why the agency operates as it does, and perhaps how he or she can address problems related to its functioning.

The outline that follows provides another, more detailed means of assessing one's agency. This outline contains a set of questions to help the social worker become familiar with the agency's mission, major programs, client population,

Large size/Tall hierarchy . . . . Small size/Flat hierarchy
Structured   Informal
(strict job descriptions) . . . . (some worker discretion)
Emphasis on outcomes . . . . Emphasis on process
Material incentives . . . . Social incentives
Concentrated power . . . . Staff empowerment
Closed system . . . . Environmental focus
Agency focus . . . . Consumer focus

F I G U R E 11.1 Dimensions of Organizations

community environment, supervisory practices, and record-keeping practices. Additionally, it helps the social worker discover how the profession is defined within the agency and what its major service gaps might be. (Because no agency has the resources to do everything it wants, all agencies have service gaps, although how these are articulated depends on the point of view of the beholder.)

The agency. What is the mission of the agency, and its various programs? What client population does the agency or program serve? What are its demographic characteristics (age, gender, race, and socioeconomic status)? What problems related to the agency mission do clients tend to experience? Do any subgroups of the client population seem to experience these problems most strongly?

The community. What geographic area does the agency (or program) serve? Where is the client population located within that community? What major challenges (that may not be directly related to agency mission) affect the client population in the community? What other community agencies and groups provide services to the client population?

Service gaps. Are there any services not being provided, or not being provided adequately, to the client population with regard to original agency intent? How did these service gaps develop? Are they due to agency or community limitations? Have efforts been made by agency administrators to address service gaps?

Social work practice at the agency. What is the definition of social work practice in the agency, based on the perspectives of agency staff (social workers and others)? What are the activities of social workers within the agency? Are social workers primarily focused on service to individuals, groups, families, organizations, or the community? Highlight the major differences between social work practice and that of other services in the agency.

Supervision and evaluation. Are professional staff supervised and evaluated? How so? How often? Are there agency policies that support ongoing staff development and training? Do program standards exist to determine the quality of services? If so, who is responsible for this activity?

Record keeping. What records and statistics do social workers need to compile? Do they serve an employee accountability function? Are records used to evaluate services? If so, how?

Having considered issues relevant to agency functioning, we now turn to a discussion of ways in which social workers can intervene in their agencies, for the good of clients and, hopefully, the staff.

AGENCY INTERVENTION

The focus of this chapter has thus far been on organizational theory and assessment. Using this information as a basis to make decisions about agency-level intervention, we note here that change can be categorized into the following three types (Meenaghan, Gibbons, & McNutt, 2005):

People-focused change refers to changes made in the values, knowledge, and skills of agency staff. One example is the instituting of a monthly professional development series for all social workers at an agency. There could be many good reasons for such a program; one might be management's desire to enhance the quality of work being provided by the agency social workers.

Technological change refers to the process of service delivery, and often involves material adjustments. An example is the introduction of standardized charting checklists on computers for social workers to use after their client visits. This change might be implemented to increase the efficiency of charting activities and allow social workers to have more time to spend with clients.

Structural change refers to the ways in which agency units interact. An example is the establishment of regular interdepartmental team meetings among professional staff, implemented for the better coordination of services to the clients they share.

A social worker may also attempt to implement changes at any of three organizational levels (Netting, Kettner, & McMurtry, 2004). Generally speaking, the *broader* the scope of the proposed change, the *more difficult* it will be, since more people and more interests will be drawn into the process. Thus, *policy* changes that apply to all staff and all programs in an agency are the most difficult to realize. Examples of policy changes include changing an agency's hours of operation, requiring all staff to work evenings or weekend hours, changing the criteria for annual evaluations, and mandating the adoption of a short-term intervention model by all professional staff.

Program changes are less difficult to implement as they pertain to smaller groups of staff whose interests are more common. Examples of program changes include requiring home visits by social workers in a family service department and allowing phone contacts to be counted as billable service by case managers who provide community-based interventions. *Special projects,* because they are short-term, carried out by few staff members, and usually inexpensive, tend to represent the least difficult level of agency intervention. For example, a social worker may be permitted to initiate a family support group program on a one-time-only basis to see if the idea has merit as an agency program. If it does, the project may be revisited as a program change.

Generalist practitioners have a unique holistic perspective on systems functioning and can thus act as perceptive change agents. We will focus on interventions related to small-scale research projects.

A list of agency components that may be a target of the social worker's change efforts was presented earlier.

Agency Opposition to Change

The social worker should understand that most organizations by nature tend to be resistant to change (Schmid, 2004). They represent patterned, structured sets of activities that have evolved as efficient ways to serve client populations. They feature clear specialization and separation of staff functions and programs, and strict divisions in professional roles. While it is good that organizations offer efficiency through their divisions of labor, these characteristics contribute to a slowness to change. The 10 items listed next are intended to help the social worker understand that the manner in which his or her change effort is perceived by the organization at large will have much influence on the outcome of the change effort. It will also help to illustrate why the levels of change described earlier have different chances for success.

1. Perceived advantage is important. The more people inside the agency who will benefit from the proposed change, the better its chances (but remember that administrators, middle managers, and line staff have different perspectives on "benefits").
2. The less effort (time and energy) required for the change process, the better. The fewer risks involved (how change might harm the program or agency, through lost money and other resources), the better.
3. The fewer "hidden costs" (the less-than-obvious personal and financial costs related to making a change), the better.
4. The simpler the plan (regarding comprehensiveness), the better.
5. The greater the perceived capacity of the agency or program to change (with staff and resources), the better.
6. The narrower the depth or extent of change, the better (since this represents less disruption to existing operations).
7. The closer the proximity of key administrative staff to the change initiator, the better (because administration can monitor the process).
8. The greater the consistency of the change idea with prevailing agency ideology, the better.

9. The greater the extent of staff perception of the need for change, the better.
10. The lesser degree to which the change will reverberate through the entire agency structure, the better.

In summary, the social worker always needs to consider the impact of intervention on the organization at large, asking the following questions:

- Will my change activities improve resources and service availability?
- What specifically will be changed?
- Are these resources (for clients) considered to be essential by a majority of administrators?
- How will the changes affect the total supply of agency resources and services?
- What can be predicted about the short-term and long-term impact of the proposed change?
- Who will be indirectly affected by the changes (such as staff and clients from other programs or even other agencies)?

Program and Practice Evaluation

Much agency intervention is done through program and practice evaluation. This is the application of systematic methods to measure change processes and the results of change efforts. *Process* evaluations refer to the quality of interactions between workers and clients toward the achievement of goals. *Outcome* evaluations refer to the results for clients stemming from those interactions.

Also included here is an outline for a social worker's agency research. With this tool social workers can identify and explore a perceived service gap or other agency problem issue. Remember that it is the responsibility of all social workers to make efforts to improve the services of their employing agencies (Westerfelt & Dietz, 2005). This proposal form essentially provides a step-by-step process for information gathering about an issue of concern, ideally with the support of agency administrators. The social worker must have some familiarity with basic research methods in order to use it effectively (for example, Monette, Sullivan, & De Jong, 2000).

    The problem. Present a clear, concise formulation of the practice issue (perceived service gap, problem, or topic of interest). What circumstances have contributed to the issue's development and persistence? What is the relevance of the issue for service delivery?

    Questions or hypotheses. Based on the previous discussion, compose a specific question, set of questions, or a hypothesis that your study will attempt to answer or test.

    Methods. What means will you use to gather information (such as interviews with key informants, a survey, literature review, review of existing records, and so on)? What people will be used to gather information (yourself, other staff, clients, board members, and so on)? What kinds of information will you gather (statistics, personal observations, existing written material, and so on)? How will you summarize the information you collect? What is the projected timetable for completion of your project (on a week-to-week basis)?

Strengths and limitations. Summarize the strengths of your particular research methods in producing a result that will provide useful information for the agency. All research studies have limitations. Note the limitations of your research methods for resolving the research questions or hypotheses (limitations in data collection, limited input from agency staff, a small sample, and so on).

We now present four examples of agency change activities, all of which were carried out by student social workers during their field placements.

Case Illustration: Consumers as Board Members.   Meals on Wheels (MOW) is a nationally known service designed to assist frail older adults and younger shut-ins with disabilities by providing them with a balanced nutritious diet. All MOW programs have a board of directors that work to implement and maintain facilitative policies to insure that the service is available to all qualified people in their metropolitan areas. This is an example of an agency-level intervention that occurred at one site.

At least once a month the local organization's 21-member board met to discuss financial issues, service improvements, and problems. This helped to keep the agency focused, and to solve many problems before they become serious. A concern of one social worker at this agency (Valencia) was that never during the history of this Meals on Wheels program had there been client involvement at board meetings. Although the board tried its best to act on behalf of the clients' interests, having clients attend board meetings would allow them the chance to voice concerns and ideas that the board may unknowingly overlook.

According to the local Meals on Wheels president, clients had been asked in the past to attend board meetings but showed little interest. Valencia reasoned that this could be due to a number of reasons. The types of clientele served are elderly or handicapped, and in most cases it was difficult for them to leave home. Another reason might be a lack of transportation, as most clients had no vehicle or were not able to operate one. A third reason might be a lack of interest. That is, clients may not have been made aware of the importance of their potential contributions to the board.

Valencia suggested to her supervisor that the MOW clients be made aware of the board and its operations, and that an offer be extended to them for assistance and transportation to the board meetings. She decided to pursue this issue because she thought that having no client involvement in policy making was a hindrance to the clients and to the agency as well. She felt that with a little effort the agency's stated goal of client participation might be achieved. Valencia's supervisor approved this project, seeing that it would address a problem in existing policy implementation. There was no risk and little cost associated with the project, so there was no opposition to the idea.

The question that Valencia attempted to answer was: Would the client population served by Meals on Wheels be interested in attending their monthly board meetings? Valencia gathered data by surveying 25 randomly selected MOW clients by telephone. She generated the sample from a computerized list, choosing every 10th client. Before administering the survey questions the selected clients were briefed on the purpose and activities of the Meals on Wheels board of directors. The first survey question was measured using a five-point Likert scale, ranging from a low of strongly disagree to a high of strongly agree. The following questions were asked of each participant:

- As a client, how valuable is the service that Meals on Wheels provides for you?

- Do you believe that a client has the right to be involved in the decision making at board meetings?

- Would you yourself be interested in attending board meetings?

- If yes, would you need assistance and/or transportation?

- If no, would a family member be interested in attending board meetings?

Three original participants were confused by the survey questions and could not respond. Valencia then chose the next person under their name on the sampling frame so that she secured responses from 25 clients.

The results surprised Valencia and her supervisor. An overwhelming majority of the sample was in favor of client involvement at board meetings, and about half were interested in attending. Of those wanting to attend, most would need some means of transportation and assistance. None of the respondents who did not want to attend meetings suggested a family member who would be interested in attending. All 25 clients responded that the service Meals on Wheels provides was extremely valuable to them. Neither Valencia nor her supervisor, nor any other staff at the agency, had expected such a positive response to this survey. The results had major implications for the Meals on Wheels agency. The administrators immediately recruited, with the social worker's participation, four consumers to serve on the board. With this simple study the agency had been sensitized anew to the importance of consumer participation and maintained the policy of consumer board membership with new vigor.

Case Illustration: Parent Participation at Sacred Heart Center.   Sacred Heart Center (SHC) was a community organization that attempted to improve the quality of life for residents of its surrounding neighborhoods. Although service provision was directed at families, the primary interventions occurred with children. Parent involvement in the preschool, school, after-school, and adolescent programs was often poor. Moreover, programs that targeted adults traditionally had low rates of participation despite organizational efforts at marketing. In order to help the agency fulfill its mission, a social work student named

William proposed to research factors contributing to the lack of parent participation at the agency. Until this time there had been few formal service evaluations at the 8-year-old agency. William decided that a quantitative measure of parent participation would enable the agency to better understand some factors contributing to this problem.

William set out to answer the following questions:

1. Do personal factors (such as time, transportation, finances, work, interest, and infant or toddler children) contribute to parental nonparticipation in agency programs?

2. Are parents satisfied with service provision and delivery at Sacred Heart Center?

3. Are parents motivated to provide feedback about agency programs and their participation in them?

William had more difficulty than Valencia (in the preceding example) in getting agency support for his study. His findings might have implications for agency *programming*, which is the second-most difficult area for agency change (behind policy). If the study resulted in recommendations for new or revised programs, administrative staff might be concerned about costs to the agency. On the positive side (for William), his area of interest was consistent with agency goals, was seen by many staff as advantageous and perhaps necessary for agency survival, and wouldn't overwhelm the agency's capacity to change. Further, William's supervisor was on the administrative management team, which kept him close to the executive director. On the negative side, there might be time and energy costs, extensive suggestions for change, and negative effects on other agency programs. William's supervisor ultimately supported his research, although she could not guarantee that the agency director would seriously consider his recommendations.

William prepared and distributed a survey questionnaire to gather information from the parents of children and adolescents who utilized agency programs. During its construction, the survey was presented to staff members for evaluation, revision, and approval. The final survey generated statistical data from 21 questions that measured factors contributing to parental nonparticipation. A Likert scale was used to rate client perceptions in five categories ranging from strongly agree to strongly disagree. Significant themes were then evaluated to specifically address research questions 1 and 2. For example, 7 of the 21 questions addressed the personal factor issue, while 14 spoke to parental satisfaction; this created a range of 35 and 70 points, respectively, in each category. By examining the frequency distributions in each of these areas, it was possible to determine the answers to the first two research questions. The answer to question 3 was gauged by the number of returned surveys. William decided that if the return rate fell within a predetermined range (45 percent or above), then parents would be considered to be motivated.

Teachers and their aides were utilized to distribute and collect this survey. Approximately 227 "Parental Satisfaction" surveys were distributed to parents when they came to the agency to pick up their children for the day. In the case of children transported by the agency, surveys were sent home with the children. Parents were given two weeks for survey completion and return. William sent a reminder memo to parents near the end of the second week. This memo included mention of an ice cream party for the children as an incentive for timely return.

William summarized his results in the following way:

The degree to which personal factors are influencing parental nonparticipation in agency programs. The frequency distribution in this category was concerning, as 76.2 percent of all survey respondents reported personal factors that seriously hampered (16.4 percent) or interfered (59.8 percent) with their involvement in agency programs. Only 23.8 percent of responses indicated limited interference. Thus, research question 1 was answered "yes," as the data appeared to indicate a relationship between personal factors and parental nonparticipation in agency programs.

The extent to which parents are satisfied with agency service provision and delivery. The results in this category were encouraging, as 78.7 percent of all respondents' satisfaction level was very good (49.2 percent) or excellent (29.51 percent). An additional 21.3 percent of parents rated program quality as adequate. No responses reflected a poor satisfaction level. Consequently, research question 2 was also answered "yes"; parents were satisfied with agency service provision and delivery.

The nature of personal factors indicated that time, transportation, finances, work, interest, and having infant or toddler children were factors that interfered with participation in agency programs. Slightly more than half the respondents (52.5 percent) displayed interest in Sacred Heart Center's offering more adult classes, seminars, and programs in the evening. One question revealed that a lack of time was a significant element in nonparticipation, and 49.2 percent of all respondents strongly agreed (4.9 percent) or agreed (44.3 percent) that parent leadership and parent meetings were scheduled at a time that was inconvenient. Thirty-two (32) percent of parents surveyed reported that it would be easier to participate in agency programs if SHC provided childcare services.

Research question 3 was answered by examining the survey return rate. A total of 227 surveys were distributed to parents, representing the number of individuals participating in Sacred Heart Center programs; 122 were returned. Since the measure was set at 45 percent, the return rate of 53.7 percent answered research question 3 by reflecting that parents were indeed motivated to provide feedback about agency programs and their participation in them.

This study had several implications for service provision and delivery at Sacred Heart Center. The research questions yielded data that identified personal factors as the major contributor to parental nonparticipation in agency programs. As such, these factors, which included work, interest, time, and infant or toddler children, needed to be addressed. Since clients indicated an interest in seeing an increased number of classes, seminars, and programs in the evening, the social worker recommended that the agency consider building on the few currently offered evening programs, or possibly providing new alternatives. Connected to

this issue were the problems of work and time interfering with parental participation. Finally, the infant and toddler care problem suggests that the community
and the agency might benefit from the implementation of an early childcare program. In fact, this was the one issue that the agency board decided to address,
and three months later such a program was implemented. William was pleased
that one of his important findings was used to change the center's programming.

Case Illustration: Length of Stay at the Salvation Army.   The mission of the
Salvation Army, where Latonya was placed, was to provide homeless people
with quality care in a safe, humane, Christian-centered environment. One of
the main goals of the Salvation Army was to help clients secure permanent housing. When men were accepted into the Salvation Army Shelter they were permitted an initial 14-day stay. This was not always long enough for clients to
make the transition from the shelter to permanent housing. If the client was unemployed when he came for shelter it was almost impossible to get into permanent housing within 14 days. If the client was homeless but working when he
came to the shelter, there was a possibility that two weeks would be enough
time to find permanent housing. For these reasons, the shelter gave extensions
to some clients if they needed them. An extension could be as little as one day
to as many as 14 days. The social worker decided whether an extension was
given, and for how long. An extension was only given to clients who were considered to be actively trying to better their situation. The clients must be working, following the rules of the shelter, and not causing problems among other
residents and staff.

It was the policy of the Salvation Army that once a client's time was up at
the shelter he could not return for 60 days. Further, a client could stay at the
shelter no more than three times altogether. The problem that seemed to be
occurring was that the men kept coming back. As soon as their stay was up,
they left, and 60 days later they were back again, looking for shelter.
Obviously, their housing situations had not significantly improved. A longer initial stay in the shelter was considered to be a possible answer to the problem of
recidivism.

The social work student, Latonya, selected this issue for study for two reasons. Within her own caseload, it seemed that all male clients asked for an extension to find housing. Further, agency administration was already considering
changing the number of days clients were allowed to stay in the shelter. Thus,
while this study might result in a policy change, Latonya had the backing of the
executive director. Any changes based on Latonya's study would likely be seen as
advantageous to the agency, consistent with its mission, and within its capability.

Latonya formulated two research questions, as follows:

1. Are people who stay longer than 14 days in the shelter more likely to get
    into permanent housing?

2. What number of days seems to be enough time to stay and find permanent
    housing?

Latonya first gathered information by reading case records and tracking sheets, talking to her own clients, and formulating a questionnaire. She randomly selected a sample of 58 men who had stayed or were staying at the shelter during the previous five months. She used the tracking sheets to see when the client came to the shelter and how long he stayed. Next, Latonya looked through case records to determine if the clients went into permanent housing after leaving the shelter. She analyzed the information by determining whether the percentage of the men staying in the shelter longer than 14 days and successfully obtaining permanent housing was greater than the percentage of men staying 14 days or less. In her questionnaire Latonya asked residents what they felt was enough time to stay in the shelter and be able to find permanent housing.

Latonya found that out of 58 men who stayed in the shelter, 59 percent ($n=34$) secured permanent housing. Of the 59 percent who found permanent housing, 11 did so in 14 nights or less, with 7 being the average number of nights stayed in the shelter. It took the other 23 residents more than 14 nights, with the average number of 32. Out of the 41 percent ($n=24$) of the men who did not find permanent housing, 5 stayed in the shelter 14 nights or less, with the average number being 13. Nineteen (19) of the men stayed at the shelter more than 14 nights, with an average of 44 nights. Of the 58 men in the sample, 14 of them were bell ringers or monitors, a group that is automatically given a longer initial stay of up to 3 months. Eight (8) of them found permanent housing during an average stay of 47 nights, while the other 6 residents stayed an average of 61 nights and did not find housing.

Latonya had a return rate of 13 out of 25 questionnaires distributed. Seven of those clients were working and the others were unemployed but looking for work. Four of the men received public assistance in the form of food stamps. Not one of the respondents had yet found housing. When answering the question about how long they thought was enough time to find permanent housing, the answers ranged from 14 to 90 days, with an average of 30 days.

The results showed that staying at the shelter for longer than 14 nights did help some people get into permanent housing, but did not help others. The answer to the second question (regarding the number of days that seems to be enough time to find permanent housing) ranged from 30 to 90 days for current residents. Among men who had found permanent housing (and the bell ringers/monitors) the average length of stay was 40 nights.

The results of this study helped the Salvation Army decide to make several changes to its program. Staff conducted further studies of the types of clients who tended to move quickly or more slowly through the program (such as age, demographic, health, and mental health characteristics). They adjusted the policy of the 14-day limit so that case managers could more flexibly set discharge goals for clients during the assessment process. A result of this study, then, was a greater individualizing of client care.

Case Illustration: "Gender Suitability" of Staff at a Homeless Shelter.   Social workers need to be sensitive to issues of gender and clients' perceptions of gender roles in an agency. If social workers allow or ignore gender stereotyping, they are contributing to the same oppression that they are fighting against. Thus, social welfare agencies need to be especially aware of issues of gender, even among an agency's staff. The silent message that is sent simply by the composition of staff may not be a message that social workers support or even intended to send. What follows is one social work student's (Serena's) story of assessing client perceptions of appropriate gender roles at her agency.

At the Metropolitan House Community Homeless Shelter (MHCHS) there were two types of staff—support services staff and general shelter staff. Support staff performed case management services; they acted as brokers, linking clients to resources in the community, providing support as clients make the transition from homelessness to a housing situation, and teaching clients new life skills. General shelter staff remain at the shelter overnight to ensure that agency policies and procedures were followed. They kept order in the shelter and ensured the safety of residents.

While looking at the gender distribution of shelter staff, Serena noticed that the entire support staff was female, and the entire general staff was male. Traditionally, in American society, there is a prevailing cultural belief that men and women are different. A common assumption is that men are by nature active, aggressive, rational, and concerned with autonomy, while women are passive, nurturing, emotional, verbal, and concerned with relationships (Bonvillain, 2007). The gender dynamics of the MHCHS staff were demonstrative of these assumptions. The support staff, which was concerned with developing relationships with clients and offering them support, performed a role that is similar to the traditional female role in society while the general shelter staff, who enforced rules and maintained order, performed a role similar to the traditional male role in society. Thus, the social worker decided to examine the gender dynamics among staff as a social work practice issue.

While the gender dynamics of the staff at the MHCHS had always been consistent with this pattern, it is unclear how this pattern persisted. The executive director contended that gender dynamics occurred accidentally. Still, if clients perceived that only one gender was appropriate in a particular staff position, then they would experience a lower level of comfort interacting with a staff person whose gender was not congruent with that traditional gender.

The purpose of Serena's project was to determine whether clients perceived that staff roles were directly linked to gender. Serena talked with her supervisor about the fact that her findings might have implications for agency policy (hiring practices and staffing patterns). The supervisor approved the study but advised Serena that the administration and board members may not act on any recommendations, given that the director had already concluded that the staffing issue did not present a problem for the agency.

Serena proceeded, and attempted to test the following hypotheses:

- Clients will perceive that one gender is better suited for each staff position.
- Clients will feel a low level of comfort interacting with a staff person whose gender is not congruent with the traditional gender norms of that position.

Serena gathered data relevant to her research questions with a survey questionnaire composed of closed-ended questions. She chose to use closed-ended questions because these tend to produce data that is simpler to analyze. She created her own research instrument, utilizing staff and a panel of experts to ensure its validity. Serena composed a list of potential questions and presented them to staff at the shelter as well as faculty at her School of Social Work. She utilized shelter staff to help administer the survey to the 40 shelter residents.

Thirty-two (32) out of 40 residents at the shelter participated in this project. Of the 32 responses, 11 (34.4 percent) were answered partially or incorrectly, and thus only partial information could be obtained from them. Twenty-five (25) percent of the respondents were females and 75 percent were males. As for the racial composition of the sample, 65.6 percent were African American, 28.1 percent were European American (white), 3.1 percent were Native American, and 3.1 percent were biracial (Native American and African American). Twelve (12) percent of the sample were between the ages of 20 and 30 years, 40.6 percent were between 31 and 40 years old, 31.3 percent were 41 to 50, 12.5 percent were between 51 and 60, and 3.1 percent were between 61 and 70. The largest portion of respondents was African American males between the ages of 31 and 40, who account for 31.3 percent of the sample.

The first portion of the survey was concerned with determining what clients perceived the duties of both types of staff to be. When asked about the role of support services, 43.8 percent of the respondents viewed the position to involve more feminine than masculine qualities, 40.6 percent viewed the position to involve more masculine than feminine duties, and 15.6 percent viewed the position to involve an equal number of masculine and feminine duties or qualities. As for the role of the night staff, 12.5 percent viewed the position to involve more feminine than masculine qualities, 68.8 percent viewed the position to involve more masculine than feminine duties, and 18.8 percent viewed the position to involve an equal number of masculine and feminine qualities.

The next part of the survey inquired about the most suitable gender to perform each type of staff duties. For the role of support services, 9.4 percent viewed males to be best suited to fill the role, 9.4 percent viewed females to be best suited to fill the position, and 81.3 percent viewed both genders to be equally qualified for the position. As for the role of general shelter staff (night staff), 31.3 percent viewed males to be most qualified to fill the role, 9.4 percent viewed females to be best suited to fill the position, and 59.4 percent viewed both genders to be equally qualified.

The remainder of the survey sought to determine the level of comfort clients would feel interacting with staff people who were not of the gender traditionally employed in that position. When asked to rate their comfort level for interacting with a female night staff person, 12.5 percent did not provide an answer, 9.4 percent indicated that they were not at all comfortable, 21.9 percent indicated they were somewhat comfortable, 15.6 percent indicated a high level of comfort, and 40.6 percent indicated that they were totally comfortable. As for the level of comfort interacting with a male support services staff person, 12.5 percent did not provide an answer, 3.1 percent stated that they were not at all comfortable, 3.1 percent would experience a low level of comfort, 12.5 percent indicated that they were somewhat comfortable with the idea, 18.8 percent indicated a high level of comfort, and 50.0 percent stated that they would be totally comfortable interacting with a male case manager.

The research hypotheses were not supported by the findings. The majority of clients indicated that they perceived both genders to be equally qualified to fill the roles of both support services and general shelter staff. Further, the majority of the respondents stated that they would be totally comfortable interacting with a staff person whose gender was not congruent with the traditional gender that was employed in that position. Thus, the majority of the residents at the shelter did not feel that the staff positions were linked to gender.

The data analysis did yield findings that may have implications for the agency, however. For instance, while a significant majority of the respondents did not perceive the role of case management to involve mostly feminine qualities and duties, 68.8 percent of respondents, a clear majority, did view the role of general shelter staff (night staff) to involve mostly masculine qualities. Additionally, while the majority of respondents indicated that either gender would be equally qualified to perform the role of night staff, a large number, 31.3 percent of respondents, did indicate that they perceived males to be best qualified. Further, more clients indicated that they would be totally comfortable with a male support services staff person than indicated comfort with a female night staff. Thus, there seemed to be a strong belief among a large number of respondents that the role of general staff was better performed by, and suited for, males. Thus, clients seem more receptive to the notion of accepting support from males than accepting discipline and order from females.

It was important for the agency administrators to note this finding because it was the role of all staff to enforce guidelines and to discipline clients when rules have been broken. Fortunately, the administration did take this finding to heart. As a direct result of this study, staff incorporated more information about staff duties during its client orientations, including an active de-emphasis of gender differences. Serena's work did have a positive effect at the program level in these ways.

The previous illustrations have included a variety of examples of social workers being effective change agents within their own agencies. Now we turn to a consideration of two common ethical dilemmas that can occur in agency practice.

ETHICAL DILEMMAS IN ORGANIZATIONAL PRACTICE

Value Principle: Service

Many clients of social service agencies must survive on low incomes. Thus, clients may be charged nothing (in some cases) for agency services or an amount that is relative to their income levels. This money, modest as it may be, is nonetheless critical to the agency budget. Agencies typically have policies stating that clients must pay for services either at the time the service is rendered, or on some regular basis. It may be the social worker's responsibility to collect those fees. For clients who fall behind on their payments there may be policies regarding an eventual termination of services.

A related element of agency solvency is the notion of billable hours. For agencies that receive external funding based on numbers of clients served, practitioners need to produce a certain number of billable hours each year in the form of face-to-face and sometimes phone contact with clients. Supervisors usually break this figure down into some weekly total so that social workers can track how successfully they are meeting their productivity expectations. Clearly, when scheduled clients cancel or do not show up for their appointments, the social worker suffers in the sense that he or she may not be able to meet those performance expectations. The social worker's consistent failure to produce a required number of billable hours may result in disciplinary action or a poor performance evaluation. Again, to minimize the prevalence of this problem the agency may have policies about terminating clients who no-show for a certain number of appointments. These practices are part of the realities of agency life, but a related ethical dilemma is: How can a client with significant needs, or who is at-risk for dangerous and perhaps life-threatening behavior, be terminated from service because of his or her income problems or difficulties with time organization?

Shawntee was a social worker who was having trouble meeting her billable hour expectations due to client no-shows, and many of her clients were far behind on their bill payments as well. Shawntee, who was one of three social workers in the adolescent services department of her agency, felt that agency termination policies regarding these practices were unfair to her and her clients because adolescents were inherently at-risk for missing appointments and payments. She argued that adolescents are often ambivalent about services, are often coerced by their parents into coming for services, and are forgetful by nature. Shawntee observed that social workers in other departments, specifically older adults and adult outpatient therapy, did not face the same risks. Agency administrators expressed empathy about Shawntee's situation but they did not want to begin making exceptions for individual staff or programs, fearing that doing so would result in ceaseless arguments among staff about differential expectations. Further, her supervisor felt that Shawntee could be more aggressive in confronting her clients about keeping their appointments and paying for their services each week. Shawntee disagreed with this assessment of her practice.

Shawntee did not want to terminate clients whom she felt needed social work intervention, and as a result she made several decisions that eventually cost her the job. She tried to collect fees, but when unsuccessful she did not terminate those clients from her caseload. She worked with those clients about developing acceptable payment plans, but she often went beyond permissible agency timelines in this regard. Further, Shawntee held onto most of her clients who no-showed beyond the prescribed limit. She continued to rationalize that these clients were good people doing their best with agency expectations. Shawntee's billable hours and collection rates were consistently low in the agency, and she faced occasional reprimands about her practices. She continued to advocate for adjustments to be made for staff in her program, but these were denied. Shawntee ultimately lost her job when it was discovered that she was padding her billing of Medicaid clients. That is, in order to partially make up for her no-shows, Shawntee overstated (and thus overbilled) the amount of time she was spending with those clients who paid nothing out of their own pockets. This was clearly cheating the government funding body. Shawntee left the agency feeling disillusioned, believing that agency policies were enforcing staff demands that were incompatible with the needs of certain clients.

Value Principle: Dignity and Worth of the Person

Social workers "respect the inherent dignity and worth of the person" (NASW, 1999, p. 5). They treat *every* person with care and respect, are mindful of differences and diversity, promote self-determination, and enhance all people's opportunities to meet their needs. Social workers need to be cognizant of their dual responsibility to individual clients and the larger society and work to resolve any related conflicts in a responsible manner. This is an overarching value principle that is inherent in almost all of the code's ethical standards, including those related to the agency context of practice. Value-based rationales for agency intervention may include increasing service accessibility for clients and enhancing client dignity with respect to how they are treated within agencies. The social worker may wish to ensure equitable amounts and quality of services for all types of agency clients.

A social work student named Carolyn advocated for agency change in a way that provides a simple, effective example of supporting client dignity. Carolyn was placed in a community agency that provided many programs to the rural county population. Some of these featured case management, or community-based assessment and linkage activities, while others featured psychotherapy, in which social workers spent more time with clients in their offices for problem-solving activities. All staff and students were expected to attend weekly case conferences in which practitioners had a chance to present their challenging clients for educational and help-seeking purposes. Carolyn noticed that the case management clients, such as her own from the older adults program, were never scheduled for presentations at these conferences. When she asked why, Carolyn was told that these clients "only required service linkages" and thus did not feature the complexity of other agency clients that provided for interesting learning experiences. Carolyn objected, respectfully arguing that all agency clients deserved the best service possible, and that case managers might have difficult situations to discuss with other staff regarding relationship development, dealing with uncooperative clients, setting limits, making thorough assessments, and deciding on appropriate linkages. Carolyn surveyed the other case managers and a consensus emerged supporting her point of view. Soon afterward the agency supervisors began reserving time for case managers to make presentations at the case conferences.

Social workers may be taking serious risks when they attempt to make changes within their agencies that are resisted by significant others, whether agency managers or members of other professions. Even when a social worker feels strongly about an ethical issue, he or she may be reluctant to act for fear of experiencing negative formal or informal sanctions.

SUMMARY

The employing agency is the context in which all social work practice takes place. While all agencies strive to fulfill missions that are intended to benefit certain client populations, the nature of organizational life is such that policies and procedures might at times hinder, as well as facilitate, the provision of effective social work practice. The social worker has an ethical obligation to both understand and intervene within his or her own agency to insure that the mission is appropriately formulated and addressed. This may be difficult, in that organizations tend not to change quickly, and also because agency assessment and intervention strategies may put the social worker in opposition to some of his or her coworkers and supervisors. Included in this chapter have been four examples of agency-level interventions that demonstrate how single social work students can successfully develop projects with concrete benefits for the agency and its clients.

TOPICS FOR DISCUSSION

1. Describe an organization you have worked for in the past, and which organizational theory best describes it. What characteristics of the agency lead you to your conclusions?

2. How can interprofessional teams work more productively for the benefit of clients? In your experiences, what appear to be the strongest obstacles toward that end?

3. Describe examples of agency leaders with whom you have been affiliated. What are the characteristics of the better and worse leaders? How can staff be trained to become good leaders?

4. One example was included in this chapter of how the dignity and worth of clients might be violated. What are some other examples of this process? How is it that many of these situations occur without intent?

5. Identify and discuss examples from your own agencies where change activities might be beneficial to clients and/or staff. Think about how your change ideas might benefit some clients or staff, and at the same time work against the interests of other clients or staff.

6. Consider the issues raised in the "Agency Opposition to Change" section of this chapter. Share examples of how you have seen these processes develop

in your agency, and how they were (or could have been) managed so that the change process could proceed.

ASSIGNMENT IDEAS

1. Assess your field agency (or another one with which you are familiar) with the outline provided in this chapter.

2. Develop an agency research proposal based on your agency assessment or other learning experiences.

3. Select any of the four case illustrations included in this chapter. Devise one alternative means of answering the research question. Compare the strengths and limitations of both procedures toward achieving a result that would be beneficial to clients.

4. Interview a social worker who is either the executive director of a social service agency or a department head. Ask the person to describe two agency procedures that may get in the way of social workers providing good client service. Find out what a social worker can do to minimize the possibility of these experiences, and how a social worker can generally best intervene in the agency toward the end of resolving an agency issue.

Chapter 12

Community Interventions

JENNIFER HAUSE CROWELL,
M. LORI THOMAS, AND
JOSEPH WALSH

The broadest level of intervention in generalist practice is community intervention. In community practice, the social worker's target population includes all members of a neighborhood, a city, and sometimes a state or the nation (in the context of social policy work). Community interventions can range from the social worker's participating with a neighborhood civic association on a children's recreation committee to participating in the development of a statewide antipoverty program. Community work requires that the generalist practitioner be able to work with small and large teams of other professionals and citizens toward some common goal. Interpersonal, political, and often leadership skills are important. This kind of work is never done alone! The purpose of this chapter is to review the purposes of community intervention, explore the types of assessment and interventions used at this level, and consider three examples of generalist community practice.

To review briefly from Chapter 7, a *community* consists of people bound together by geography or network links who share common ties and interact with one another (Hutchison, 2003). There are many types of communities, and they may be territorial (based on geography) or relational (based on interactions). Two theories of human behavior development with relevance to community practice are social learning theory (people learn to behave by seeing how the behavior of others is reinforced) and social exchange theory (people give to others so that they may receive in turn). Four possible perspectives of client groups on their communities include the community as a set of geographic relationships, a place where conflict occurs, a harmonious social system, or a place where holistic social bonding can occur. All communities exist to provide their participants with so-cial support—relationships that provide citizens with actual assistance or feelings of attachment to other people (Hobfoll, Freedy, Lane, & Geller, 1990). Communities may not, however, always fulfill these desired functions. As articu-lated in the PIE assessment system (see Chapter 1), social systems where problems may be located include the economic, health, education, legal, and affectional systems.

The roles of the social worker in community practice include those of *prob-lem assessor, broker of clients* with existing resources, *broker of resource providers* with one another toward better service coordination, *advocacy,* and *service evaluation.* Three general types of community intervention are described in this chapter, in-cluding *neighborhood and community organizing, program development,* and *political or social action.*

A COMMUNITY ASSESSMENT OUTLINE

The following assessment topics can help generalist practitioners to examine a potential community-based problem or need and determine whether it merits addressing (Netting, Kettner, & McMurtry, 2004).

Characteristics of the community population(s). This refers to the demographics of the community, and includes the boundaries of a perceived client population within the community (that is, whether they are concentrated or scattered). Census bureau information can be helpful in this regard, as it provides data about small tracts of a locality with regard to such variables as family size, employment, income levels, and ethnicity.

Problem profile. A social worker who initiates a community assessment proba-bly has a potential problem in mind for which he or she is seeking information. In this step the social worker should assess (through a broad or limited survey) the assumed client population's perceptions of their needs, and their perceptions of the community-at-large's responsiveness to them. (The target population may well include people other than social services clients.) Archival data from agen-cies where members of the client population receive services can also be helpful in providing this information. Strict confidentiality needs to be observed when seeking this type of data, of course. The social worker can also review agency and government policies to determine if there is additional support for the client population's perceptions of their needs.

Differences in community participation among community groups. The social worker needs to determine if there are any barriers that inhibit the client population from participating in aspects of community life, as well as whether there is evidence of discrimination, and what groups exist in the community (who may comprise the target system) to advocate for or oppose the client population.

Community values related to dealing with the presenting issue. This may be evidenced by the different perspectives held by community actors and the sources of formal decision-making power within the community. More broadly, the social worker can examine existing community norms about giving and receiving help, and whether the client population can participate in decisions that affect the area.

Social organizations within the community, including other community agencies that are major service providers to the target population. The social worker can examine formal social and material support resources that are available for community use, public and private resources that exist to deal with community member needs, and what other resources may be needed in the community, from the perspectives of various groups.

Location of power. This issue refers to which people or groups control the resources (financial, informational, and social) required for making changes. It also pertains to the roles of citizens and consumers in service control, who makes decisions in the community, whether power is localized or spread among many people and groups (depending, perhaps, on the issue), and the extent to which community members have access to the decision-making process.

For all of these activities, the social worker may consult a variety of data sources in addition to those already mentioned. *Key informants* are community members who have some awareness of the problem situation. They may include business leaders, social agency leaders, educators, leaders of charitable organizations, church ministers, and perhaps other well-known personalities in the area. They also include people recognized by those who experience a problem as having relevant knowledge and influence. The social worker can determine the identities of key members of a community by informally asking questions of colleagues such as "Who runs the town?" "Who are the most economically powerful people?" and "Who is influential because of the high regard people have for him or her?" The social worker can *attend any public forums* where the issue of concern is discussed. These include meetings of the school board, city council, neighborhood associations, and others. Finally, through *surveys of community residents* the social worker can gather data from a cross-section of residents. This process yields rich data but can be time consuming and expensive.

Following the assessment process, the social worker should be ready to *specify a topic for analysis* and select appropriate goals and intervention strategies.

TYPES OF COMMUNITIES

As the social worker becomes familiar with the community, he or she may be able to categorize it as one of six types. This step can be helpful in determining interventions that are most likely to be helpful to the target population (Meenaghan, Gibbons, & McNutt, 2005):

- Integral—characterized by a high level of resident participation in community affairs both in that community and in surrounding areas.

- Parochial—a self-contained community where there is interaction and stability but no external focus.

- Stepping stone—a "high participation" community where there is also high turnover because of residents' moving away when they reach a certain income level or their children reach a certain age.

- Transitory—characterized by a high rate of change and instability, as residents frequently move in and out.

- Anomic—little cohesion is evident among members of the population.

- Diffuse—there is minimal interaction in the internal life of the community.

Community intervention always involves bringing together members of a community. A sense of community "type" thus helps the social worker understand how residents interact with one another, and in what circumstances they do so, so that coalition building can be organized in a manner that is appropriate.

Following community assessment, the social worker may select one of the broad intervention strategies described next.

INTERVENTION STRATEGIES

The social worker may or may not seek official sanction for his or her community interventions. The practitioner may be working in opposition to existing community norms and practices (bucking the system, so to speak), and if so he or she will establish legitimacy from members of the client and action populations, as well as the NASW Code of Ethics. If the practitioner is working in collaboration with members of powerful community systems, however, he or she may seek an official sanction for investigating the problem. This sanction could be provided by an administrator from the social worker's agency or from another agency interested in the problem issue. Sanctioning is often secured by the formal designation of a task force including community leaders who can lend support to the assessment effort.

The three major general intervention strategies in community practice are as follows (Fellin, 2000).

Collaboration

Members of the client system, target system (those from whom change is sought), and action system (all who participate in the change effort) agree about the issue of concern. The social worker can thus engage in a collaborative process of problem solving with members of all three groups. An example of this is when the physically disabled members of a school system (and their families) indicate a need for greater access to school buildings, and the school board and administrators agree that such changes should be made. Intervention will not necessarily be easy, but it will include participants who can work collaboratively about the basic issue.

Campaign

The client, target, and action systems communicate well and have positive regard for one another, but lack consensus about the problem issue. The social worker's change tactics in this situation will include education, persuasion, and lobbying for greater consensus. An example is older adults who want transportation services to visit their spouses who experience extended stays in a physical rehabilitation facility. The program funders are sympathetic to the issue but do not believe that demand for the service justifies the financial investment, given the organization's other needs. In this situation the social worker will perhaps try to help the members of the action system understand the presenting issue more thoroughly, so that they will make it a greater priority for their financial support. Members of the client population will of course have an active role in this campaign process. This process may include conflict, depending on the receptiveness of the target system to the educational efforts.

Contest

The target and action systems are in opposition to each other about the presenting issue. The social worker, who supports the position of the client population and opposes that of the action system, must then initiate bargaining, negotiation, and perhaps confrontation tactics. As one example, the major funding body of a community mental health center made a decision to change its service orientation from one of "general adult counseling" to assisting clients with severe mental disorders. This change had drastic implications for staff (and existing clients) at the agency and was opposed by many of them. The social workers, as well as other staff participating in the contest, became highly confrontational through the process, participating appropriately in the series of planning meetings with county administrators but consistently presenting opinions and data to oppose the changes.

SOCIAL ADVOCACY

Social advocacy, with which the social work profession is closely identified, can be done at any level of generalist practice, but is often associated with community intervention. This is a process in which the social worker confronts the community's status quo toward initiating changes that will benefit some oppressed or disadvantaged group (Schneider & Lester, 2001). Social action activities usually occur in a context where the proposed change effort is anticipated as difficult and likely to encounter significant opposition. It is sometimes a long-term process and requires the social worker's persistence in the face of opposition and the slow pace of change. There are usually many people involved in a social advocacy effort (if it has a chance to succeed) and there are many ways for generalist practitioners to participate. One example of a social advocacy intervention was the collective efforts of faculty members at a School of Social Work to have gay and lesbian partners included in the university's formal statement of nondiscrimination.

There are many ways in which a social worker can engage in social advocacy, including:

- Gathering comprehensive information about an issue of concern

- Conferring with staff from other agencies about the needs of the client population

- Participating with interagency committees to generate broad support for an issue

- Providing expert testimony as requested

- Educating relevant segments of the community about the issue

- Contacting public officials and legislators for their education and to solicit support

- Organizing client groups to advocate on their own behalf

We now turn to an examination of three community intervention efforts by social workers.

COMMUNITY INTERVENTION: THREE
ILLUSTRATIONS

Described next are three examples of community-level intervention for generalist practice. The first example features a largely *collaborative* strategy, while the other two illustrate other guiding strategies of *campaign* and *contest*.

A Partnership with the Community Mental Health Association

One summer a group of four social workers came together, in conjunction with the local mental health center of a midsize city in the southeastern United States, to attempt to better understand the issue of postpartum depression and its impact on women in their community. This began as an informal observation by several staff social workers of clients who had experienced the problem but had little awareness of how to deal with it. The director of the mental health center had conducted an informal analysis of the resources and barriers women experiencing postpartum depression encountered in the community. What she found troubled her greatly. The response to postpartum depression in the community was fragmented and lacked consistency, with some agencies offering support groups and educational materials for women, and others not even addressing the issue.

A graduate of the local school of social work, the director turned to the school for assistance in formulating a response to the apparent need she had discovered. She and several graduate students came together to form a community task force around the issue of postpartum depression.

Community Assessment.   The first item of business for the task force was to conduct an assessment of the current barriers to education and treatment women experiencing postpartum depression faced in the community. The group interviewed 20 women who had received help for postpartum depression to become more thoroughly sensitized to their needs. Two of these women accepted invitations to become members of the task force. Next, the group identified local organizations and agencies that were most likely to come into contact with pregnant women or women with infants—agencies such as the health department, family planning centers, maternity centers, obstetric clinics, and hospitals. A representative from each agency was interviewed by a task force member and asked whether his or her agency addressed the issue of postpartum depression and, if so, in what manner.

The task force found that many agencies reported discussing postpartum depression with consumers, while others offered some literature on the issue in the form of brochures or fliers. A small number of agencies addressed postpartum depression through referrals to practitioners who were equipped to treat depression. Lastly, one agency conducted an in-house support group for women with postpartum depression. The materials each agency used were different, providing clients inconsistent information related to postpartum depression. The group also found that the state department of health, who maintained a web-based resource with fact sheets on various health issues, did not include postpartum depression on its website.

In addition to interviewing agency representatives, the task force examined local media reports related to postpartum depression. The results were disappointing. At that time, the two major newspapers in the city had never covered the issue, and no major news stories concerning postpartum depression had been reported on network television.

The task force was troubled by the discovery that prevention, screening, and treatment for postpartum depression varied depending on the agency or program a mother utilized. There was no central referral source or support group open to all members of the community. The task force discovered that barriers to addressing postpartum depression in the community included inconsistency in pre- and postnatal education programs, inadequate screening for depression, and a lack of detailed knowledge related to postpartum depression on the part of service providers. After assessing the state of affairs related to postpartum depression in the community, the task force was ready to take action.

Task Force Objectives and Intervention Tactics.   The task force determined that the overall goal of their efforts would be to increase awareness of postpartum depression in the community. After a detailed examination of the research they had done in the community, as well as the professional literature, the group came to the conclusion that they would concentrate on education as a means of increasing the community's awareness related to postpartum depression. The education efforts of the group would be three-fold, including efforts to reach expectant and new mothers, their partners, and their families. Finally, the group chose to target improvement in both the amount and the quality of the postpartum depression educational materials health care providers were able to access.

The intervention tactics chosen to accomplish each of the task force's objectives were evaluated in terms of:

- Their ability to reach the target audience (in this case mothers and health care practitioners)

- Their cost, measured in both time and money

- The degree and amount of contact necessary to accomplish the intervention (for instance, would a member of the task force need to make a phone call to accomplish the goal, or would sustained face-to-face contact in the form of weekly meetings be necessary?)

Finally, a social justice perspective was utilized in selecting intervention tactics in order to better understand issues related to access, equitability, and the utility of each tactic for diverse community groups.

Interventions.   The task force was able to rely on collaboration and campaign strategies in its work. Its educational efforts centered on creating and distributing a brochure that included a brief description of postpartum depression and the symptoms associated with it. The brochure also included a short list of resources specific to the area, such as the local mental health center, that women could contact for further information or assistance. The creation of the brochure was key to accomplishing the goal of increased awareness related to postpartum depression as it allowed the group to reach a large audience of women who may, at one point or another, suffer from the disorder. Further, the creation of the brochure was a significant contribution toward unifying ongoing efforts in the community. That is, those clinics and agencies that were addressing postpartum depression in one way or another now all had access to the same materials. Lastly, the brochure was an inexpensive and feasible means of contributing to existing efforts. The task force distributed the brochure to area clinics and agencies. The state department of health was the only agency to refuse acceptance, stating that it was required to use informational materials that had undergone an in-house approval process.

The second tactic used to help in providing community-wide education was the creation of a link on the state health department's website that, when used, could provide the reader with information about the signs and symptoms of postpartum depression. Again, the addition of the link to the existing website was seen by the group as a relatively inexpensive and feasible means of providing an educational resource to the community. The group was unsuccessful, however, in its efforts to have the state department of health create a fact sheet on postpartum depression, due to state department regulations about such activities.

Despite this setback, the nurses and nurses' aids in the prenatal care clinic agreed to continuously request that more information be made available to the women seeking care from the health department.

The third tactic chosen by the group was the creation and submission of an op-ed article to the two local papers that had the highest levels of readership and circulation in the area. The op-ed piece was designed to call attention to the issue of postpartum depression in the area. The ultimate objective of the submission was to bring more attention to the issue as well as to the efforts of the task force. This attention, the group hoped, would perhaps spur people to learn more about postpartum depression or at the very least put it somewhere on the community radar screen, perhaps leading to an article or editorial in the paper. The article was accepted for publication in one of the newspapers. The task force members agreed to periodically submit additional op-ed pieces in the future.

Fourth was the creation of a resource list for use by the Mental Health Association in referring consumers for assistance with postpartum depression. The association director was very interested in maintaining a list of area mental health practitioners who were trained or specialized in treating mothers suffering from postpartum depression. In order to create such a list, the task force members made hundreds of calls to area practitioners in order to learn, first, whether they were trained and comfortable treating women suffering from postpartum depression, and second, whether they were interested in receiving referrals for the treatment of the disorder. The result was an electronic database maintained by the Mental Health Association with a list of over 100 area practitioners who were interested in receiving referrals.

Finally, and most significantly, the task force, in cooperation with the local Mental Health Association, organized a meeting of local practitioners and agency representatives who were in contact with pregnant or recently delivered mothers in order to coordinate front-line efforts in addressing postpartum depression. Representatives from each of the major area hospital labor and delivery departments were present, as was a representative from a private birthing center, a state health department official, a reproductive health clinic representative, and the mental health association staff. This meeting was productive in that it resulted in a shared sense of purpose and a better understanding of what each service was doing to address the issue of postpartum depression. The participants shared stories of clients who had experienced postpartum depression and affirmed their commitment to better educating women and their families about the disorder. Further, the meeting allowed participating clinic and agency representatives to see how they might better coordinate their efforts for the good of the community as a whole. For instance, the group began discussing the potential for a community-wide support group for women with postpartum depression. The practitioner group and task force agreed to continue meeting on a regular basis in order to assist one another in the development of the brochure and the resource list of practitioners.

In reviewing their efforts, the members of the task force noted that some of their tactics were successful and others were not, at least not in the way the group had intended. For instance, the creation of the link to a fact sheet about postpartum depression on the state health department website did not materialize. Still, in reaching out and communicating with nurses and health care practitioners in that department, the group raised awareness about the issue, demonstrated community support for improved services for women, and encouraged the practitioners to pursue change through official channels. Additionally, an unintended consequence of the group's making such a large number of calls to area mental health practitioners was an increase in the practitioners' awareness about the issue of postpartum depression. The primary objective was to create a resource list, but in discussing the issue and the aims of the task force with the mental health practitioners, the group furthered their overall objective of greater community awareness. Overall, the group considered their efforts successful and some portion of the task force still maintained contact with regular meetings.

The Cobblestone Controversy Revisited

The following example of a university system was initially presented in Chapter 7 as a type of community. Here it is described in more detail how social workers were able to organize and implement a successful intervention with regard to an identified community problem. This is an example of the *conflict* strategy.

Officials at an urban university, one square mile in size and serving 15,000 students, embarked one summer on a campus beautification effort. This involved, in part, replacing several of the major pedestrian asphalt walkways that ran through the campus with new cobblestone streets. It is sometimes difficult for universities that emerge within urban environments to look attractive and distinct from the surrounding office buildings and neighborhoods, and university administrators were attempting to bring greater coherence, atmosphere, and architectural unity to the university landscape. These two walkways ran for approximately one-half mile and intersected at the midpoint of the campus.

The street renovations were done during the summer, when relatively few students were present on campus. The university planners had apparently not considered that these new walkways would be problematic for students with certain physical handicaps who required walkers and wheelchairs. When classes resumed in the fall, three incidents occurred during a two-week span in which students with disabilities fell due to the (intentionally) rough street surfaces. Fortunately, none were seriously injured, but the incidents occurred at a time when the university was attempting to come into greater compliance with state legislation about disability accommodations. Concern developed among some members of the student body (the incidents came to the attention of undergraduate student government) that the university was becoming *less* rather than more accessible to people with disabilities. One person who noticed the problem with the new walkways, even before learning of the three reported incidents, was a member of the faculty of the School of Social Work, who himself had a physical disability that required the use of a walker.

The faculty member decided to offer this perceived problem to students within his School of Social Work as an issue for advocacy intervention. Students in the school were required to take a course in social justice and many of them often expressed interested in participating in related activities. The school also had an ongoing Social Justice Committee, the role of which was to inform the student body of social justice issues in the area and to organize student participation in addressing some of them. The faculty member attended a meeting of this committee (which included about 12 members) and presented the issue. Many students were eager to work toward the goal of making the walkways safer. They were especially interested in this issue because it was relevant to an oppressed population within their immediate community environment.

Community Assessment.   The students and faculty members of the Social Justice Committee hoped that a "collaboration" strategy would be sufficient to resolve the issue with relevant university administrators. With that in mind, the participants undertook two actions. They:

- Contacted the university's Office of Students with Disabilities to (1) see if any additional reports of accidents had been reported, and (2) alert the staff at that office about the issue and solicit their participation in the problem-solving effort.

- Contacted university administration (the Facilities and Operations department, in the president's office) to alert them of the perceived problem and raise their awareness that some adjustments need to be made.

The Office of Students with Disabilities had received one additional report of a student in a wheelchair having difficulty managing the walkway. However, the director of the office agreed that the problem was significant for many other students and agreed to cosign any correspondence with university administrators about the issue, and to attend any meetings that might be held as part of the process. The second part of this strategy did not unfold so smoothly. While the Facilities and Operations administrators expressed sincere regret that some accidents had occurred, and admitted that some students might be "at risk" for accidents in the future, they reported that the risk was minimal in the larger context of student life, and that budgetary concerns precluded the paving project to be revisited at this time.

Objectives and Intervention Tactics.   At this point the committee decided that the "collaboration" strategy had not been effective, and that a "campaign" strategy was called for. That is, the committee felt that all university members were probably sympathetic to the needs of people with physical disabilities, but perhaps due to their limited awareness of the nature and scope of the problem, they needed to be educated. Thus the committee formulated the following additional strategies:

- Send three student representatives to a School of Social Work faculty assembly meeting to encourage the faculty to draft a formal letter to the university president and vice presidents, informing them of the concerns and requesting action.

- Arrange for three student representatives to accompany the two elected faculty members to a faculty senate meeting to make a presentation about the issue and request senate support in requesting action from the president's office.

- Send three students to an undergraduate student government meeting to educate student leaders about the issue, enlist their help in gathering more information, publicizing the issue through ongoing attention at its meetings, and possibly requesting action from university administrators.

- One member would contact the campus newspaper (published twice weekly) and encourage staff to devote an article to the issue and how it was being addressed.

Interventions. As a result of these efforts, a variety of relevant campus groups, including the Social Workers with Disabilities Association, the undergraduate student government, the faculty of the School of Social Work, and the faculty senate joined forces to petition the university administration to amend their mistake. Prior to this petition, members of the Social Justice Committee and Office of Students with Disabilities collected a great deal of information about the nature and effects of physical disabilities, the special challenges faced by these students, ways in which these challenges had been addressed at other campuses around the country, and trends in recent legislation regarding people with disabilities. This information was shared with all relevant target groups to help raise their awareness about the importance of amending the current problem with the walkways. The university was initially reluctant to make additional changes to the streets because of the financial cost, but a compromise was eventually reached in which 10-foot brick strips (also decorative) were installed in the middle of the cobblestone streets. The process took almost one year to complete, partly because the nature of the university bureaucracy was such that all processes of this sort moved very slowly. Many of the students involved expressed frustration with the slow pace of change, but the problem was satisfactorily resolved.

"Housing First"

In this third example of a community-level intervention, the stages of assessment, planning, and intervention are difficult to distinguish. This is partly because many of the activities were pursued within a local community in response to a federal initiative. The guiding intervention strategy is one of *campaign*.

Zarasun was hired in a midsize city (population 200,000) to participate in a project with a local nonprofit organization that provided transitional and permanent supportive housing for individuals and families who were homeless or at risk of becoming homeless. As her first project, she was assigned to participate in the coordination of a broad community initiative to introduce a new model of homeless services called Housing First. The project had started over a year earlier and involved a number of community organizations including other nonprofit homeless service providers, state government housing officials, state government mental health and substance abuse officials and service providers, state department of social services officials, local community service board service providers, local real estate experts, and local elected officials. This was truly a broad-based community development effort. Zarasun joined the project after an advisory committee and several subcommittees were formed. She would be one of dozens of people, professional and otherwise, participating in this project.

Housing First is a housing and service model for homelessness that emphasizes providing permanent housing before tackling other issues a person or family might face. Such programs generally secure housing early in a relationship with a homeless client and then provide other necessary support services, such as vocational training. The model of intervention stood in contrast to the predominant model of the time that provided services before a person is ready for independent and permanent housing. This predominant model was called Continuum of Care and began in cities throughout the United States in response to legislation initiated during the Clinton administration that required a continuum of services in order to receive federal funds for homelessness programs.

Community Assessment.   The Housing First model had proven to be effective in other parts of the country in providing housing and services for homeless individuals with severe mental illnesses and substance abuse problems. The Housing First advisory committee had considered two different models of Housing First, one that provides housing in a congregate setting (similar to an SRO, or single-room occupancy) and one that provided housing in apartments scattered throughout the city (scattered site housing). Because Zarasun's organization specialized in SROs, her advisory committee chose to use the congregate model and began searching for a site to convert into a Housing First building. This decision had already been made when she was hired.

Objectives and Intervention Tactics.   Zarasun discovered that the project had stalled because the Site Selection Subcommittee had not been able to locate a suitable property for a Housing First building. While the subcommittee continued its work, Zarasun sought to become better educated about the Housing First model and the target population. Through literature searches and informal interviews with key community informants, she was able to accomplish four things, including:

- Gaining a deeper understanding of how the Housing First model had been successful in other parts of the country
- Understanding the chronology of the model's development in her city and the influential people and organizations that were involved in the process
- Determining that there was a significant need in her city for such a model
- Beginning to build relationships with members of the community who would make possible the collaboration needed to implement the model

After gaining a greater understanding of the model and its initial development in her city, Zarasun began working with another local homelessness agency to better understand the problems faced by chronically homeless people and the problems the service delivery system faced in serving them. Together, Zarasun and a researcher from the local agency began to gather information that would serve as the basis for educational materials used to raise money to support the project.

Interventions.   Zarasun and her advisory group also participated in a series of meetings to discuss the differences between the Housing First and the Continuum of Care models with organizational leaders. While a majority of the leaders had agreed that the city needed help serving the chronically homeless who were severely mentally ill, the advisory group was concerned about the differences in the models and the conflict those differences might cause among the organizations serving the homeless population. In response to this threat, Zarasun helped plan a series of meetings as a means of educating and persuading organizational leaders about the importance of the Housing First model. This proved helpful, as a majority of the Continuum of Care providers became active supporters of the new model.

As a result of Zarasun's (and the task force's) efforts, the following goals were achieved.

A change to the Housing First model. A member of the site location committee approached Zarasun to share her concerns about the delay in finding a congregate housing site. Through conversations with this and other committee members, Zarasun convinced the advisory committee members to invite a proponent of the scattered site Housing First model to speak about the advantages and disadvantages of that model. The scattered site model was eventually adopted as preferable.

Productive advocacy with public officials and other service providers. Zarasun was faced with the task of explaining the logic behind putting a homeless person in a house without first requiring him or her to access services. The persuasiveness of Zarasun's points provided the task force with opportunities to confront some prevailing and stigmatizing assumptions about people who are mentally ill and homeless.

Fundraising advances. The social worker and an influential advisory committee member created a fundraising committee that led to sufficient funds to start a Housing First program in the city and support it for three years. The fundraising committee also created a plan that led toward the long-term sustainability of the Housing First project.

Within 18 months of Zarasun's involvement as the Housing First project coordinator, the first 10 chronically homeless individuals were housed in scattered sites throughout the city.

ETHICAL DILEMMAS IN COMMUNITY PRACTICE

Community practice is an arena in which all of social work's value principles can be supported. The case studies described in this chapter have illustrated how the participating social workers were helping people in need, addressing social problems, challenging social injustices, respecting the dignity and worth of all people, and recognizing the central importance of human relationships. Still, social workers quite often will face ethical dilemmas at this level of practice, especially when conflict tactics are utilized, around issues (for example) of confidentiality, competence to engage in certain kinds of activities, and interdisciplinary collaboration. The following is an example of a social worker's ethical dilemma related to a dispute with a colleague.

During one sensitive phase of the "cobblestone controversy" described earlier, a faculty member of the School of Social Work entered into a dispute with the university's director of the Office for Students with Disabilities. These two people had worked together in the past on several projects in which their interests were compatible, and their interactions had proceeded productively and congenially. The director had, as one example, been instrumental in the university's installation of electronic door openers at the main entrances to all buildings on the campus. The current dispute arose over a fundamental disagreement about the extent of the director's advocacy responsibilities with university officials for students with physical disabilities. The faculty member felt that the director was not assertive enough in pressuring university administrators to enact certain changes to the campus's walkways. The faculty member attempted to resolve this conflict with the director in a private meeting but eventually recognized, following a consultation with several other colleagues, that the director was in fundamental disagreement with his conflict tactics.

As a result of this impasse, the faculty member began speaking out publicly against the position of the director in the context of the current issue. He made her, in essence, part of the problem in the university's initial failure to respond in favor of the school's requests for corrections to the university's major walkways. He had to confront the director openly in several meetings and discourage her from further attendance at the task force's strategic meetings. This was a stressful interpersonal development for both people, but especially the director, who felt that a friend had betrayed her. She went to the dean of the School of Social Work to report her feelings and to request his assistance in mediating the dispute. The faculty member refused to do so until after the controversy was resolved. Afterward he approached the director to make amends, but this was not successful. The director felt that he had been unfair to her and was not willing to resume their former congenial relationship. While disappointed, the faculty member believed that his earlier decision to confront her office had been appropriate, given what was at stake for the university's students with disabilities.

SUMMARY

In most forms of community-level intervention the generalist practitioner is one member of a project team, and he or she may play a central or more of a peripheral role. Regardless of the social worker's position, the contributions from all members of the team are essential toward realizing the project goal. There are many specific interventions that a generalist practitioner may implement in community work, but these may be summarized into the categories of conflict, cooperation, or campaign. In most cases, elements of all three strategies will be utilized, although one is usually prominent. The three illustrations in this chapter have shown the generalist practitioner in the roles of primary task force member, leader of the change effort, and, in a less visible sense, one member of a subcommittee. In each case the social worker needed to demonstrate knowledge of the community, knowledge about the issue of concern, and the ability to work cooperatively with many types of community players, in order to be an effective change agent.

TOPICS FOR DISCUSSION

1. Review the steps involved in community assessment as presented in this chapter. Would they be feasible in the geographic community where you live or work? Would you add any steps to the assessment process?

2. What are some ways that a social worker might become engaged in agency or community assessment? In those examples, how can the social worker achieve credibility with the people or agencies that should be included in the assessment?

3. Describe some specific examples of social welfare problem issues in communities where you have lived or worked. Would they likely call for collaboration, campaign, or conflict intervention strategies? Why?

4. Using the previous examples, describe the different skills that would be required of social workers. What themes seem to emerge in considering these skills?

5. Regarding professional values, how can social workers be accountable to clients when their interventions are made at such a broad level? Use the examples from this chapter as a basis for this discussion.

6. Describe some examples of successful and unsuccessful social advocacy you have observed or participated in. For what reasons did the efforts succeed or fail?

ASSIGNMENT IDEAS

1. Devise a strategy for evaluating the effectiveness of any of the three community-level interventions discussed in this chapter.

2. On a sheet of paper, draw a chart (an eco-map) showing the relationship of your field placement agency to three other agencies in the community that are most relevant to yours in serving the same or similar populations. Then, address the following questions:

- Is your agency a voluntary, public, or for-profit agency? Describe the other three agencies in these same terms. Does this characteristic affect the nature of agency interactions in any observable ways?

- What types of linkages exist, formally or informally, between your agency and the others (communication, cooperation, coordination, and collaboration)?

- Note any *power* and *dependency* relationships between organizations that affect the quality of their interactions.

- Identify and discuss any issues of "turf" issues among agencies and any problems that stem from them.

- Are there service gaps that result from the particular types of organizational relationships?

3. Several years ago the nation was shocked by the terrible impact of Hurricane Katrina on the people of New Orleans. While this was a great tragedy, perhaps it can provide lessons for social workers. It may suggest ideas for how social workers could respond to such an event, to minimize the physical and emotional damage done and to facilitate the recovery process. The situation in New Orleans was one in which a generalist approach to social work practice would be highly applicable.

   Try to assume the perspectives of three types of social workers in New Orleans, from the *school system,* department of *social services,* and department of *corrections.* How would you organize and implement one intervention strategy for New Orleans from each of the five "levels" of generalist practice? Be sure to articulate your target population(s) while doing so. Draw on specific theories or intervention strategies you have learned in this textbook to support your decisions about intervention strategies.

References

Abbott, A. A. (2003). Understanding transference and countertransference: Risk management strategies for preventing sexual misconduct and other boundary violations in social work practice. *Psychoanalytic Social Work, 10*(2), 21–41.

Adams, R. (1996). *Social work and empowerment.* London: Macmillan.

Ahern, S., & Bailey, K. G. (1996). *Family-by-choice: Creating family in a world of strangers.* Minneapolis, MN: Fairview Press.

Allen-Meares, P. (2003). *Intervention with children and adolescents: An interdisciplinary perspective.* New York: Prentice Hall.

Anderson, J. (1997). *Social work with groups: A process model.* White Plains, NY: Longman.

Angrosino, H. V. (2004). *The culture of the sacred: Exploring the anthropology of religion.* Prospect Heights, IL: Waveland.

Aponte, H. J., & DiCesare, E. J. (2000). Structural theory. In F. M. Dattilio & L. J. Bevilacqua (Eds.), *Comparative treatments for relationship dysfunction* (pp. 45–57). New York: Springer.

Backlar, P. (1996). The three Rs: Roles, relationships, and rules. *Community Mental Health Journal, 32*(5), 505–509.

Bal, S., Crombez, G., & Oost, P. V. (2003). The role of social support in well-being and coping with self-reported stressful events in adolescents. *Child Abuse & Neglect, 27*(12), 1377–1395.

Bandura, A. (1977). *Social learning theory.* Englewood Cliffs, NJ: Prentice Hall.

Banyard, V. L., & Graham-Bermann, S. A. (1993). A gender analysis of theories of coping with stress. *Psychology of Women Quarterly, 17,* 303–318.

Barkley, R. A. (2000). Commentary: Issues in training parents to manage children with behavior problems. *Journal of the American Academy of Child & Adolescent Psychiatry, 39*(8), 1004–1007.

Barlow, C. A., Blythe, J. A., & Edmonds, M. (1999). *A handbook of interactive exercises for groups.* Needham Heights, MA: Allyn & Bacon.

Barrera, M., & Ainlay, S. L. (1983). The structure of social support: A conceptual and empirical analysis. *Journal of Community Psychology, 11,* 133–143.

Basham, K. (2004). Multiculturalism and the therapeutic process. *Smith College Studies in Social Work, 72*(4), 457–462.

Beck, A. T. (1967). *Depression: Clinical, experimental, and theoretical aspects.* New York: Hoeber.

Beck, A. T. (1976). *Cognitive therapy and the emotional disorders.* New York: International Universities Press.

Beck, J. S. (1995). *Cognitive therapy: Basics and beyond.* New York: Guilford.

Bellah, R. N., Madsen, R., Sullivan, W. M., Swindler, A., & Tipton, S. M. (1985). *Habits of the heart: Individualism and commitment in American life.* New York: Perennial.

Berlin, S. B. (2002). *Clinical social work practice: A cognitive-integrative perspective.* New York: Oxford.

Bertolino, B., & O'Hanlon, B. (2002). *Collaborative, competency-based counseling and therapy.* Boston: Allyn & Bacon.

Best, S., & Kellner, D. (1991). *Postmodern theory: Critical interrogations.* New York: Guilford.

Bloomquist, M. L. (2006). *Skills training for children with behavior problems: A parent and practitioner guidebook* (Rev. ed.). New York: Guilford.

Bonvillain, N. (2007). *Women and men: Cultural constructs of gender.* Upper Saddle River, NJ: Prentice Hall.

Bransford, C., & Bakken, T. (2001). Organization theory and the utilization of authority in social work. *Social Work and Social Sciences Review, 9*(1), 3–21.

Brody, E. M., & Farber, B. A. (1996). The effects of therapist experience and patient diagnosis on countertransference. *Psychotherapy, 33*(3), 372–380.

Bruggemann, W. G. (2002). *The practice of macro social work* (2nd ed.). Belmont, CA: Brooks/Cole.

Bruhn, J. G., Levine, H. G., & Levine, P. L. (1993). *Managing boundaries in the helping professions.* Springfield, IL: Charles C. Thomas.

Burbach, R. (1998). The (un)defining of postmodern Marxism: On smashing modernization and narrating new social and economic actors. *Rethinking Marxism, 10*(1), 52–65.

Burckell, L. A., & Goldfriend, M. R. (2006). Therapist qualities preferred by sexual minority individuals. *Psychotherapy: Theory, Research, Practice, Training, 43*(1), 32–49.

Burt, S., & Minor, M. J. (1983). *Applied network analysis: A methodological approach.* Beverly Hills, CA: Sage.

Caplan, G. (1989). Recent developments in crisis intervention and the promotion of support service. *Journal of Primary Prevention, 10*(1), 3–25.

Caplan, G. (1990). Loss, stress, and mental health. *Community Mental Health Journal, 26*(1), 27–48.

Carey, T. A., & Mullan, R. J. (2004). What is Socratic questioning? *Psychotherapy: Theory, Research, Practice, Training, 41*(3), 217–226.

Carroll, K. (1998). *A cognitive-behavioral approach: Treating cocaine addiction.* Retrieved August 28, 2001, from http://www.drugabuse.gov/TXManuals/CBT/CBT1.html

Carroll, K. M. (1995). Methodological issues and problems in the assessment of substance use. *Psychological Assessment, 7*(3).

Cassel, J. (1976). The contribution of the social environment to host resistance. *American Journal of Epidemiology, 104,* 107–123.

Chang, E. C., D'Zurilla, T. J., & Sanna, L. J. (Eds.) (2004). *Social problem solving: Theory, research, and training.* Washington, DC: American Psychological Association.

Charon, J. M. (1992). *Symbolic interactionism: An introduction, an interpretation, an integration* (3rd ed.). Englewood Cliffs, NJ: Prentice Hall.

Cobb, S. (1976). Social support as a moderator of life stress. *Psychosomatic Medicine, 38,* 300–314.

Cohen, S., Underwood, L. G., & Gottlieb, B. H. (2000). *Social support measurement and intervention: A guide for health and social scientists.* New York: Oxford.

Cohen, S., & Willis, T. A. (1985). Stress, social support, and the buffering hypothesis. *Psychological Bulletin, 98*(2), 310–357.

Coleman, H. (1992). "Good families don't . . ." (and other family myths). *Journal of Child and Youth Care, 7*(2), 59–68.

Collins, S., & Long, A. (2003a). Too tired to care? The psychological effects of working with trauma. *Journal of Psychiatric Nursing and Mental Health Services, 10*(1), 17–27.

Collins, S., & Long, A. (2003b). Working with the psychological effects of trauma: Consequences of mental health care workers: A literature review. *Journal of Psychiatric Nursing and Mental Health Services, 10*(4), 417–424.

Connors, G., Donovan, D., & DiClemente, C. (2001). *Substance abuse treatment and stages of change: Selecting and planning interventions.* New York: Guilford.

Cooper, B. (2002). Constructivism in social work: Towards a participative practice viability. *British Journal of Social Work, 31*(5), 721–738.

Corcoran, J. (2000). Brief solution-focused therapy. In N. Coady & P. Lehman (Eds.), *Theoretical perspectives in direct social work practice: An eclectic-generalist approach* (pp. 326–343). New York: Springer.

Corcoran, J. (2006). *Cognitive-behavioral methods for social workers: A workbook.* Boston: Allyn & Bacon.

Cordova, J. V., & Scott, R. L. (2001). Intimacy: A behavioral interpretation. *Behavior Analyst, 24*(1), 75–86.

Corey, M. S., & Corey, G. (2006). *Groups: Process and practice* (7th ed.). Belmont, CA: Brooks/Cole.

Curtis, L. C., & Hodge, M. (1994). Old standards, new dilemmas: Ethics and boundaries in community support services. In *Introduction to psychiatric rehabilitation* (pp. 340–354). Columbia, MD: International Association of Psychosocial Rehabilitation Services.

Davis, M., Eshelman, E. R., & McKay, M. (2000). *The relaxation and stress workbook* (5th ed.). New York: MJF Books.

Deal, J. E. (1996). Marital conflict and differential treatment of siblings. *Family Process, 35*(3), 333–346.

DeJong, P., & Berg, I. K. (2002). *Interviewing for solutions* (2nd ed.). Pacific Grove, CA: Brooks/Cole.

Dolgoff, R., Loewenberg, F. M., & Harrington, D. (2005). *Ethical decisions for social work practice* (7th ed.). Itasca, IL: F. E. Peacock.

Donaldson, L. (2001). *The contingency theory of organizations.* Thousand Oaks, CA: Sage.

Doreen, C. (1998). Knowing patients: How much and how well? In P. Griffiths & J. Ord (Eds.), *Face to face with distress: The professional use of self in psychosocial care* (pp. 135–146). Oxford, England: Butterworth-Heinemann.

Dziegielewski, S. F., & Montgomery, D. H. (1999). Gender issues in family therapy. In C. Franklin & C. Jordan (Eds.), *Family practice: Brief systems methods for social work* (pp. 321–340). Pacific Grove, CA: Brooks/Cole.

Ehin, C. (2004). *Hidden assets: Harnessing the power of informal networks.* Boston: Kluwer.

Ehrenreich, J. H. (1985). *The altruistic imagination: A history of social work and social policy in the United States.* Ithaca, NY: Cornell University Press.

Ellis, A. (1962). *Reason and emotion in psychotherapy.* New York: Stuart.

Farber, N. J., Novack, D. H., & O'Brient, M. K. (1997). Love, boundaries, and the patient-physician relationship. *Archives of Internal Medicine, 157*(20), 2291–2295.

Fellin, P. (2000). *The community and the social worker.* Itasca, IL: F. E. Peacock.

Figley, C. R. (2002). Compassion fatigue: Psychotherapist's chronic lack of self care. *Journal of Clinical Psychology, 58*(11), 1433–1441.

Fischer, C. S. (1982). *To dwell among friends.* Chicago: University of Chicago Press.

Fischer, J. (1978) Does anything work? *Journal of Social Service Research, 1*(3), 215–243.

Flicker, S. M. (2005). The relationship between ethnic matching, therapeutic alliance, and treatment outcome with Hispanic and Anglo adolescents in family therapy. *Dissertation Abstracts International, 65* (8), 4282B.

Fong, R., & Furuto, S. (Eds.) (2001). *Culturally competent practice: Skills interventions, and evaluations.* Boston: Allyn & Bacon.

Foster, S. L., & Crain, M. M. (2002). Social skills and problem-solving training. In F. W. Kaslow & T. Patterson (Eds.), *Comprehensive handbook of psychiatry: Cognitive-behavioral methods, Vol. 2* (pp. 31–50). Hoboken, NJ: Wiley.

Frank, J. D., & Frank, J. B. (1993). *Persuasion and healing: A comparative study of psychotherapy* (3rd ed.). Baltimore: Johns Hopkins University Press.

Frankel, A. J., & Gelman, S. R. (2004). *Case management* (2nd ed.). Chicago: Lyceum.

Frankl, V. E. (1988). *The will to meaning: Foundations and applications of logotherapy.* New York: Meridian.

Franklin, C., & Corcoran, K. (2003). Quantitative clinical assessment methods. In C. Jordan & C. Franklin (Eds.), *Clinical assessment for social workers: Quantitative and qualitative methods* (2nd ed., pp. 71–96). Chicago: Lyceum.

Franklin, C., Hopson, L., & Barge, C. T. (2003). Family systems. In C. Jordan & C. Franklin (Eds.), *Clinical assessment for social workers: Quantitative and qualitative methods* (2nd ed., pp. 255–311). Chicago: Lyceum.

Freud, S., & Krug, S. (2002a). Beyond the Code of Ethics, part I: Complexities of ethical decision making in social work practice. *Families in Society, 83*(5–6), 474–482.

Freud, S., & Krug, S. (2002b). Beyond the Code of Ethics, part II: Dual relationships revisited. *Families in Society, 83*(5–6), 483–492.

Gabbard, G. O. (1995). Countertransference: The emerging common ground. *International Journal of Psychoanalysis, 76,* 475–485.

Gambrill, E. (1990). *Critical thinking in clinical practice.* San Francisco: Jossey-Bass.

Garcia-Preto, N. (1996). Puerto Rican families. In M. McGoldrick, J. Giordano, & J. Pearce (Eds.), *Ethnicity and family therapy* (2nd ed.). New York: Guilford.

Gardner, H. (1999). *Intelligence reframed: Multiple intelligences for the 21st century.* New York: Basic Books.

Garreau, J. (1991). *Edge city: Life on the new frontier.* New York: Doubleday.

Germain, C. B., & Gitterman, A. (1996). *The life model of social work practice: Advances in theory and practice* (2nd ed.). New York: Columbia University Press.

Ginsberg, L., Nackerud, L., & Larrison, C. (2004). *Human biology for social workers: Development, ecology, genetics, and health.* Boston: Allyn & Bacon.

Goffman, E. (1963). *Stigma: Notes on the management of spoiled identity.* Englewood Cliffs, NJ: Prentice Hall.

Goldberg, C. (2001). The constructive use of countertransference in family psychotherapy. *Journal of Family Psychotherapy, 12*(2), 75–81.

Goldsmith, D. J. (2004). *Communicating social support.* New York: Cambridge University Press.

Granvold, D. K. (Ed.) (1994). *Cognitive and behavioral treatment: Methods and applications.* Pacific Grove, CA: Brooks/Cole.

Green, J. W. (1999). *Cultural awareness in the human services: A multi-ethnic approach* (3rd ed.). Boston: Allyn & Bacon.

Greene, J. O., & Burleson, B. R. (Eds.) (2003). *Handbook of communication and social interaction skills.* Mahwah, NJ: Lawrence Erlbaum Associates.

Gutheil, T. G., & Gabbard, G. O. (1998). Misuses and misunderstandings of boundary theory in clinical and regulatory settings. *American Journal of Psychiatry, 155*(3), 409–414.

Guy, J. D., & Norcross, J. C. (1998). Therapist self-care checklist. In G. P. Koocher, J. C. Norcross, & S. Hill (Eds.), *Psychologists' desk reference.* London: Oxford University Press.

Harper, K. V., & Lantz, J. (2007). *Cross-cultural practice: Social work with diverse populations* (2nd ed.). Chicago: Lyceum.

Harrigan, M. P., Fauri, D. P., & Netting, F. E. (1998). Termination: Extending the concept for macro social work practice. *Journal of Sociology and Social Welfare, 25*(4), 61–80.

Hatchet, G. T., & Park, H. L. (2004). Revisiting relationships between sex-related variables and continuation in counseling. *Psychological Reports, 94*(2), 381–386.

Hawton, K. (1989). Suicide and the management of suicide attempts. In K. R. Herbst & E. S. Paykel (Eds.), *Depression: An integrative approach* (pp. 197–215). Halley Court, Jordan Hill, Oxford: Heinemann.

Helgeson, V. S. (2003). Social support and quality of life. *Quality of Life Research: An International Journal of Quality of Life Aspects of Treatment, Care & Rehabilitation, 12*(Suppl. 1), 25–31.

Hennessey, B. A. (2007). Promoting social competence in school-aged children: The effects of the Open Circle Program. *Journal of School Psychology, 45*(3), 349–360.

Hepworth, D., Rooney, R., Rooney, G. D., Strom-Gottfried, K., & Larsen, J. (2006). *Direct social work practice: Theory and skills* (7th ed.). Belmont, CA: Brooks/Cole.

Herlihy, B., & Corey, G. (1997). *Boundary issues in counseling: Multiple roles and responsibilities.* Alexandria, VA: American Counseling Association.

Hermansson, G. (1997). Boundaries and boundary management in counseling: The never-ending story. *British Journal of Guidance and Counseling, 25*(2), 133–146.

Hewitt, J. P. (1997). *Self and society: A symbolic interactionist social psychology.* Boston: Allyn & Bacon.

Hobfoll, S., Freedy, R., Lane, C., & Geller, P. (1990). Conservation of social resources: Social support resource theory. *Journal of Social and Personal Relationships, 7,* 465–478.

Hobfoll, S., & Vaux, A. (1993). Social support: Social resources and social context. In L. Goldberger & S. Breznitz (Eds.), *Handbook of stress: Theoretical and clinical aspects* (2nd ed., pp. 685–705). New York: Free Press.

Hutchison, E. D. (2003). *Dimensions of human behavior: Person and environment* (2nd ed.). Thousand Oaks, CA: Sage.

Hutchison, E. D. (2008). *Dimensions of human behavior: Person and environment* (3rd ed.). Los Angeles: Sage.

Ito, K. L., & Marimba, G. G. (2002). Therapeutic beliefs of Asian American therapists: Views from an ethnic-specific clinic. *Transcultural Psychiatry, 39*(1), 33–73.

Jacobs, T. J. (1999). Countertransference past and present: A review of the concept. *International Journal of Psychoanalysis, 80,* 575–594.

James, R. K., & Gilliland, B. E. (2001). *Crisis intervention strategies* (4th ed.). Pacific Grove, CA: Brooks/Cole.

Janzen, C., & Harris, O. (1997). *Family treatment in social work practice* (3rd ed.). Itasca, IL: F. E. Peacock.

Johnson, A. K. (2004). Social work is standing on the legacy of Jane Addams: But are we sitting on the sidelines? *Social Work, 49*(2), 319–322.

Kadushin, A., & Kadushin, G. (1997). *The social work interview.* New York: Columbia University Press.

Kanter, J. (1989). Clinical case management: Definition, principles, components. *Hospital and Community Psychiatry, 40,* 361–368.

Kanter, J. (1996). Case management with long-term patients: A comprehensive approach. In S. M. Soreff (Ed.), *Handbook for the treatment of the seriously mentally ill* (pp. 257–277). Seattle: Hogrefe & Huber.

Kanter, J. (1999). Clinical issues in delivering home-based psychiatric services. In A. Menikoff (Ed.), *Psychiatric home care: Clinical and economic dimensions* (pp. 19–37). San Diego, CA: Academic Press.

Karls, J. M. (2002). Person-in-environment system: Its essence and applications. In A. R. Roberts &

G. J. Greene (Eds.), *Social workers' desk reference* (pp. 194–198). New York: Oxford.

Karls, J. M., & Wandrei, K. E. (Eds.) (1994). *Person-in-environment system: The PIE classification system for social functioning problems.* Washington, DC: National Association of Social Workers.

Kazdin, A. (2000). *Behavior modification in applied settings* (6th ed.). Pacific Grove, CA: Brooks/Cole.

Keidel, G. C. (2002). Burnout and compassion fatigue among hospice caregivers. *American Journal of Hospice & Palliative Care, 19*(3), 200–205.

Killick, S., & Allen, C. (1997). "Shifting the Balance"—Motivational interviewing to help behaviour change in people with bulimia nervosa. *European Eating Disorders Review, 5*(1), 35–41.

Kilpatrick, A. C., & Holland, T. P. (Eds.) (2006). *Working with families: An integrative model by level of need* (4th ed.). Boston: Allyn & Bacon.

Kirst-Ashman, K. K., & Hull, G. H. (1997). *Generalist practice with organizations and communities.* Chicago: Nelson-Hall.

Kocan, M. (1988). *Transference and countertransference in clinical work.* Workshop sponsored by the American Healthcare Institute.

Krohn, M. D., & Thornberry, T. P. (1997). Network theory: A model for understanding drug abuse among African-American and Hispanic youth. *Substance Use and Misuse, 32*(12–13), 1931–1936.

Lantz, J. (1996). Cognitive theory and social work treatment. In F. J. Turner (Ed.), *Social work treatment* (4th ed., pp. 94–115). New York: Free Press.

Lantz, J., & Pegram, M. (1989). Casework and the restoration of meaning. *Social Casework, 70,* 549–555.

Lantz, J., & Walsh, J. (2007). *Short-term existential intervention in clinical practice*. Chicago: Lyceum.

Lazarus, R. S. (1993). Coping theory and research: Past, present, and future. *Psychosomatic Medicine, 55,* 234–247.

Lazarus, R. S. (1999). *Stress and emotion: A new synthesis.* New York: Springer.

Lazarus, R. S., & Lazarus, B. N. (1994). *Passion and reason: Making sense of our emotions.* New York: Oxford University Press.

Leahy, R. L. (1996). *Cognitive therapy: Basic principles and applications.* Northvale, NJ: Jason Aronson.

Lee, J. A. B. (2001). *The empowerment approach to social work practice: Building the beloved community* (2nd ed.). New York: Columbia University Press.

Lee, M. (2000). Understanding Chinese battered women in North America: A review of the literature and practice implications. *Journal of Ethnic and Cultural Diversity in Social Work, 8,* 215–241.

Lee, M. (2002). *Working with Asian American populations: A treatment guide.* Columbus, OH: Asian American Community Services.

Lee, R. M. (1997). The role of social connectedness in the social support process and small group interactions. *Dissertation Abstracts International, 57* (8), 5390B.

Leigh, J. W. (1998). *Communicating for cultural competence.* Boston: Allyn & Bacon.

Levine, S. S., & Kurzban, R. (2006). Explaining clustering in social networks: Towards an evolutionary theory of cascading benefits. *Managerial & Decision Economics, 27*(2–3), 173–187.

Lewinsohn, P. M., Clarke, G. N., Rohde, P., & Hops, H. (2001). A course in coping: A cognitive–behavioral approach to the treatment of adolescent depression. In E. D. Hibbs & P. S. Jensen (Eds.), *Psychosocial treatment for child and adolescent disorders* (pp. 109–135). Washington, DC: American Psychiatric Press.

Lincoln, K. D. (2000). Social support, negative social interactions, and psychological well-being. *Social Service Review, 74*(2), 231.

Liu, H. C. S. (2004). Client perceptions of seeking counseling as a function of counselor ethnicity, counselor acculturation, counselor gender, and client gender. *Dissertation Abstracts International, 64* (9), 3203A.

Lloyd, C., King, R., & Chenowith, L. (2002). Social work, stress, and burnout. *Journal of Mental Health, 11*(3), 255–266.

Loeber, R., Green, S. M., Lahey, B. B., Frick, P. J., & McBurnett, K. (2002). Findings on disruptive behavior disorders from the first decade of the Developmental Trends Study. *Clinical Child and Family Psychology Review, 3,* 37–60.

Long, D. D., Tice, C. J., & Morrison, J. D. (2006). *Macro social work practice: A strengths perspective.* Belmont, CA: Brooks/Cole.

Lubart, T. I., & Mouchiroud, C. (2003). Creativity: A source of difficulty in problem solving. In J. E. Davidson and R. J. Sternberg (Eds.), *The psychology of problem solving* (pp. 127–148). New York: Cambridge University Press.

Lum, D. (1999). *Social work practice and people of color.* Pacific Grove, CA: Brooks/Cole.

Macgowan, M. J. (2004). Prevention and intervention in youth suicide. In P. Allen-Meares & M. W. Fraser (Eds.), *Intervention with children and adolescents: An interdisciplinary perspective* (pp. 282–310). Boston: Allyn & Bacon.

Maguire, L. (1991). *Social support systems in practice: A generalist approach.* Silver Spring, MD: NASW.

Maguire, L. (2002). *Clinical social work practice: Beyond generalist practice with individuals, groups, and families*. Pacific Grove, CA: Brooks/Cole.

Maier, H. W. (1978). *Three theories of child development* (3rd. ed.). New York: Harper & Row.

Manns, W. (1988). Supportive roles of significant others in Black families. In H. P. McAdoo (Ed.), *Black families* (2nd ed., pp. 270–283). Thousand Oaks, CA: Sage.

Marlow, C. (1998). *Research methods for the generalist practitioner* (2nd ed.). Pacific Grove, CA: Brooks/Cole.

Maslow, A. H. (1968). *Toward a psychology of being*. New York: Van Nostrand Reinhold.

McClam, T., & Woodside, M. (1994). *Problem solving in the helping professions*. Pacific Grove, CA: Brooks/Cole.

McFarlane, A. H., Neale, K. A., Norman, G. R., Roy, R. G., & Streiner, D. L. (1982). Methodological issues in developing a scale to measure social support. *Schizophrenia Bulletin, 7,* 90–100.

McGoldrick, M., Gerson, R., & Shellenberger, S. (1999). *Genograms: Assessment and intervention* (2nd ed.). New York: W. W. Norton.

McGoldrick, M., Heiman, M., & Carter, B. (1993). The changing family life cycle: A perspective on normalcy. In F. Walsh (Ed.), *Normal family processes* (pp. 405–443). New York: Guilford.

McMillen, J. C., Morris, L., & Sherraden, M. (2004). Ending social work's grudge match: Problems versus strengths. *Families in Society, 85*(3), 317–325.

Meacham, J. A., & Emont, N. C. (1989). The interpersonal basis of everyday problem solving. In J. D. Sinnott (Ed.), *Everyday problem solving: Theory and applications* (pp. 7–23). New York: Praeger.

Meenaghan, T. M., Gibbons, W. E., & McNutt, J. G. (2005). *Generalist practice in larger settings: Knowledge and skill concepts* (2nd ed). Chicago: Lyceum.

Meichenbaum, D. (1999). *Cognitive-behavior modification: An integrative approach*. Cambridge, MA: Perseus.

Merton, R. K. (1994). Social structure and anomie. In S. H. Traub and C. B. Little (Eds.), *Theories of deviance* (4th ed., pp. 114–148). Itasca, IL: F. E. Peacock.

Miller, W. R., & Rollnick, S. (2002). *Motivational interviewing: Preparing people for change* (2nd ed.). New York: Guilford.

Minuchin, S. (1974). *Families and family therapy*. Cambridge, MA: Harvard University Press.

Minuchin, S. (1984). *Family kaleidoscope*. Cambridge, MA: Harvard University Press.

Minuchin, S., & Fishman, H. (1981). *Family therapy techniques*. New York: Harvard University Press.

Minuchin, S., Lee, W., & Simon, G. M. (1996). *Mastering family therapy: Journeys of growth and transformation*. New York: Wiley.

Minuchin, S., Montalvo, B., Guerney, B., Rosman, B., & Schumer, F. (1967). *Families of the slums*. Cambridge, MA: Harvard University Press.

Monette, D. R., Sullivan, T. J., & De Jong, C. R. (2000). *Applied social research: Tools for the human services*. Belmont, CA: Brooks/Cole.

Moyers, T., & Rollnick, S. (2002). A motivational interviewing perspective on resistance in psychotherapy. *JCLP/In Session: Psychotherapy in Practice, 58,* 185–193.

Murphy, C. D., & Dillon, C. (2003). *Interviewing in action: Relationship, process, and change* (2nd ed.). Pacific Grove, CA: Brooks/Cole.

Myer, R. A. (2001). *Assessment for crisis intervention: A triage assessment model.* Belmont, CA: Wadsworth.

National Association of Social Workers. (1999). *Code of ethics.* Washington, DC: Author.

Negy, C. (2004). Therapy with dissimilar clients: Issues to consider along this road more traveled. In C. Negy (Ed.), *Cross-cultural psychotherapy: Toward a critical understanding of diverse clients* (pp. 3–22). Reno, NV: Bent Tree Press.

Netting, F. E., Kettner, P. M., & McMurtry, S. L. (2004). *Social work macro practice* (3rd ed.). Boston: Allyn & Bacon.

Neugeboren, B. (1996). *Environmental practice in the human services: Integration of micro and macro roles, skills, and contexts.* New York: Haworth.

Nichols, M. P., & Fellenberg, S. (2000). The effective use of enactments in family therapy: A discovery-oriented process study. *Journal of Marital & Family Therapy, 26*(2), 143–152.

Nichols, M. P., & Schwartz, R. C. (2007). *The essentials of family therapy* (3rd ed.). Boston: Allyn & Bacon.

O'Hanlon, W. H., & Weiner-Davis, M. (1989). *In search of solutions: A new direction in psychotherapy.* New York: Norton.

Ouchi, W. G. (1981). *Theory Z: How American business can meet the Japanese challenge.* Reading, MA: Addison-Wesley.

Parker-Sloat, E. L. (2003). Client-therapist ethnicity and gender matching as predictors of length of treatment and goal completion at a practicum training clinic. *Dissertation Abstracts International, 64* (6), 2934B.

Parsons, R. J. (1991). Empowerment: Purpose and practice principle in social work. *Social Work with Groups, 14*(2), 7–21.

Pavlov, I. P. (1927). *Conditioned reflexes.* London: Oxford.

Perkins, D. V., Hudson, B. L., Gray, D. M., & Stewart, M. (1998). Decisions and justifications by community mental health providers about hypothetical ethical dilemmas. *Psychiatric Services, 49*(10), 1317–1322.

Petronio, S., Ellemers, N., Giles, H., & Gallois, C. (1998). (Mis)communicating across boundaries: Interpersonal and intergroup considerations. *Communication Research, 25*(6), 571–595.

Piaget, J. (1967). *The child's conception of the world.* Totawa, NJ: Littlefield.

Pimentel, E. E. (1996). Effects of adolescent achievement and family goals on the early adult transition. In J. T. Mortimer & M. D. Finch (Eds.), *Adolescents, work, and family: An intergenerational developmental analysis: Vol. 6. Understanding families* (pp. 191–220). Thousand Oaks, CA: Sage.

Piselli, F. (2007). Communities, places, and social networks. *American Behavioral Scientist, 50*(7), 867–878.

Porter, L. W., & Bigley, C. A. (1995). *Human relations: Theory and development.* Brookfield, VT: Dartmouth University Press.

Potts, K. (1997). Social support and depression among older adults living alone: The importance of friends within and outside of a retirement community. *Social Work, 42*(4), 348.

Prochaska, J., & Norcross, J. (1994). *Systems of psychotherapy: A transtheoretical analysis* (3rd ed.). Pacific Grove, CA: Brooks/Cole.

Procidano, M., & Heller, K. (1983). Measures of perceived social support from friends and family: Three validation studies. *American Journal of Community Psychology, 11,* 1–24.

Rampersad, H. K. (2001). *Total quality management: An executive's guide to continuous improvement*. New York: Springer.

Reamer, F. G. (1998). The evolution of social work ethics. *Social Work, 43*(6), 488–500.

Reamer, F. G. (2003). Boundary issues in social work: Managing dual relationships. *Social Work, 48*(1), 121–133.

Reid, K. E. (1997). *Social work practice with groups: A clinical perspective* (2nd ed.). Pacific Grove, CA: Brooks/Cole.

Reid, W. J. (2000). *The task planner*. New York: Columbia University Press.

Reid, W. J., & Epstein, L. (1972). *Task centered casework*. New York: Columbia University Press.

Reid, W. J., & Fortune, A. E. (2002). The task centered model. In A. R. Roberts & G. J. Greene (Eds.), *Social workers' desk reference* (pp. 101–104). New York: Oxford.

Richman, J. M., Rosenfeld, L. B., & Hardy, C. (1993). The social support survey: A validation study of a clinical measure of the social support process. *Research on Social Work Practice, 3*, 288–311.

Roberts, A. R. (2000). An overview of crisis theory and crisis intervention. In A. R. Roberts (Ed.), *Crisis intervention handbook: Assessment, treatment, and research* (2nd ed., pp. 3–30). New York: Oxford.

Rooney, R. H. (1992). *Strategies for work with involuntary clients*. New York: Columbia University Press.

Rose, S. M. (1990). Advocacy/empowerment: An approach to clinical practice for social work. *Journal of Sociology and Social Welfare, 17*(2), 41–51.

Saleebey, D. (1996). The strengths perspective in social work practice: Extensions and cautions. *Social Work, 41*(3), 296–305.

Saleebey, D. (Ed.) (2002). *The strengths perspective in social work practice* (3rd ed.). Boston: Allyn & Bacon.

Sarason, B. R., & Sarason, I. G. (2001). Ongoing aspects of relationships and health outcomes: Social support, social control, companionship, and relationship meaning. In J. Harvey and A. Wenzel (Eds.), *Close romantic relationships: Maintenance and enhancement* (pp. 277–295). Mahwah, NJ: Lawrence Erlbaum.

Saunders, T., Driskell, J. E., Hall, J., & Salas, E. (1996). The effect of stress inoculation training on anxiety and performance. *Journal of Occupational Health Psychology, 1*, 170–186.

Schmid, H. (2004). Organization-environment relationships: Theory for management practice in human service organizations. *Administration in SocialWork, 28*(1).

Schneider, R. L., & Lester, L. (2001). *Social work advocacy: A new framework for action*. Belmont, CA: Brooks/Cole.

Schoenwolf, G. (1993). *Counterresistance: The therapist's interference with the therapeutic process*. Northvale, NJ: Jason Aronson.

Segal, E. A., Gerdes, K. E., & Steiner, S. (2007). *An introduction to the profession of social work: Becoming a change agent* (2nd ed). Belmont, CA: Brooks/Cole.

Selye, H. (1991). History and present status of the stress concept. In A. Monat & R. S. Lazarus (Eds.), *Stress & coping: An anthology* (3rd. ed., pp. 21–35). New York: Columbia University Press.

Sherman, E. M. (2000). An analysis of variables influencing student therapists' and clients' ratings of session satisfaction. *Dissertation Abstracts International, 60* (8), 4251B.

Skinner, B. F. (1953). *Science and human behavior*. New York: Macmillan.

Sori, C. F. (2006). Reflections on children in family therapy: An interview with Salvador Minuchin. In C. F. Sori (Ed.), *Engaging children in family* therapy: Creative approaches to integrating theory and research in clinical practice (pp. 21–35). New York: Routledge/Taylor & Francis Group.

Streeter, C. L., & Gillespie, D. F. (1992). Social network analysis. Journal of Social Service Research, 16.

Taylor, R. J., Chatters, L. M., Hardison, C. B., & Riley, A. (2001). Informal social support networks and subjective well-being among African Americans. Journal of Black Psychology, 27(4), 439–463.

Teram, E. (1999). A case against making the control of clients a negotiable contingency for interdisciplinary teams. Human Relations, 52(12), 263–276.

Thompson, M. S., & Peebles-Wilkins, W. (1992). The impact of formal, informal, and societal support networks on the psychological well-being of black adolescent mothers. Social Work, 37, 322–328.

Thyer, B. A., & Bursinger, P. (1994). Treatment of clients with anxiety disorders. In D. K. Granvold (Ed.), Cognitive and behavioral treatment: Methods and application (pp. 272–284). Pacific Grove, CA: Brooks/Cole.

Thyer, B. A., & Myers, L. L. (1998). Social learning theory: An empirically based approach to understanding human behavior in the social environment. Journal of Human Behavior in the Social Environment, 1(1), 33–52.

Thyer, B. A., & Wodarski, J. S. (Eds.) (1998). Handbook of empirical social work practice. Vol. 1: Mental disorders. New York: Wiley.

Thyer, B. A., & Wodarski, J. S. (Eds.) (2007). Social work in mental health: An evidence-based approach. Hoboken, NJ: Wiley.

Toseland, R. W., & Rivas, R. F. (2005). An introduction to group work practice (5th ed.). Boston: Allyn & Bacon.

Traub, S. H., & Little, C. B. (Eds.) (1994). Theories of deviance (4th ed.). Itasca, IL: F. E. Peacock.

Treasure, J., & Ward, W. (1997). A practical guide to the use of motivational interviewing in anorexia nervosa. European Eating Disorders Review, 5, 102–114.

Turner, F. J. (Ed.) (1996). Theory and social work treatment. In F. J. Turner (Ed.), Social work treatment (4th ed., pp. 1–17). New York: Free Press.

Turner, J., & Jaco, R. M. (1996). Problem-solving theory and social work treatment. In F. J. Turner (Ed.), Social work treatment (4th ed., pp. 503–522). New York: Free Press.

Tyrrell, C. L., Dozier, M., Teague, G. B., & Fallot, R. D. (1999). Effective treatment relationships for persons with serious psychiatric disorders: The importance of attachment states of mind. Journal of Consulting and Clinical Psychology, 67(5), 725–733.

Van Voorhis, R. (1998), "Culturally relevant practice: A framework for teaching the psychosocial dynamics of oppression" Journal of Social Work Education, 34, 121–133.

Vaux, A. (1992). Assessment of social support. In H. O. Veiel & U. Baumann (Eds.), The meaning and measurement of social support (pp. 193–216). Washington, DC: Hemisphere Publishing.

Walitzer, K., Dermen, K., & Conners, G. (1999). Strategies for preparing clients for treatment: A review. Behavior Modification, 23, 129–151.

Wallace, A. C. (1997). Setting psychological boundaries: A handbook for women. Westport, CT: Bergin & Garvey.

Walsh, F. (2006). Strengthening family resilience (2nd ed.). New York: Guilford Press.

Walsh, J. (2000a). Clinical case management with persons having mental illness: A *relationship-based perspective*. Belmont, CA: Brooks/Cole.

Walsh, J. (2000b). Recognizing and managing boundary issues in case management. *Journal of Case Management, 9*(2), 79–85.

Walsh, J. (2003a). The psychological person: Cognition, emotion, and self. In L. Hutchison, *Dimensions of Human Behavior: Person and environment* (2nd ed., pp. 151–182). Thousand Oaks, CA: Sage.

Walsh, J. (2003b). The psychological person: Relationship, stress, and coping. In L. Hutchison, *Dimensions of human behavior: Person and environment* (2nd ed., pp. 185–218). Thousand Oaks, CA: Sage.

Walsh, J. (2006). *Theories for direct social work practice*. Pacific Grove, CA: Brooks/Cole.

Walsh, J. (2007). *Endings in clinical practice: Securing closure across diverse service settings* (2nd ed.). Chicago: Lyceum.

Walsh, J., & Connelly, P. R. (1996). Supportive behaviors in natural support networks of people with serious mental illness. *Health and Social Work, 21*(4), 296–303.

Walsh, J., & Harrigan, M. P. (2003). The termination stage in structural family intervention. *Family Therapy, 30*(1), 13–26.

Walsh, J., & Meyersohn, K. (2001). Ending clinical relationships with people with schizophrenia. *Health and Social Work, 26*(3), 188–195.

Waring, S. P. (1991). *Taylorism transformed: Scientific management since 1945*. Chapel Hill: University of North Carolina Press.

Watson, J. B. (1924). *Psychology from the standpoint of a behaviorist*. Philadelphia: J. D. Lippincott.

Webster-Stratton, C. (2001). Incredible years parents and children training series. Seattle, WA: Incredible Years.

Retrieved from www.incredibleyears .com

Wellman, B., & Berkowitz, S. D. (Eds.) (1988). *Social structures: A network approach*. New York: Cambridge University.

Westerfelt, A., & Dietz, T. J. (2005). *Planning and conducting agency-based research* (3rd ed.). Boston: Allyn & Bacon.

Wetchler, J. L. (2003). Structural family therapy. In L. L. Hecker & J. L. Wetchler (Eds.), *An introduction to marriage and family therapy* (pp. 63–93). Binghamton, NY: Haworth Clinical Practice Press.

Whitfield, K. E., & Wiggins, S. (2002). The influence of social support and health on everyday problem solving in adult African Americans. *Experimental Aging Research, 29*(1), 1–13.

Widegren, O. (1997). Social solidarity and social exchange. *Sociology, 31*(4), 755.

Willer, D., & Anderson, B. (Eds.) (1981). *Networks, exchange, and coercion: The elementary theory and its applications*. New York: Elsevier.

Wilson, G. T. (2000). Behavior therapy. In R. J. Corsini & D. Wedding (Eds.), *Current psychotherapies* (6th ed., pp. 205–240). Itasca, IL: F. E. Peacock.

Wodarski, J. S., & Bagarozzi, D. A. (1979). *Behavioral social work*. New York: Human Sciences Press.

Wong, Y., & Hillier, A. (2001). Evaluating a community-based homelessness prevention program: A geographic information systems approach. *Administration in Social Work, 25*(4), 21–45.

Wuthnow, R. (1998). Loose connections: Joining together America's fragmented communities. Cambridge, MA: Harvard University Press.

Yan, M. C., & Wong, Y. R. (2005). Rethinking self-awareness in cultural competence: Toward a dialogic self in cross-cultural social work. *Families in Society, 86*(2), 181–188.

Young, T. R. (1999). Marxism and social movements: Theory and practice for social justice. *Contemporary Sociology, 28*(3), 268–270.

Zastrow, C. H. (2006). *Social work with groups: A comprehensive workbook* (6th ed.). Belmont, CA: Brooks/Cole.

Index

CPSIA information can be obtained
at www.ICGtesting.com
Printed in the USA
FFOW03n1414121213
2725FF